For the Love
of Psychoanalysis

For the Love of Psychoanalysis

The Play of Chance in Freud and Derrida

Elizabeth Rottenberg

FORDHAM UNIVERSITY PRESS
New York 2019

Fordham University Press gratefully acknowledges financial assistance and support provided for the publication of this book by DePaul University.

Copyright © 2019 Fordham University Press

All rights reserved. No part of this publication may be reproduced, stored in a retrieval system, or transmitted in any form or by any means—electronic, mechanical, photocopy, recording, or any other—except for brief quotations in printed reviews, without the prior permission of the publisher.

Fordham University Press has no responsibility for the persistence or accuracy of URLs for external or third-party Internet websites referred to in this publication and does not guarantee that any content on such websites is, or will remain, accurate or appropriate.

Fordham University Press also publishes its books in a variety of electronic formats. Some content that appears in print may not be available in electronic books.

Visit us online at www.fordhampress.com.

Library of Congress Cataloging-in-Publication Data available online at https://catalog.loc.gov.

Printed in the United States of America

21 20 19   5 4 3 2 1

First edition

for Avivi

CONTENTS

Abbreviations of Works Cited   ix

Introduction: *Freuderrida*   1

Part I   FREUDERRIDA

1. Psychoanalysis and Neuroscience (Foreign Bodies I)   9
2. Traumatic Temporalities: Freud's Other Legacy   24
3. Is There Such a Thing as a Psychical Accident?   35
4. What Are the Chances? Psychoanalysis and Telepathy (Foreign Bodies II)   47
5. The Speculative Turn: Plato's Place in the Theory of the Drives   68

Part II   FREUDERRIDA

6. For the Love of Psychoanalysis: Deconstruction and Psychoanalysis   101
7. Cruelty and Its Vicissitudes   120
8. The "Question" of the Death Penalty   139
9. A New Primal Scene: Derrida and the Scene of Execution   151

Appendixes   CRIB NOTES

A. What Is at Play in Play? Derrida's *Fort/Da* with Freud's *Fort/Da*   179
B. Devouring Figures: Little Red Riding Hood and the Final Seminars of Jacques Derrida   190

Acknowledgements 199
Notes 201
Index 243

ABBREVIATIONS OF WORKS CITED

Works by Sigmund Freud

GW *Gesammelte Werke.* 18 vols. Frankfurt am Main: Fischer, 1940–1968.
N   *Gesammelte Werke, Nachtragsband, Texte aus den Jahren 1885 bis 1938.* Ed. Angela Richards in collaboration with Ilse Grubrich-Simitis. Frankfurt am Main: Fischer, 1987.
SE *The Standard Edition of the Complete Psychological Works of Sigmund Freud.* 24 vols. Trans. James Strachey in collaboration with Anna Freud, assisted by Alix Strachey and Alan Tyson. London: Hogarth, 1953–1974.

Works by Jacques Derrida

"AI"   "Autoimmunity: Real and Symbolic Suicides—a Conversation with Jacques Derrida." Trans. Pascale-Anne Brault and Michael Naas. In *Philosophy in a Time of Terror*, ed. Giovanna Borradori, 85–136. Chicago: University of Chicago Press, 2003. "Auto-immunités, suicides réels et symboliques." In *Le "concept" du 11 septembre*, 133–196. Paris: Éditions Galilée, 2003.
"BPP" "Beyond the Power Principle." Trans. Elizabeth Rottenberg. *The Undecidable Unconscious* 2, no. 1 (2015): 7–17. "Au-delà du principe de pouvoir." *Rue Descartes* 82, no. 3 (2014): 4–13.
BS1   *The Beast and the Sovereign, Volume I: Seminar of 2001–2002.* Trans. Geoffrey Bennington. Chicago: University of Chicago Press, 2009. *Séminaire La bête et le souverain, Volume I (2001–2002).* Ed. Michel Lisse, Marie-Louise Mallet, and Ginette Michaud. Paris: Éditions Galilée, 2008.
BS2   *The Beast and the Sovereign, Volume II: Seminar of 2002–2003.* Trans. Geoffrey Bennington. Chicago: University of Chicago Press, 2011. *Séminaire La bête et le souverain, Volume II*

	(*2002–2003*). Ed. Michel Lisse, Marie-Louise Mallet, and Ginette Michaud. Paris: Éditions Galilée, 2010.
"CHM"	"Cogito and the History of Madness." In *Writing and Difference*, 31–63. "Cogito et histoire de la folie." In *L'écriture et la différence*, 51–97.
"DoA"	"Deconstruction of Actuality." In *Negotiations: Interventions and Interviews, 1971–2001*, ed., trans., and intro. Elizabeth Rottenberg, 85–116. Stanford, CA: Stanford University Press, 2002.
DP1	*The Death Penalty, Volume I: Seminar of 1999–2000*. Trans. Peggy Kamuf. Chicago: University of Chicago Press, 2014. *Séminaire La peine de mort, Volume I (1999–2000)*. Ed. Geoffrey Bennington, Marc Crépon, and Thomas Dutoit. Paris: Éditions Galilée, 2012.
DP2	*The Death Penalty, Volume II: Seminar of 2000–2001*. Trans. Elizabeth Rottenberg. Chicago: University of Chicago Press, 2017. *Séminaire La peine de mort, Volume II (2000–2001)*. Ed. Geoffrey Bennington and Marc Crépon. Paris: Éditions Galilée, 2015.
"Env"	"Envois." In *The Post Card*, 3–256. "Envois." In *La carte postale*, 7–273.
EO	*The Ear of the Other: Otobiography, Transference, Translation*. Ed. Christie V. McDonald. Trans. Peggy Kamuf and Avital Ronell. New York: Schocken, 1985. *L'oreille de l'autre: otobiographies, transferts, traductions*. Ed. Claude Lévesque and Christie V. McDonald. Montréal: VLB Éditeur, 1982.
"FSW"	"Freud and the Scene of Writing." In *Writing and Difference*, 196–231. "Freud et la scène de l'écriture." In *L'écriture et la différence*, 293–340.
"FV"	"Le facteur de la vérité." In *The Post Card*, 411–96. "Le facteur de la vérité." In *La carte postale*, 441–524.
FWT	*For What Tomorrow . . . A Dialogue*. With Élisabeth Roudinesco. Trans. Jeff Fort. Stanford, CA: Stanford University Press, 2004. *De quoi demain . . . Dialogue*. With Élisabeth Roudinesco. Paris: Libraire Arthème Fayard et Éditions Galilée, 2001.
"Geo"	"Geopsychoanalysis 'and the rest of the world.'" Trans. Peggy Kamuf. In *Psyche 1*, 318–43. "Géopsychanalyse 'and the rest of the world.'" In *Psyché*, tome 1, 327–52.
"Imp"	"Implications: Interview with Henri Ronse." In *Positions*, 1–14. "Implications: Entretien avec Henri Ronse." In *Positions*, 9–24.

Abbreviations   xi

"K"   "*Khōra*." Trans. Ian McLeod. In *On the Name*, 87–127. *Khōra*.
         Paris: Éditions Galilée, 1993.
"LL"   "For the Love of Lacan." In *Resistances*, 39–69. "Pour l'amour
         de Lacan." In *Résistances*, 55–88.
LLF   *Learning to Live Finally: The Last Interview*. Trans. Pascale-Anne
         Brault and Michael Naas. Hoboken, NJ: Melville House, 2007.
         Apprendre à vivre enfin: Entretien avec Jean Birnbaum. Paris:
         Éditions Galilée/Le Monde, 2005.
"LNF"   "Let Us Not Forget—Psychoanalysis." Trans. Geoffrey
         Bennington and Rachel Bowlby. *Oxford Literary Review* 12,
         nos. 1–2 (1990): 3–7.
LVLM   *Séminaire La vie la mort (1975–1976)*. Ed. Pascale-Anne Brault
         and Peggy Kamuf. Paris: Éditions du Seuil, 2019. *Life Death,
         Seminar of 1975–1976*. Trans. Pascale-Anne Brault and
         Michael Naas. Chicago: University of Chicago Press, 2020.
"MC"   "My Chances/*Mes chances*: A Rendezvous with Some Epicurean
         Stereophonies." Trans. Irene Harvey and Avital Ronell. In
         Psyche 1, 344–76. "Mes chances: Au rendez-vous de quelques
         stéréophonies épicuriennes." In *Psyché*, tome 1, 353–84.
MO   *Monolingualism of the Other; or, The Prosthesis of Origin*. Trans.
         Patrick Mensah. Stanford, CA: Stanford University Press, 1998.
         Le monolinguisme de l'autre: ou la prothèse d'origine. Éditions
         Galilée, 1996.
"MP"   "Me—Psychoanalysis." Trans. Richard Klein. In *Psyche 1*,
         129–42. "Moi—la psychanalyse." In *Psyché*, tome 1, 145–58.
ON   *On the Name*. Ed. Thomas Dutoit. Stanford, CA: Stanford
         University Press, 1993.
PC   *The Post Card: From Socrates to Freud and Beyond*. Trans. Alan
         Bass. Chicago: University of Chicago Press, 1987. *La carte
         postale: de Socrate à Freud et au-delà*. Paris: Flammarion, 1980.
"PMS"   "Peine de mort et souveraineté (pour une déconstruction de
         l'onto-théologie)." *Divinatio* 15 (2002): 13–38.
PoF   *Politics of Friendship*. Trans. George Collins. New York: Verso,
         1997. *Politiques de l'amitié*. Paris: Éditions Galilée, 1994.
Pos   *Positions*. Trans. Alan Bass. Chicago: University of Chicago
         Press, 1981. *Positions*. Paris: Éditions de Minuit, 1972.
"Pos"   "Positions: Interview with Jean-Louis Houdebine and Guy
         Scarpetta." In *Positions*, 37–96. "Positions: Entretien avec Jean-
         Louis Houdebine and Guy Scarpetta." In *Positions*, 51–133.
"PSS"   "Psychoanalysis Searches the States of Its Soul: The Impossible
         Beyond of a Sovereign Cruelty." Trans. Peggy Kamuf. In

	Without Alibi, 238–80. *États d'âme de la psychanalyse: L'impossible au-delà d'une souveraine cruauté*. Paris: Éditions Galilée, 2000.
Psy1	*Psyche 1. Inventions of the Other*. Ed. Peggy Kamuf and Elizabeth Rottenberg. Stanford, CA: Stanford University Press, 2007. *Psyché: Inventions de l'autre*. Tome 1. Éditions Galilée, 1987–1998.
Psy2	*Psyche 2. Inventions of the Other*. Ed. Peggy Kamuf and Elizabeth Rottenberg. Stanford, CA: Stanford University Press, 2008. *Psyché: Inventions de l'autre*. Tome 2. Éditions Galilée, 1987–2003.
R	*Rogues: Two Essays on Reason*. Trans. Pascale-Anne Brault and Michael Naas. Stanford, CA: Stanford University Press, 2005. *Voyous*. Paris: Éditions Galilée, 2003.
Res	*Resistances of Psychoanalysis*. Trans. Peggy Kamuf, Pascale-Anne Brault, and Michael Naas. Stanford, CA: Stanford University Press, 1996. *Résistances: de la psychanalyse*. Paris: Éditions Galilée, 1996.
"Res"	"Resistances." In *Resistances*, 1–38. "Résistances." In *Résistances*, 13–53.
"SoF"	"To Speculate—on 'Freud.'" In *The Post Card*, 257–409. "Spéculer—sur 'Freud.'" In *La carte postale*, 277–437.
"Tel"	"Telepathy." Trans. Nicholas Royle. In *Psyche 1*, 227–61. "Télépathie." In *Psyché*, tome 1, 237–69.
"UWC"	"The University without Condition." Trans. Peggy Kamuf. In *Without Alibi*, 202–37. *L'université sans condition*. Paris: Éditions Galilée, 2001.
WA	*Without Alibi*. Ed., trans., and intro. Peggy Kamuf. Stanford, CA: Stanford University Press, 2002.
WD	*Writing and Difference*. Trans. Alan Bass. Chicago: University of Chicago Press, 1978. *L'écriture et la différence*. Paris: Éditions du Seuil, 1967.

Psychoanalysis brings out the worst in everyone . . .

—SIGMUND FREUD, "On the History of the Psychoanalytic Movement"

INTRODUCTION

Freuderrida

> Psychanalyse et déconstruction: double modalité de l'inoriginaire.
> —JEAN-LUC NANCY, "Double plongée aux abîmes"

I would like to begin this book with an anecdote of a slightly confessional nature. If I mention this anecdote, it is because it came to me *by chance* as an association to what French analyst and philosopher Monique David-Ménard calls "positive contingency" or the "positive aspect of chance,"[1] what in colloquial English we would call a "happy accident."

So here is the association. For reasons I cannot fully explain, the therapist I was seeing in graduate school encouraged me to take the Minnesota Multiphasic Personality Inventory test (the MMPI, as it's called), a widely used psychometric test of adult personality and psychopathology. The test involved hundreds of simple, inoffensive questions, questions like "do you read all the editorials in the newspaper every day?"[2] and it took me hours to complete. A week or so after taking the test, I met with my therapist, and we went over the results together. According to the test (which, interestingly, takes into account even the performative aspects of test-taking), I had answered all the questions in such a way as to appear neither excessively good nor excessively bad; that is, I had answered all the questions honestly and consistently. As far as psychopathology was concerned, my answers showed few signs of hypochondriasis, hysteria, psychopathy, schizophrenia, or hypomania. On the other hand, when it came to depression, paranoia, psychasthenia, and social introversion, my scores were a little higher, and a shockingly high percentage of my answers reflected "stereotypical masculine interests/behaviors." None of this seemed to worry my therapist in the least. The only thing she pointed to were my "odd answers" (the MMPI also has a special category for odd answers—which, presumably, correspond to the answers of academics). She wondered about my answer to this question in particular: "Do you see people or animals or things that other people don't see?" "You answered 'yes' to that question," she said. "I don't understand. Why would you answer 'yes'? You're not psychotic." I explained that I had read the "or"—do you see people OR animals OR things that other people don't see—as a disjunctive rather than a conjunctive OR. "So, yes, when I read texts, sometimes I see things that other people don't see." At the time, of course, I wasn't thinking of Gilles Deleuze's "contingent reason" or of his account of the inventive power of disjunctive synthesis. And I certainly wasn't thinking that my figurative reading of *seeing*, my misreading of *seeing*, my seeing in *seeing* something that my therapist did not, was indicative of the essential and indeterminable contingencies of reading (of grammar and semantics). No, I was only giving what I took to be a perfectly accurate description of the *déformation professionnelle* that belongs to academics or to anyone who is a stickler for grammar, a positive *déformation*, I might add.

This association immediately led me to another (contingent?) association, this time to Freud and to Freud's astonishment before the transformative power of Jean-Martin Charcot's dazzling, clinical insight. Although Freud was at times critical of Charcot, he never questioned his X-ray vision of things:

> [Charcot] . . . had the nature of an artist—he was, as he himself said, a *"visuel,"* a seer [*ein Seher*]. Here is what he himself told us about his method of working. He used to look again and again at the things he did not understand, to deepen his impression of them day by day, till suddenly [*plötzlich*] an understanding of them dawned on him. . . . He might be heard to say that the greatest satisfaction a person could have was to see something new—that is, to recognize it as new; and he remarked again and again on the difficulty and value of this kind of "seeing." He would ask why it was that in medicine people only see what they have already learned to see. (SE 3:12 / GW 1:22–23, modified)[3]

Or a few pages later:

> Charcot ... never tired of defending the rights of purely clinical work, which consists in seeing ... against the encroachments of theoretical medicine. On one occasion there was a small group of us, all students from abroad, who, brought up on German academic physiology, were trying his patience with our doubts about his clinical innovations. "But that can't be true," one of us objected, "it contradicts the Young-Helmholz theory." He did not reply "So much the worse for the theory, clinical facts come first" ... but he did say something which made a great impression on us: *"La théorie, c'est bon, mais ça n'empêche pas d'exister* [Theory is good, but it doesn't prevent things from existing]." (SE 3:13 / GW 1:23-24)

Freud sees in Charcot a form of vision—of sight and insight—that is bound up with another kind of contingency. He sees an innovative vision that disturbs, disrupts, and resists the saturation of the natural world by theoretical medicine. Charcot's insight appears suddenly, out of the blue, by chance, *plötzlich*. It is something one doesn't see coming. What *strikes* Charcot and what *leaves an impression* on his students also calls for a movement of appropriation (description, determination, knowledge). But this appropriation does not reduce the insight. Rather it leads to the enrichment or advancement of theoretical medicine: "No physician needs to be told what a wealth of forms were acquired by neuropathology through him [Charcot], and what increased precision and sureness of diagnosis were made possible by his observations" (SE 3:13 / GW 1:23).

Now if I have insisted on the positive function of contingency, it is because a happy accident lies at the heart of this book: the historic coupling of Freud and Derrida. The two men never met, of course (Derrida was nine in 1939 at the time of Freud's death), but they form a couple, precisely because of this, because of their "singular anachrony" ("Env" 191/206). Freud's dazzling insight leaves its indelible mark on Derrida; Freud is, for Derrida, along with Heidegger, one of the "two great ghosts of the 'great epoch'" ("Env" 191/206). But the reverse is also true: Derrida's mode of seeing has utterly transformed the way we—or at least some of us—read Freud today. In order to capture this "singular anachrony," I have decided to conjoin the two names. With different emphases, both parts of this book are called *Freuderrida*. I should say, however, that this word-name did not originate with me; it is the invention of Hélène Cixous, who uses it in her book *Philippines: Prédelles* (2009), a book that is about twins or "double almonds [*amandes jumelles*]."⁴ And though it appeared to me in a way that was purely serendipitous, its appearance in a literary work was perhaps no accident. Indeed, if literature also plays an important role in this book, it is because literature lends itself, often in an exemplary way, to the contingencies of the relation between reading and theory, that is, to those contingencies that make Charcot, Freud, and Derrida so remarkably insightful.

Thus, I have used the title *Freuderrida* to set the stage for "the mock battle of the Titans, which does not oppose but rather brings together Freud and Derrida" (P 13/26, modified). Brings them together in such a way as to keep the tension between them alive. As Cixous says: "they *steal the show from each other*" (P 13/26). Coiled around the letter *d* like a spiral ladder, the single-double word-name *Freuderrida* revealed to me the structure or *DNA* of the present book. Not only could I see the two names ("Freud" "Derrida") as strands, but I could also see the two strands being held together by a series of bases or bonds—the building blocks of the "living matter," or material life, of *Freuderrida*.

Freud and Derrida are thus bonded, in life and letter(s). But they are also implicated in a death that has, by chance, left its mark on this book. All of the chapters in this volume were written following the death of Jacques Derrida. And if I mark this death as a kind of starting point, it is because, in its own way, this book is driven by the question of the secret *affinity*, the secret *proximity*, between destructive and affirmative contingencies, between the destructive role of contingency in a trauma and the affirmative role of contingency in an analytic or deconstructive reading. Is it even possible, this book asks, to think the transformative potential of analysis, let alone what Derrida calls "the worldwide-ization of psychoanalysis" (DP2 134/184, 159/215), without at the same time taking this proximity into account? Is it not "precisely in the *proximity* of destruction that new articulations of desire can take place" (EHVS 296, my emphasis)?

For the Love of Psychoanalysis is a book about what exceeds or resists calculation—in life and in death. It is a book that takes us from what is "inside outside" the psyche to what is "inside outside" the theoretical framework of any single discipline. It is a book about what emerges, and perhaps only emerges, from the difference between psychoanalysis and deconstruction. In order "to say and to think what can barely be said and thought" (DP2 30/55), new terms are needed . . . terms such as *Freuderrida* or, as the book suggests (since there is never just one *Freuderrida*): *Freud*errida and Freu*derrida*.

Part I: "*Freud*errida" opens with a *différant* Freud, a Freud associated not with sexuality, repression, unconsciousness, and symbolization but with accidents and chance. It begins, that is, with the accidents both in and of Freud's writing, the unexpected insights that simultaneously produce and disrupt our received ideas of psychoanalytic theory. Whether this disruption is figured as a "foreign body," as "traumatic temporality," as "spatial unlocatability," or as the "death drive," it points to something, I will argue, that is neither simply inside nor simply outside the psyche, neither psychically nor materially determined. But if I have written *différant* with an "a," it is not only because Freud's legacy is split and double; it is also because the resistances of psychoanalysis will have had a powerful and lasting effect on Derrida.

Where Part I: "*Freu*derrida" *leaves us open* to the accidents of psychoanalytic writing, Part II: "Freu*derrida*" addresses itself to what transports us back and *limits the openness* of our horizon. The second part of this book begins, then, not with Derrida's thinking of openings or openness but with those moments where openness comes to a close. And here the example par excellence is the death penalty and the cruelty of its calculating decision:

> I would like to go with you in a single stroke [*trait*], step [*pas*], or shot [*flèche*] toward what it is that makes putting to death, the will or the desire to kill, the death drive intolerable. . . .
>
> It's because the death that one makes or that one lets come . . . is not the end of this or that, of this being or that being, of someone or something *in the world*. Every time it dies [*ça meurt*], it's the end of the world. Not of a world but of the world, of the whole of the world, of the infinite opening of the world. And this is the case for every living being: from the tree to the protozoa, from the mosquito to the human, death is infinite; it is the end of the infinite [*la fin de l'infini*]. The finite of the infinite [*le fini de l'infini*] . . . wherever there is death, the world closes itself [*le monde se ferme*]. The infinite makes itself finite, it comes to an end [*l'infini se finit*]. (DP2 80–81/118–19)

What is intolerable and unthinkable and thus, for Derrida, the "only thing worthy of being thought" (DP2 82/120) is the *end*: the closure of the infinite opening of the world. But what *precipitates* this end—both rhetorically and politically—is the death penalty, the calculating decision of the death penalty. If "Freu*derrida*" insists on the death penalty, if it returns to it compulsively (via the question of the question and the question of cruelty), it is not only because its "insuring and calculating drive" (DP2 157/213) is inseparable from the history of reason as philosophical reason. It is also because the death penalty provides us with one of the most spectacular and spectacularly obscene expressions of Freud's death drive. But let there be no mistake: If "Freu*derrida*" takes this death drive to heart, it is because, without it, there is no way forward, no way to think the *propulsive force* of Derrida's—and Freud's—"unconditional affirmation of life" (LLF 51/54).

In the end, you might say that *For the Love of Psychoanalysis* sees contingency with open eyes. With contingency comes risk, and we must never minimize this risk. Here I return to my original association, to the happy chance, the "positive contingency" of reading. What if my therapist, the one who asked me to take the MMPI, had been unable to read my figurative reading of *seeing* ("I see things that other people don't see")? What if this therapist had misread my (mis)reading? What if she had insisted on her literal reading, her normative reading of *seeing*? Who knows? Things might have gotten *positively dicey*. I might have ended up on a psych ward and not at my desk writing these words of introduction. Fortunately for me, my therapist took a chance . . . she took a chance and read *seeing* otherwise.

This book is not about my good luck with therapy, however. It is about the extraordinary chance that is ours—a chance that marks us *for life*—in the wake of *Freuderrida*.

PART I

*Freud*errida

CHAPTER I

Psychoanalysis and Neuroscience
(Foreign Bodies I)

The Oedipal Question

I should not have been so surprised by the question. After all, it came at a moment when "new materialisms" were all the rage in continental philosophy. And yet, when a graduate student asked me about the intersections of psychoanalysis and neuroscience, I flinched. Yes, I flinched. But probably not for the reasons you imagine. As an analyst and a feminist, it's true, I tend to be wary of discourses that, consciously or unconsciously, turn science into a phallic supplement—phalloscientific discourses in which neuroscience suddenly appears as a knight in shining armor capable of restoring a delicate and vulnerable psychoanalysis to its former glory by reaching out its helping hand. "Our aim," write Kaplan-Solms and Solms in their *Clinical Studies in Neuro-Psychoanalysis*, is "to supplement the traditional viewpoints of metapsychology with a new, *'physical'* [i.e., observable and measurable] *point of view*."[1] According to such discourses, psychoanalytic knowledge would be "far less secure than that of neuroscience."[2] What this means, predictably, is that psychoanalysis needs the big strong arms of neuroscience to set its traditional concepts on a "firm, organic foundation," a "new, and more secure, scientific footing" (BIW 104, 289). Psychoanalytic claims cannot be securely grounded until they have been *correlated* (and this is the magic word for "neuro-psychoanalysis")[3] with "concrete neurological mechanisms" (CS 147). Only when psychoanalysis has been joined with neuroscience in a *"lawful relationship"* (CS 260) can it become "a psychoanalysis that retains its pride of place as the science of human *subjectivity"* (BIW 314). But analysts be warned. If psychoanalysis pays neuroscience no heed, if it rejects the hand of this neuroscientific suitor, it will lose not only its "standing in the public sphere" (CS 249) but also its future: "This situation represents something of a crossroads for psychoanalysis. Psychoanalysts can choose to remain aloof from neuroscience . . . but . . . in the long term, a comprehensive neuroscience of subjective experience will be developed, *with or without* psychoanalysis" (BIW 314, my emphasis).

Now I would not want to reduce the exploration of the neural underpinnings of mental phenomena to a mere phalloscientific discourse (and though I have quoted, rather ungenerously, from the neuro-psychoanalytic literature, I do not think neuro-psychoanalysis can or should be reduced to this discourse). In fact, I find it hard to imagine that anyone interested in hysteria or psychosis would not also be interested in the neurodynamics of these phenomena—or that those who interpret dreams would not be curious to discover the physiological processes that occur in the tissues of our brains when we dream. But then again, this does not mean that I would want our literature departments, for example, to devote themselves to split-brain research because it can be shown that the "creative, narrative talent," the "interpreter mechanism," that is, the very capacity for fabulation, belongs to the left hemisphere.[4]

No, if I flinched, it was for another reason. I flinched because my father is a neurologist. He is the author of papers such as "Mapping Cerebral Blood Flow during Speech Production in Hereditary Ataxia" (2006), "Are Brain Functions Really Additive?" (1999), and "Abnormal Cerebral Glucose Metabolism in HIV-1 Seropositive Subjects with and without Dementia" (1996). If I flinched, it was because the intersections of psychoanalysis and neuroscience go straight to the heart of my family romance. "Neurology" and "psychoanalysis" are the signposts of my Oedipal crossroads. A further irony in this Oedipal story of *fons et origo* is that I had enlisted my father to help me retranslate Freud's 1891 monograph *On Aphasia* a few years ago only to discover that Mark Solms, Mr. Neuro-psychoanalysis, had already retranslated it. Curious about this new translation, I immediately wrote Solms and received the following reply:

Dear Dr. Rottenberg, I did indeed complete the authorized new translation of that book many years ago, as part of the four-volume edition of Freud's complete neuroscientific works. The publication was however delayed.... I'd be glad to send you a copy of my translation of the aphasia book for your private use, and I would also be delighted to have any comments you and your father might want to make on it.... With all good wishes, Mark Solms... PS: Do you know the origin of your family name? My family owned vineyards on the Rothenberg, in Nackenheim near Mainz, from the 1550s to [the] 1830s!

If I confess all of this in writing, it is not only to point to the amusing way in which my personal history is situated at the crossroads of psychoanalysis and neuroscience. It is also to suggest that one always, inevitably, raises the question of origins, indeed an Oedipal question, when one speaks of the intersections of psychoanalysis and neuroscience. For there is no way around it: What has been called for more than one hundred years now "psychoanalysis" was, in its founding moment, a deviation or departure from neurology. Whether we understand this departure as the radical rejection of localizationalism in classical German neurology[5] or as the revolutionary turn to a notion of psychical—as opposed to anatomical or physiological—reality, one thing is clear: Psychoanalysis had to throw off the tutelage of neurology in order to become itself, in order to become psychoanalysis.

So the question, the Oedipal question, remains. If the psychoanalytic revolution goes against a certain history of neurology, if its indispensable audacity of thought consists in—and I will quote Derrida here—"writing, inscribing, signing theoretical 'fictions' in the name of a knowledge without alibi" (FWT 173/281), then isn't this desire *to correlate* the phenomena of mental life with the structures and functions of the brain, isn't this desire to find a *neurological* alibi for psychoanalysis, a *neuroscientific* alibi for what "would be another name for the 'without alibi'" ("PSS" 240/13), isn't this desire a wish to return to a primal scene of separation in order to triumph over a Freud who was unable to achieve intersection with neuroscience, a wish to cancel out and thereby overcome the father's *correlatio interrupta*? Let me quote Mark Solms again (and I am quoting here from the final paragraphs of his book *The Brain and the Inner World*):

> Psychoanalysts can choose to remain aloof from neuroscience ... but ... in the long term, a comprehensive neuroscience of subjective experience will be developed, with or without psychoanalysis.

The high road for psychoanalysis is to engage with the neuroscientific issues that should now directly interest it. This will not be an easy task. Most psychoanalysts are unfamiliar with the complexities of neuroscience.... Some psychoanalysts today are, however, keen to rise to the challenge.... If a critical mass of psychoanalysts should choose this path, there is much to be gained.... A radically different psychoanalysis will emerge. It will be a psychoanalysis that retains its pride of place as the science of human subjectivity.... But its claims will be far more securely grounded.... And in the end, we believe, we shall be able to say with confidence at last: this is how the mind *really* works. (BIW 314–15)

In other words, we will be *free at last* of the great father figure who could tell us only how the mind *seemed* to work, whereas the neuro-psychoanalysts of tomorrow will be able to tell us how the mind *really* works. A new breed of psychoanalysts will emerge: a breed of superpsychoanalysts, neuro-psychoanalysts, able to rise to the challenge of neuroscience in a single bound and carry psychoanalysis to safety (where its "claims will be far more securely grounded").

To rephrase my question, then: To what extent does the drive to reconcile psychoanalysis with neuroscience risk participating (whether consciously or not) in a movement of appropriation, an attempt to reduce the *event* of psychoanalysis by innocently assuming, for example, Freud's departure from neurology to be but a temporary and remediable fact, an unfortunate accident resulting from the very inadequate state of neurological and physiological understanding at the time? Indeed, how not to suspect a movement of appropriation (or even a re-medicalization of psychoanalysis) when the very language of reconciliation (namely, "correlation") already, historically, belongs to one of the parties in question: "When Freud decided to specialize in neurology," write Kaplan-Solms and Solms, "it was still a relatively young discipline, which rested almost entirely on one scientific method. That was the method of *clinico-anatomical correlation*" (CS 6)?

In what follows, therefore, I would like to return to the "crossroads" of psychoanalysis and neuroscience in order to revisit an early but transitional moment in the history of psychoanalysis. As we will see, Freud's break with the French neurologist Jean-Martin Charcot, an Oedipal break avant la lettre, begins by underscoring a point of *noncorrelation* or *co-resistance* between organic and hysterical paralyses. But it does not end there. Rather, Freud's rejection of cerebral localization,[6] his rejection of the clinico-anatomical method of correlation in neurology, goes hand in hand with another kind of rejection, a rejection of another order or of another order of localization: the rejection of the strict localization of *psychical* suffering. For what we see emerge in Freud's early work on hysteria is a kind of *spatial unlocatability*.[7] Psychical suffering can never simply be located inside (in a material lesion, for example), nor can it simply be located outside (in an actual external event, no matter how catastrophic). What we find, in other words, or at least such will be my contention, is that, unlike neurology, which has traditionally tried to locate traumatic events in what Catherine Malabou calls "cerebral laws,"[8] psychoanalysis has always advanced another, more radical thinking of trauma, according to which there remains an essential unlocatability at the heart of any trauma. One might wonder, then, to what extent the neuro-psychoanalytic "quest to correlate psychoanalysis with neuroscience" (CS 235) is not, in the end, an attempt to correlate unlocatability with locatability, a kind of superlocalization (or "dynamic localization," as Kaplan-Solms and Solms call it). What I will try to show is that the neuro-psychoanalytic attempt to locate a psychoanalytic understanding of the mind *in* the brain does not, in fact, end up correlating psychoanalysis with neuroscience. Instead, I will argue, it points to another, less conciliatory model for their relationship.

Hysteria and the Question of Spatial Unlocatability

In his 1893 essay "Some Points for a Comparative Study of Organic and Hysterical Motor Paralyses [*Étude comparative des paralysies motrices organiques et hystériques*]" (1883 [1888–1893]), Freud points to an intriguing noncorrelation between organic and hysterical paralyses. A hysterical paralysis, he explains, is characterized by a paradox in organic terms. On the one hand, a hysterical paralysis is *precisely limited*: "It is not bound by the rule, which applies regularly to organic cerebral paralyses, that the distal segment is always more affected than the proximal one. In hysteria, the shoulder or thigh may be more paralyzed than the hand or the foot. Movements may appear in the fingers while the proximal segment is still absolutely inert" (SE 1:163/GW 1:43); "Next to an absolutely insensitive area of skin there will be one of absolutely normal sensibility. Along with a totally paralyzed arm there will be a perfectly intact leg on the same side" (SE 1:48/N 80). On the other hand, a hysterical paralysis is *absolute* to the most extreme extent: "The [hysterical] aphasic utters not a word, whereas the organic aphasic almost always retains a few words, 'yes' or 'no,' a swearword [*un juron*], etc." (SE 1:164/GW 1:45). In other words, by being both precisely limited and excessively intense, hysterical paralyses "diverge" (SE

1:166/GW 1:47) from organic cerebral paralyses, which "*cannot at the same time become absolute and retain [their] delimitation*" (SE 1:165/GW 1:45).⁹

This divergence will lead Freud to questions of etiology. As to the causes of organic motor paralysis, there is not the slightest doubt. To explain organic paralysis, one need only point to "the *facts* of anatomy [*les* faits *de l'anatomie*]," that is, to "the construction of the nervous system and the distribution of its vessels—and the relation between these two series of *facts* and the circumstances of the lesion" (SE 1:166/GW 1:47–48, my emphasis). These facts are what set neurology on the firm ground of reality: "Every detail of the cerebral paralyses is the clinical expression of *a fact* of anatomy [*l'expression clinique d'*un fait *anatomique*]" (SE 1:167/GW 1:49, my emphasis). Gone are the facts in hysteria. Hysterical paralyses and anesthesias of the various parts of the body are, on the contrary, "demarcated according to the popular idea of their limits and not according to anatomical facts" (SE 20:14/GW 14:38). Thus, Freud came to the conclusion (somewhere between 1888 and 1893, when he completes his comparative study) that an explanation for the clinical symptoms of hysteria would never be found in pathological anatomy: "I . . . assert that the lesion in hysterical paralyses must be completely independent of the nervous system, since *in its paralyses and other manifestations hysteria behaves as though anatomy did not exist or as though it had no knowledge of it*" (SE 1:169/GW 1:50–51).

In this way, Freud and Breuer's "Preliminary Communication" (1893),¹⁰ published in the same year as Freud's "Some Points for a Comparative Study of Organic and Hysterical Motor Paralyses," marks what is perhaps the most important terminological shift in Freud's thinking about the etiology of hysteria. For this is the text in which one finds the famous line: "*Hysterics suffer mainly from reminiscences*" (SE 2:7/GW 1:86). That is, the term "reminiscences" designates the (nonsomatic) *lesion*¹¹ that produces functional or dynamic alterations in hysteria. Hysterical lesions can no longer be understood as physical damage to the brain. Rather they result from another kind of mental disturbance, namely, the disturbance of memory.¹² Indeed, what "reminiscences" are in the context of hysteria and how they differ from normal memories becomes the subject of investigation not only in *Studies on Hysteria* but also in all of Freud's lectures and writings in the 1890s.¹³ The word "reminiscences," which translates the German word "Reminiszenzen," comes from the Latin verb *reminiscor*: "*to recall to mind, recollect, remember*" (Lewis and Short). Hysterics suffer from their memories. But the choice of the word "reminiscences," as opposed to the more colloquial "memories" or "recollections" (*Erinnerungen*), already tells us that what is at issue in hysteria is a particular and quite special sort of memory.

As Freud and Breuer explain, two features distinguish "reminiscences" from normal memories. On the one hand, reminiscences are precisely those memories that hysterical patients *cannot* remember. Or rather, what they remember is remembered unconsciously—in their bodies or through their bodies, *somatically*. Thus, the "Preliminary Communication" begins, in its opening paragraph, not with memory but with Freud and Breuer's observation of their patients' *inability* to remember:

> In the great majority of cases it is not possible to establish the point of origin [of the illness] by a simple interrogation of the patient. . . . This is in part because what is in question is often some experience which the patient dislikes discussing; but principally because he is genuinely unable to recollect it and often has no suspicion of the causal connection between the precipitating event and the pathological phenomenon [*den ursächlichen Zusammenhang des veranlassenden Vorganges und des pathologischen Phänomens nicht ahnen*]. (SE 2:3 / GW 1:81)

In other words, Freud and Breuer's patients' *inability* to remember—their inability both to recollect the point of origin of their illness and to establish a causal link between precipitating factors and pathological symptoms—*is* their illness. On the one hand, therefore, a hysterical memory is unremembered in the usual sense.

On the other hand, however, and this is where the irony of unremembered memories leads to something of a paradox: Hysterical memories are *unforgettable*. Indeed, the language of the "Preliminary Communication" attests to the surprise of this particular discovery. What is so striking about memories that have become the determinants of hysterical phenomena is their astonishing vividness, their remarkable clarity: "One of our patients reproduced . . . with hallucinatory vividness [*mit halluzinatorischer Lebhaftigkeit*] everything that had excited her on the same day the previous year"; another patient "re-lived with hallucinatory clarity [*mit halluzinatorischer Deutlichkeit*] all the events . . . which she had passed through ten years earlier" (SE 2:9 / GW 1:88). Memories that date back a quarter-century remain "astonishingly intact"; they possess "remarkable sensory force" and act "with all the affective strength of new experiences" (SE 2:9–10 / GW 1:89).

Just as traumatic dreams will disrupt the theory of dreams as wish fulfillment in *Beyond the Pleasure Principle* (as we will see in Chapter 2), so too hysterical reminiscences disrupt a theory of normal memory. Hysterical memories persist with such freshness and affective strength because they occupy an exceptional position with regard to the normal wearing-away of memories. Hysterical memories have not been disposed of by "abreaction" or by associative thought-activity (the way normal memories have). They have remained in a kind of limbo or dissociated state and have therefore become pathological. Without even going into Freud and Breuer's theory of repression, strangulated affect, and split-off psychical groups, it is clear that what causes hysterics to suffer is *a memory*, a particular and quite special kind of memory, an unremembered and unforgettable memory.[14]

But we might inflect this differently. What causes hysterics to suffer is *a memory* and not an experience or an event: "Hysterics suffer mainly from *reminiscences*." Indeed, we might be tempted to hear in the language of reminiscence a *prequel* to the abandonment of the seduction theory, a *d*eemphasis of external events in favor of internal or fantasied reality. And yet, I would contend, the language of "reminiscence" is what will allow Freud and Breuer not only to provide a new mechanism for hysterical phenomena but also to break with a medical tradition that regards hysteria as a "hereditary nervous taint" (SE 3:144/GW 1:408), a sign of "mental degeneracy" (SE 3:146/GW 1:411), an internal or "innate weakness" (SE 3:46/GW 1:60). I will suggest that the language of "reminiscence" is first and foremost a rethinking of the structure of what Freud called "traumatic neurosis," of the causal relation between external and internal events, between accidents and symptoms.

And more specifically it is a critique of the etiology put forward by Charcot in which the accident, the extrinsic and contingent event, plays a merely incidental or secondary role, is nothing but a trigger or *agent provocateur* in the determination of a hysteria:

> Charcot put forward a simple formula for [the etiology of hysteria]: heredity was to be regarded as the sole cause. Accordingly, hysteria was a form of degeneracy, a member of the *"famille névropathique."*[15] All other aetiological factors played the part of incidental causes, of *"agents provocateurs."* (SE 3:21/GW 1:33)

> The role attributed in [Charcot's] theory to nervous heredity is well known: it is the sole true and indispensable cause of neurotic affections, and the other aetiological influences can aspire only to the name of *agents provocateurs*. (SE 3:143/GW 1:407)

> As you know, in the view of the influential school of Charcot heredity alone deserves to be recognized as the true cause of hysteria, while all other noxae of the most various nature and intensity only play the part of incidental causes, of *"agents provocateurs."* (SE 3:191/GW 1:426)

The attention of physicians has remained dazzled [*éblouie*] by the grandiose prospect of the aetiological precondition of heredity. (SE 3:146/GW 1:410)

In spite of Freud's many encomia to Charcot (and Freud did, after all, name his oldest son after Charcot), his criticism here is obvious. Charcot greatly overestimated heredity as a causative agent in hysteria and in so doing left no room for acquired disorders, that is to say, disorders whose mechanism was *psychical* and not *hereditary* (SE 3:23/GW 1:35), *acquired* and not *dispositional* (SE 2:12/GW 1:92).[16]

Freud will go so far as to say that "heredity could have done nothing [*l'hérédité n'aurait pu rien faire*]" (SE 3:145/GW 1:410) had it not been for accidental factors and external events. To speak of a "disposition" or a "proclivity" to acquire hysteria is thus only to speak ex post facto: "Previously there was no evidence of [the] existence [of this proclivity]" (SE 2:122/GW 1:180–81).[17] Instead the "Preliminary Communication" singles out the accident. It emphasizes a *primary* relation, a *necessary* relation to contingent, external events:

> Accidental factors [*das akzidentelle Moment*] determine the pathology of hysteria to an extent far greater than is known and recognized. It is of course obvious that . . . what provokes the symptoms is the accident [*der Unfall*].[18] (SE 2:4/GW 1:82, modified)[19]

In other words, Freud and Breuer break *radically* with Charcot when they insist on the necessary causal connection between, on the one hand, the "accident" (SE 2:4/GW 1:82), the "precipitating event" (SE 2:3/GW 1:81), and, on the other, the symptoms or pathology of hysteria. "How greatly the claims of hereditary disposition are diminished," Freud writes, "by the establishment . . . of accidental aetiological factors [*der akzidentellen ätiologischen Momente*]" (SE 3:163/GW 1:381). Where Charcot minimizes the accidental factor in hysteria, Freud and Breuer make it a central causative agent.

What we see, finally, in the language of "reminiscence" is thus neither a retreat to interiority nor a simple positing of exteriority. It is a little as if Freud and Breuer's phrase "hysterics suffer mainly from reminiscences" were the response to a kind of spatial questioning. It is as if they were asking the question: Where does the trauma come from? Does the trauma come from the inside, from a place of pure interiority? Is it endogenous to the sufferer in its origin and its cause? To which the answer would be no, as we have seen. Then does the suffering come from the outside, from a place of pure exteriority? Is it external to the sufferer in its origin and its cause? Again the answer would have to be no. What the "Preliminary Communication" and *Studies on Hysteria* provide us with, in other words, is a way of thinking the spatial structure of trauma as *neither inside nor outside*. "Psychical trauma" (SE 2:6/GW 1:84) would come from an "inside outside" or an "outside inside."[20] And to a certain extent, it remains there, on this unlikely, unsettling boundary of the inside outside or the outside inside.

This is why Freud and Breuer offer us a new figure—a spatial figure—for the kind of causation involved in hysteria: the figure of the foreign body (*Fremdkörper*). This figure is meant to replace Charcot's *agent provocateur*, which appears in every text of Freud's in which the etiology of hysteria is discussed (one might even say that Charcot's French locution is already something of a foreign body in Freud's German text):

> The causal relation between the determining psychical trauma and the hysterical phenomenon is not of a kind implying that the trauma merely acts like an *agent provocateur* in releasing the symptom, which thereafter leads an independent existence. We must presume rather that the psychical trauma—or more precisely the *memory of the trauma* [thus what is traumatic, properly speaking, is not the event but the memory of the event]—acts like a *foreign body* [*nach Art eines* Fremdkörpers] which long after its entry must continue to be regarded as an agent that is still at work. (SE 2:6/GW 1:85, my emphasis) [Later, as we will see in Chapter 2, this will also become a temporal issue.]

> There is another kind of causation. . . . We can elucidate this from the picture of a foreign body [*durch das Bild des Fremdkörpers*], which continues to operate unceasingly as a stimulating cause of illness until it is gotten rid of. (SE 3:35/N 191)

Neither appropriable by the inside nor assimilable to the outside, the foreign body remains at the boundary of the inside outside. *It is the figure of psychical trauma as a figure of spatial unlocatability*. On the one hand, it cannot be reduced to biology or to fantasy (on the side of the internal). On the other hand, it cannot be reduced to bad external events (no matter how catastrophic), for *there is no such thing as an event that would be traumatic in and of itself; there is no such thing as a "traumatic event" if by this we mean that everyone will be traumatized by it.*[21]

Let me conclude this section by jumping to the last mention of the foreign body in *Studies on Hysteria*. In the very last chapter of this book (of which the "Preliminary Communication" is the first chapter), Freud refigures or rather disfigures this figure:

> We have said that [the memory of the trauma] behaves like a foreign body [*wie ein Fremdkörper*], and that the treatment, too, works like the removal of a foreign body from the living tissue. We are now in a position to see where this comparison fails. A foreign body does not enter into relation with the layers of tissue that surround it. . . . Our pathogenic psychical group, on the other hand, does not admit of being cleanly extirpated from the ego. Its external strata *pass over in every direction* into portions of the normal ego; and indeed they belong to the latter just as much as to the pathogenic organization. . . . The interior layers of the pathogenic organization are increasingly alien to the ego, but once more *without there being any visible boundary* at which the pathogenic material begins. In fact the pathogenic organization does not behave like a foreign body, but far more like an infiltrate [*wie ein Infiltrat*]. (SE 2:290/GW 1:294–95, my emphasis)

In the end, says Freud, there can be no clean boundaries between inside and outside. Even the foreign body loses its spatial delimitation and becomes an infiltrate. The line at which the pathogenic material passes over into portions of the normal ego does not take the form of a solid front (or confrontation); the lines between ego and alien remain undecided, indeterminable. And it is this theoretical insight that will lead Freud to reformulate his conception of the analytic process. Psychoanalytic treatment will no longer be about the removal or excision of what is pathological. It will be about the establishment of conditions that enable movement or circulation in areas that have been cut off.[22]

The Lesion as Site of Unlocatability

I would like to turn now to several clinical examples from the neuropsychoanalytic literature. In Chapter 8 of their *Clinical Studies in Neuro-Psychoanalysis*, Kaplan-Solms and Solms describe a series of patients who have sustained damage to the perisylvian region of the right cerebral hemisphere[23] and with whom they have also worked psychoanalytically. In all of these cases, they are seeking "the physical correlates of psychoanalytic knowledge" (CS 57). That is, they are seeking to map their psychoanalytic knowledge onto the neurological lesions in questions (lesions that can be dynamically located, even reproduced in images). One might say that they are trying to locate psychoanalysis *in* neurology. Yet, as we will see, it is precisely the differential emotional responses of these right-hemisphere patients that will lead them back to the basic concepts of psychoanalysis (and not the other way around). Here, for example, is how Oliver Sacks describes the symptomatic responses of these patients in his Foreword to *The Brain and the Inner World*:

> There are almost incredible states that . . . go with massive right-hemisphere lesions, where half the body may be neglected, disowned, or attributed preposterously to someone else—and such syndromes (it has seemed to neuroscientists like V. S. Ramachandran as well as to Solms) . . . involve a form of repression, and not just neural disconnection. (BIW x)

Indeed, much of the clinical work with right-hemisphere patients—patients whose unawareness of their illness is the cardinal symptom of their illness—would seem to contradict or at least to complicate certain rather provocative claims made by Catherine Malabou[24] in *Ontology of the Accident*:

> The denial [*dénégation*] that accompanies anosognosia—a brain pathology whereby patients are unable to recognize themselves as ill—is not a denial in the Freudian sense. When the patient does not see that his left side is paralyzed, when he feels neither pain nor anxiety after a major brain injury, he is not responding to an affective imperative . . . one that would be unconsciously calculated. He doesn't see because he can't see, end of story [*c'est tout*]. (OA 89, modified)

As Kaplan-Solms and Solms's clinical examples show, however, this is hardly the end of the story. In the case of Mrs. A, for example, we have the "paradoxical coexistence" (CS 175) of severe anosognosia, on the one hand, and profound depression, on the other: "We are thus faced with a paradoxical situation in which Mrs. A was depressed about the very events that she simultaneously denied had ever happened in the first place" (CS 177). How can a patient with a full-blown right-hemisphere syndrome (a patient who has no conscious awareness of her impairment) be at the same time severely, even suicidally, depressed about her impairment?

The answer, given by Kaplan-Solms and Solms, is *denial in the Freudian sense*:

> Here . . . the concept of unconscious knowledge is indispensable to us. This concept allows us to say that Mrs. A's depression . . . was a reaction to *knowledge that she was defending herself against*. This loss . . . could . . . only be experienced *indirectly*, by way of conscious derivatives of her disavowed knowledge. Thus, whenever her therapist attempted to

explore analytically what it was that Mrs. A . . . had lost, she responded by telling him about all manner of *minor losses*, which seemed totally out of proportion to her depth of feeling. For example, she frequently said in this connection that she had lost her spectacles, or that somebody had stolen her cigarettes, and then she would burst into tears. (Incidentally, the reason why she kept losing these things was because she was hemianopic and topographically amnesic.) (CS 177)

As a result of their analytic work with right-hemisphere patients, Kaplan-Solms and Solms conclude that "negative emotions are not absent in these cases but, rather, *dynamically suppressed*" (CS 175, my emphasis). Indeed, it is a little as if the very foundational concepts of psychoanalysis (in this case, repression) were emerging for neurology at the very site of a material lesion, as if right-hemisphere lesions had, paradoxically, become the locus of neurology's resistance to its own empirico-localizationist tendencies. Over and over again these clinical examples testify to a fact, the basis of which is no longer simply neurological: the fact that (unconscious) negative affect can "break through"[25] into the consciousness of patients who are neurologically incapable of (conscious) negative affect. What this means, ironically, is that it is no longer hysterical patients but neurological patients with right-hemisphere lesions who are here behaving "*as though anatomy did not exist or as though [they] had no knowledge of it*" (SE 1:169/GW 1:50–51).

But this is not all. For not only do we have right-hemisphere patients who are capable of negative affect in spite of a "literal deficiency" (CS 174); we also have patients who present a "paradoxical form of neglect" (CS 152). Instead of ignoring the left-hand side of their bodies, these patients become obsessed with it: "This variation on neglect," write Kaplan-Solms and Solms, "has not been adequately integrated into contemporary neuropsychological models of the mechanisms underlying the [right-hemisphere] syndrome" (CS 152). Take, for example, Mr. D, another right-hemisphere patient, whose paradoxical "neglect" has taken the form of a near-psychotic hatred of his left hand:

> I can't live like this. . . . I'll *smash* this hand into a *million* pieces. . . . I'm giving my hand six months and if it has not improved, I will come back and ask for an artificial claw. . . . I can't live like this; I'm going to have it amputated. . . . When I first came into this hospital I *bit* my hand and *spat* the pieces of meat out, because I *can't* stand it! (CS 190–91)

Mr. D's left hand has literally become a *Fremdkörper*, a foreign body, an object foreign to his body. It must be smashed, amputated, bitten, spat out, or replaced by an artificial claw. If he does not pulverize and expel this hand from his body, it will destroy him: "I can't live like this," "I *can't* stand it." What is a part of his body must be removed from his body in order for his body to remain his own. It is as if Mr. D's left hand had triggered an autoimmune response, as if his body had turned on itself, mistaking a part of itself for a loathsome and repulsive other: "I'll *smash* this hand into a *million* pieces"; "I'm going to have it amputated." Thus, what we have in the mangled, dislocated image of Mr. D's left hand is not only the symptom of another right-hemisphere patient (of the "cerebral laws" involved in right-hemisphere damage) but also the singular—projective, defensive, even paranoid—response to the event of a right-hemisphere lesion.

Inexplicably, then, "*the same lesion site* can produce . . . opposite emotional reactions: unawareness of a limb and denial of its deficits, versus obsessive hatred of a limb and its imperfections" (BIW 269). What this means is that the psychical response to the same neurological event ("*the same lesion*" [CS 195], "*the same lesion site*" [BIW 269]) is never determined solely by the organic lesion. If "*the same lesion can produce two diametrically opposite emotional states*" (CS 195), then there always remains something accidental—beyond the accident of the neurological event—about the emotional state to which the organic lesion gives rise.

Psychoanalysis as Foreign Body

As we have seen, neurology's appeal to psychoanalysis raises the problem of locatability once again. In the psychoanalytic concept of repression, neurology encounters a *Fremdkörper*, something unassimilable to its inside, something forever "inside outside" any neurological theory of trauma. This *Fremdkörper* prevents neurology from reducing neurological traumas to mere cerebral laws (according to which the same neurological events would be the same for all brains). *It is what makes every neurological trauma traumatic in its own way.*

Thus, as we have seen, both the figure of the "foreign body" and the clinical, neuropsychoanalytic studies of right-hemisphere patients point to the spatial unlocatability of trauma. And, although there can be no clean boundaries between space and time, I would like to shift to the question of *temporal* unlocatability in trauma. Indeed, I will suggest in Chapter 2 that it is by thinking spatial and temporal unlocatabilities together that psychoanalysis raises a new—and singularly incisive—question about the accident and the possibility of "accidental structures."

And this returns me to my student's question and to the phalloscientific discourses with which I began. Instead of trying to "supplement the traditional viewpoints of metapsychology with a new, '*physical*' *point of view*" (CS 251), instead of trying to bolster and fortify the psychoanalytic viewpoint with "neurochemical correlates" (CS 237), we ought perhaps to take Mr. D's wayward appendage to heart—and to remember that psychoanalysis may always *bite* the hand that feeds it.

CHAPTER 2

Traumatic Temporalities
Freud's Other Legacy

> It may be that we have studied the sexual impulses too exclusively,
> and that we are in the position of a mariner whose gaze
> is so concentrated on the lighthouse that he runs on to the rocks
> in the engulfing darkness.
>
> —D. M. THOMAS, *The White Hotel*

A Necessary Detour

What do we hear when we hear the name "Freud"? What do we associate with this venerable legacy? As it happens, I have conducted this little experiment with my undergraduate students at DePaul University. In fact, every time I teach a "Topics in Psychoanalysis" class, I ask my students this question. Although most undergraduates have never read a word of Freud, their *associations* to the name "Freud" are remarkable not only for their abundance and diversity but also for their historical-mindedness, which is quite astonishing given my students' usual fuzziness about history. In less than ten minutes, the blackboard will be filled with words like "dream interpretation," "sexuality" (one time I even got "polymorphously perverse sexuality"), "libido," "hysteria," the "unconscious," the "id," the "ego," the "superego" . . . but also "cocaine addiction." In the years immediately following the release of David Cronenberg's film *A Dangerous Method* and Mark St. Germain's play *Freud's Last Session*, the words "sado-masochism," "oral pleasure," and "jaw cancer" also appeared on the board.

If I mention this little experiment, it is not only to regale you with my students' amusing associations. It is also to mark some glaring omissions, namely, those features of Freud's legacy that have been left out of this associative network. Indeed, the Freud I will explore in this chapter, like the Freud of Chapter 1, is not the Freud of our familiar associations but another Freud—the Freud associated not with sexuality and wish fulfillment but with trauma and the peculiar temporality of *Nachträglichkeit* (often translated as "deferred action," "belatedness," "afterwardsness," or *après coup* in French). One might say, of course, as some do say and will continue to say until their dying day, that even when Freud speaks of trauma really what he is speaking of is sexuality, that what Freud calls the "death drive" is in fact nothing but a reiteration of the destructive and self-destructive aspects of sexuality, that the "death drive" is simply the death drive *of* sexuality (a "sexual *death* drive" as opposed to a "sexual *life* drive").[1]

In this chapter I would like to inflect the Freudian heritage *otherwise* and say, not exactly the opposite (not, that is, that sexuality is *trauma* or an allegory of trauma), but rather that sexuality was from the start a privileged place from which to talk about *trauma*. "The sexual element," says Freud in *Studies on Hysteria*, is "more liable than any other to provide occasion for traumas [*Anlaß zu Traumen gibt*]" (SE 2:103 / GW1:160). And this language of vulnerability, a vulnerability to trauma, persists. In his *Three Essays on the Theory of Sexuality*, Freud maintains that "sexuality remains the weak spot [*schwache Punkt*]" in the "process of human cultural development" (SE 7:149/ GW 5:48). Shifting the emphasis from sexuality to trauma, then, this chapter will argue that for twenty-seven years, from the "Preliminary Communication" to *Beyond the Pleasure Principle*, from 1893 to 1920, this "weak spot"—sexuality—served as a kind of necessary detour for thinking about *trauma*. It was necessary for *The Interpretation of Dreams* to establish a theory of dreams as wish fulfillment in order for Freud to be "astonished" by the dreams occurring in traumatic neuroses. It was necessary for psychoanalytic theory to be founded on repression, unconsciousness, and symbolization in order for trauma to be recognized as constituting a rupture in the symbolic system. Just as there can be no Freudian legacy of trauma without the legacy of sexuality, no rupture of the symbolic system without the symbolic system, so too can there be no truly *Freudian* heritage, I will argue, without the legacy of trauma, traumatic temporality, and, as I will propose at the very end of this chapter, the strange and counterintuitive notion of an *accidental structure*.

Thus, although it is true that one might speak of the irreducibly traumatic nature of sexuality, trauma and sexuality will not be the topic of this chapter. Rather I will argue that it is *precisely* when we forget that trauma is not limited to sexuality (or sexual trauma) that we miss something essential in Freud's thinking and writing about trauma. In other words, this chapter will move away from sexuality in order to read trauma in its relation to accidentality. Because sexuality is *constitutive* of the human—because it is a kind of *necessary* accident—it prevents us from thinking the true radicality of the traumatic accident in Freud.

In Chapter 1, I pointed to the figures of the "foreign body" (*Fremdkörper*) and the "infiltrate" (*Infiltrat*) in order to address *the question of spatial unlocatability* in trauma: Does the traumatic event come from the inside or the outside? In this chapter—notwithstanding that there can be no clean boundaries between space and time (we speak of "space-time")—I would like to shift the question to that of *temporal unlocatability* in trauma. The aim of this chapter is to connect Freud's early emphasis on the accidental factor in hysteria in *Studies on Hysteria* to his notoriously controversial speculation on the death drive in *Beyond the Pleasure Principle*. Indeed, if I turn to this second moment in Freud's discussion of trauma, it is because *Beyond* is magnetized by questions whose particular theoretical (but also clinical) significance still requires clarification:

1. *The question of temporal unlocatability*: What does it mean for an event to be missed?
2. *The structural question*: Are we all traumatizable? And if the answer is no, as I think Freud thinks it is (and as all empirical studies show it to be), must we not rethink the question of structure through the accident: Can a structure—namely, that which makes possible a trauma—simply be an accident?[2]

(De)location, (De)location, (De)location

When one of my colleagues first heard me use the term "delocation" (an ugly term I used to characterize Freud's departure from the localizationist tradition of nineteenth-century neurology), he immediately intoned: "location, location, location."[3] And it is true. In Freud's thinking of trauma, it is all about "(de)location, (de)location, (de)location," and this from the very beginning. As we saw in Chapter 1, psychoanalysis was, in its founding moment, a deviation or departure from the localizationist tradition of neurology. More specifically, it was a deviation or departure from theories of hysteria that tried to *locate* hysteria in a dynamic lesion. Charcot always believed that hysterical symptomology had a physiological explanation.

Although no anatomical lesion could be found in patients with hysterical paralyses, Charcot remained convinced that there must be a lesion, a "dynamic lesion,"[4] located in that part of the brain where an anatomical lesion would be in the case of an organic paralysis. Charcot believed it was at least theoretically possible to locate hysterical pathology in neuroanatomical regions.[5]

If psychoanalysis's first "delocation" was its departure from the localizationist tradition of nineteenth-century neurology, its second "delocation" was more internal. It was internal to Freud's early psychoanalytic theories according to which trauma could be located *in* the actual seduction of a child by an adult. Indeed, one must remember that when Freud shifts the ground of hysteria away from Charcot—from heredity to sexuality—he does so in two stages. In Chapter 1, I emphasized the question of spatial unlocatability in *Studies on Hysteria*, but I ignored the specificity of *sexual* trauma in favor of the more general *psychical* trauma. I also avoided Freud's early, programmatic statements about the place of precocious sexual experience in hysteria (what is often referred to as the "seduction theory"). For Freud insists, in his early texts, on the sine qua non of precocious sexual experience in the etiology of hysteria, to the point of turning precocious sexual experience into the new "heredity": "For [*Charcot*] nervous heredity occupied the place which *I* claim for the precocious sexual experience [*la place que* je *réclame pour l'expérience sexuelle précoce*]" (SE 3:155 / GW 1:420, my emphasis).[6] If I did so, it is not only because Freud found himself "dazzled" for a time by the grandiose prospect of the seduction theory.[7] It is also because I wanted to underscore the question of unlocatability that occupies Freud in all of his writing on trauma. That is, from the earliest days of the seduction theory, in the days when Freud still believed in his "*neurotica*,"[8] there was always another "delocation" at work in Freud's thinking of trauma, namely, the temporal delocation or dislocation that goes by the name of *Nachträglichkeit*.

Before we look at *Beyond the Pleasure Principle*, therefore, I would like to turn briefly to this term, which is used by Freud specifically in the context of sexual trauma. The term *nachträglich* or *Nachträglichkeit* is a term that has been discussed at length by French analyst Jean Laplanche, who suggests that we translate it in English as "afterwards" or "afterwardsness."[9] Although the term *Nachträglichkeit* disappears from Freud's major text on trauma, it will be recast and reformulated in *Beyond the Pleasure Principle* as a *temporal* model of trauma that challenges traditional conceptions of temporality. Once again, in other words, hysteria will have been the wellspring of a double legacy in Freud: On the one hand, it leads to the seduction theory, to the abandonment of the seduction theory, to the theory of infantile sexuality and primal phantasies; on the other, it leads to a rethinking of trauma, to the hypothesis of the repetition compulsion and the death drive.

Nachträglichkeit reflects Freud's early understanding of the sexual etiology of hysteria. But it does so by emphasizing the *temporal* dimension or *temporal* complexity of trauma: "A trauma," says Laplanche, "is situated entirely in the duplicitous play producing a kind of seesaw effect between . . . two events."[10] The example par excellence is the case of Emma, a case that is mentioned only in Freud's posthumous "Project for a Scientific Psychology" (this text, written in 1895—thus at the same time as *Studies on Hysteria*—was not published until 1950). Here is Freud's description of Emma in the "Project":

> Emma is subject at the present time to a compulsion of not being able to go into shops *alone*. As a reason for this, [she produced] a memory from the time when she was twelve years old (shortly after puberty). She went into a shop to buy something, saw the two shop-assistants . . . laughing together, and ran away in some kind of *affect of fright* [Schreckaffekt]. . . . Further investigation . . . revealed a second memory. . . . On two occasions when she was a child of eight she had gone into a shop to buy some sweets, and the shopkeeper had grabbed at her genitals through her clothes. (SE 1:353–54/N 445).

As Laplanche argues in *Life and Death in Psychoanalysis*, neither of the two events is *in itself* traumatic. The first one triggers nothing: "The child, at the time she is the object of an adult assault, would not yet possess the ideas necessary to comprehend it [*ne posséderait pas encore les représentations nécessaires à sa compréhension*]" (LDP 41/73). And the second event is, if anything, even less traumatic: "What is involved . . . is a nonsexual event, a banal scene out of daily life: going into a shop in which there are two assistants, perhaps convulsed with laughter" (LDP 42/74). Yet the second scene, a nonsexual scene, awakens the memory of the first.

So how is it, Freud asks in his discussion of the case, that "a memory can arouse [awaken: *erweckt*] an affect which it did not arouse [awaken: *erweckt*] as an experience" (SE 1:356/N 447, modified)? How is it, we might ask, that an affect not experienced at the time of the "experience" is experienced belatedly, *nachträglich*, as the result of a memory? What is the cause of this "interpolated pathological process" (SE 1:356/N 447)? The simple answer, the developmental answer, is "puberty": "Here we have the case of a memory arousing an affect that it did not arouse as an experience, because in the meantime the change [brought about] by puberty had made possible a different understanding [*ein anderes Verständnis*] of what was remembered" (SE 1:356/N 447).

Only with puberty, in other words, can Emma *understand* what happened. Only with puberty can she arrive at a "different understanding of what was remembered," namely, a full understanding of the sexual nature of the assault. Thus, the first moment (when she enters the store as an eight-year old) is a moment of not understanding, a moment of incomprehension. Emma is confronted, unprepared, with a sexual act that is highly significant but whose signification she cannot understand. Left hanging, isolated, dissociated, split-off, incomprehensible, the memory of the first moment is not in itself pathogenic or traumatizing. It only becomes pathogenic or traumatizing when it is revived by a second moment that enters into association with the first. So, in the second moment, the first moment is remembered, understood (though it is not a conscious understanding), and at the same time repudiated—this is when Emma runs away in a state of fright and her hysterical symptoms begin. Thus, given the fact of the new possibilities of reaction that have arisen with puberty—"the *sexual release* [Sexualentbindung]," as Freud calls it (SE 1:356/N 447)—it is the newly revived memory (it is a new-old or an old-new memory, a *reminiscence*) that serves as the source of traumatic energy:[11] "We invariably find," writes Freud, "that a memory is repressed which has only become a trauma *nachträglich* [afterwards, belatedly]. The cause of this state of things is the retardation of puberty [*die Verspätung der Pubertät*] as compared with the rest of the individual's development" (SE 1:356/N 448).[12]

As Freud's use of the term *nachträglich* makes clear here, Emma's "trauma" is not to be located in either moment (it is not locatable in the first moment when she enters the store at eight, nor it is locatable in the second moment when sees the assistants laughing). It is not locatable in either moment but only in the relation—only in the play or the "seesaw-effect"—between the two. And maybe this is the place to recall that this *nachträglich*-effect (this afterwards or belated-effect) is the effect of the infiltrate, such that spatial and temporal unlocatabilities become expressions or versions of the same structure. I will also return, when we get to *Beyond the Pleasure Principle*, to what appears to be the *nachträglich*-affect (with an *a*, this time), namely the affect of fright (*Schreckaffekt*).

The Question of Temporal Unlocatability

But what if we extended this temporal understanding of sexual trauma to trauma in general and war trauma in particular? Indeed, what if we did so precisely on the basis of the temporal delay that seemed so clearly linked to the "retardation of puberty," that is, to the particular features of human sexuality and human sexual understanding? What if, in other words, Emma's sexual assault was traumatic not because her understanding of sexuality was delayed *by puberty* (though this was certainly the case) but because an immediate or timely understanding of what was happening to her was, in a sense, impossible? I will argue in what follows that Freud's temporal definition of trauma in *Beyond the Pleasure Principle* provides us with just such an extension of the concept of *Nachträglichkeit*. With his introduction of the temporal model of trauma in *Beyond*, as we will see, Freud transforms what was an *empirical* delay (the "retardation of puberty") into a *structural* delay—namely, an untimeliness that is (or becomes) part and parcel of Freud's definition of "trauma." Perhaps Freud also, belatedly, recognized that Emma's trauma was less a "sexual" trauma than a violence to which (her) sexuality made her particularly vulnerable.

Beyond the Pleasure Principle opens with Freud's astonishment—*his* incomprehension—before the phenomenon of repetition compulsion. The patients he observes in the wake of World War I are war veterans whose symptoms seem to defy all recuperation by the pleasure principle. Flashbacks, traumatic dreams, and the constant reliving of battlefield events are painful manifestations that can no longer be understood in terms of psychic meaning. When the repetition compulsion acts in opposition to the pleasure principle, says Freud, it gives the appearance of "some 'daemonic' force at work" (SE 18:35/GW 13:36). We see this daemonic force at work in cases where patients are repeatedly brought back to the situation of their accident:

> Dreams occurring in traumatic neuroses have the characteristic of repeatedly bringing the patient back into the situation of his accident, a situation from which he wakes up in another fright [*mit neuem Schrecken erwacht*]. This astonishes people far too little. . . . Anyone who accepts it as something self-evident that their dreams should put them back at night into the situation that caused them to fall ill has misunderstood the nature of dreams. It would be more in harmony with their nature if they showed the patient pictures from his healthy past or of the cure for which he hopes. (SE 18:13/GW 13:10)[13]

Traumatic dreams bring about the return of an unpleasurable event that forces itself upon the psyche again and again. There is something compulsively self-destructive about traumatic dreams that cannot be reconciled with the psychoanalytic theory of dreams as wish fulfillment. Instead, traumatic dreams constitute a breach in the theory of wish fulfillment. They challenge the dominance of the pleasure principle. Hence, traumatic dreams are doubly traumatic: They are traumatic for the patient who dreams them, and they are traumatic for the theory that owes its therapeutic power to the dominance of the pleasure principle. "This would seem to be the place," says Freud, "at which to admit for the first time an exception to the proposition that dreams are fulfilments of wishes" (SE 18:32/GW 13:32).

According to Freud, however, this demonic force or compulsion is linked to an attempt to protect the life of the organism. By returning to the event over and over again, consciousness tries, retrospectively, to protect the psyche, to master the stimulus, to grasp the event that was not fully grasped in the first place:

> [Traumatic] dreams are endeavoring to master the stimulus retrospectively, by developing the anxiety whose omission was the cause of the traumatic neuroses. They thus afford us a view of a function of the mental apparatus which, though it does not contradict the pleasure principle, is nevertheless independent of it and seems to be more primitive than the purpose of gaining pleasure and avoiding unpleasure. (SE 18:32 / GW 13:32)

Traumatic dreams, says Freud, have a more archaic function than wish fulfillment. They repeatedly return the dreamer to the scene of the trauma in an effort to protect her or him belatedly from the accident for which s/he was not prepared.

Here Freud is using dreams as an example of traumatic symptoms (a particularly striking example given his theory of wish fulfillment), but such symptoms are also found in (conscious) waking life (flashbacks, for example). In all of these examples, ultimately, the failure to protect the psyche, the failure to master the stimulus, reflects a failure of consciousness. And in order to understand this failure, Freud must speculate on the origin of consciousness. Consciousness arises, he speculates, out of the living organism's need for protection against stimulus coming from the outside:

> This little fragment of living substance [*dieses Stückchen lebender Substanz*] is suspended in the middle of an external world charged with the most powerful energies; and it would be killed by the stimulation emanating from these if it were not provided with a protective shield against stimuli. (SE 18:27 / GW 13:26)

Consciousness functions like a barrier protecting the organism from excessive amounts of stimulation and excluding unsuitable kinds of stimuli. Freud compares consciousness and its use of the sense organs to "feelers"

(*Fühlern*) that are always "making tentative advances towards the external world and then drawing back from it" (SE 18:28 / GW 13:27). What causes trauma, therefore, is a breach in an otherwise efficacious barrier against stimuli: "We describe as 'traumatic' any excitations from outside which are powerful enough to break through the protective shield" (SE 18:29/GW 13:29). Implicit in this breach of the stimulus barrier is a quantitative model of trauma: "The stimulus barrier protects the organism from *too much stimulus* coming from the outside."[14]

But consciousness is also what perceives, recognizes, comprehends, and interprets on the basis of a horizon of anticipation and knowledge. Hence consciousness is "a barrier of sensation and knowledge that protects the organism by placing stimulation within an ordered experience of time" (UC 61). According to this model, trauma would be a rupture in the horizon of anticipation and knowledge, a "break in the mind's experience of time" (UC 61). Thus, when Freud defines trauma in terms of "the factor of surprise [*das Moment der Überraschung*]" (SE 18:12/GW 13:9–10), "the element of fright," and the "lack of any preparedness for anxiety" (SE 18:31/GW 13:31), his model of trauma is no longer quantitative but temporal:

> We may, I think, tentatively venture to regard the common traumatic neurosis as a consequence of an extensive breach being made in the protective shield against stimuli. This would seem to reinstate the old, naïve theory of shock. . . . [It] regards the essence of shock as being the direct damage to the molecular structure . . . of the nervous system, whereas what we seek to understand are the effects produced on the organ of the mind. . . . And we still attribute importance to the element of fright. It is caused by lack of any preparedness for anxiety. (SE 18:31/GW 13:31)

It is the element of fright that distinguishes a breach in the mind from a breach in the molecular structure of the nervous system, a *psychical* trauma from a *physical* trauma. "Fright," writes Freud, "is the name we give to the state a person gets into when he has run into danger without being prepared for it; it emphasizes the factor of surprise" (SE 18:12/GW 13:9–10). What produces a traumatic neurosis, in other words, is a fundamental lack of preparedness, *a structural immaturity or vulnerability against which there can be no developmental safeguard*. What causes trauma, then, is an event that comes *too soon*, an event that we do not see coming, an event that surprises us and suspends our comprehension. And it is not only *what* we do not understand but also *that* we do not understand, the fact that we do not understand: our incomprehension.[15]

Which is another way of saying that consciousness comes too late: "The threat is recognized as such by the mind *one moment too late*" (UC 62). Or that what Freud calls "trauma" is an inherent belatedness in relation to the event. Trauma is *nachträglich* or delayed as such. It is not the event but precisely the missing of the event. *A traumatic "event" is a missed event.* Thus, in *Beyond the Pleasure Principle*, *Nachträglichkeit* is what structures the traumatic "event." For this reason *Nachträglichkeit* can no longer be linked to a specific event like the retardation of puberty. *Nachträglichkeit* becomes, rather, *the structure of delay as such*; it becomes the structure that determines a trauma.[16]

And finally it is this structural belatedness, this structure of delay, that leads Freud to his final, most radical, and most controversial hypothesis in *Beyond the Pleasure Principle*: the theory of the death drive. According to Freud's own avowedly "far-reaching" (*weitausholende*) speculation in *Beyond*, trauma must be linked, ultimately, to an originating force: the drive at the beginning of life to return the organism to an inanimate state. Like repetition compulsion (its most conspicuous expression), the death drive is an attempt to restore an earlier state of things that was disrupted as a result of "external disturbing and diverting influences" (SE 18:38/GW 13:39). In this case, however, the external disturbing and diverting influences are the *attributes of life itself*: "The attributes of life were at some time evoked [awakened: *erweckt*] in inanimate nature by the action of a force of whose nature we can form no conception. . . . The tension which then arose in what had hitherto been an inanimate substance endeavored to cancel itself out" (SE 18:38/GW 13:40). Thus, the *accident of life* would be the original missed event, a missing whose universal symptom is the death drive. In this way, the structure of delay seems to become, for Freud, the originating structure of all human experience.

Still, the question cannot fail to arise: If the structure of delay lies at the origin of life, if it is, as Freud describes it, an originating structure, would this not mean that we are all traumatized or bound to be traumatized? Would it not mean that every accident is a trauma? Would it not mean that everything is potentially traumatic and that each of us is equally traumatizable? And finally, how do we reconcile this notion of originary structure with the specificity of war trauma in *Beyond*?

Here I would like to return to the question of accidentality, for the temporality of trauma allows us to speak of another, a new order of accidentality; it allows us to speak of an accidentality to the second degree.

What emerges from *Beyond the Pleasure Principle* is a new and perhaps unresolvable tension: Is trauma defined by *a structure* (the structure of delay), or is it defined by *an event* (and Freud gives us very concrete examples of events in *Beyond*: "railway disasters," "accidents involving a risk to life," "the terrible war which has just ended" [SE 18:12 / GW 13:9])? What is the nature of the accident that becomes a trauma? And I think we can find an answer in Freud. Freud's repeated insistence, from the very beginning, from his earliest work on hysteria, his insistence on the accidental quality, the surprise, the ungraspability, indeed the *incomprehensibility* of the event hints at two very different senses of "accident." For every accident that Freud describes in *Beyond* is two things at once: (1) It is an example of an actual, concrete, life-threatening or integrity-threatening *event*, and (2) it is an example of the *structure* of traumatic accidentality, that is, it is an example of the structure of delay. Only, it would seem, when an accident is both things at once—both event and structure—does it become traumatizing. What this means, then, is that *no given event* can in advance, with certainty, necessarily, be said to produce a trauma. That is, it is always an accident *whether or not* any particular "accident" will be traumatizing (indeed, it is impossible to predict who will be traumatized after which event).[17]

In the end, then, one might say that Freud is drawing an essential distinction between two kinds of structure: a necessary structure and an accidental structure (this would be the difference between something that must occur—that is, an accident that would inevitably lead to trauma—and something that may but *may also fail to* occur).[18] Indeed, one might sum up this essential difference by recalling not only that (1) an accident may always fail to occur (we are not all the victims of trauma) but also that (2) even if an accident does occur, it does not occur for everyone. Thus, for Freud, not only are we not all traumatized (though we may all be castrated!), but we are also not all necessarily traumatizable.

Let me just conclude by saying that to think trauma as an accidental structure is in no way to diminish the emotional wounds of trauma. On the contrary, it is to begin to think the reality of traumatic experience through the unsparing effects of the accident, that is to say, through the accident's dislocations of time and space.

CHAPTER 3

Is There Such a Thing as a Psychical Accident?

The "Accidents" of Psychoanalysis

It is a well-known truism of psychoanalysis that "nothing in the mind is arbitrary or undetermined" (SE 6:242 / GW 4:270–71).[1] "There are no accidents," says my analyst whenever I make a slip of the tongue. "Everything is interpretable." Try as I might *not* to hear such statements as philosophical pronouncements about the world, my irritation sometimes gets the best of me. And in my impatience I do what someone who teaches philosophy for a living is prone to do: I deflect attention from my parapraxis and lecture my analyst on the complexities of the accident. I explain to him that he is confusing the concrete accident (in this case my parapraxis) with the concept of accidentality in general. He is confusing the *Unfall* (the accident that is, in principle, always interpretable) with the *Zufall* (the uninterpretable chance occurrence). And I tell him—just to rub it in—that Freud never made that mistake. Freud did, after all, acknowledge chance occurrences (*Zufälle, Zufälligkeiten*),[2] though, it is true, he did not believe there were any accidents in the unconscious.

So imagine my surprise when I chanced upon an opinion piece in the *New York Times* entitled "The Accidents of Psychoanalysis."[3] Finally, I thought, here is someone who is going to address the problem of accidents and accidentality in psychoanalysis. Here is an analyst who will take the accident seriously. And sure enough, Jamieson Webster begins by grappling with the accidents that have befallen her patients. Here is what she says:

> In the aftermath of what we shrinks call "August"—a euphemism for the acute clinical moments that our patients experience while we're away for the standard three to five weeks of vacation—I found myself reflecting on a series of physical accidents that befell too many of my patients during my break not to note.
>
> If two patients fall down stairs . . . one more falls off her bike and yet another suffers severe burns, what am I to make of this? Was it a coincidence? Or were their mishaps somehow a continuation of their work with me in analysis?

What gives rise to Webster's reflection on the accident are the *falls*, the literal falls, that have taken place while she was away: two patients *falling down* stairs, one patient *falling off* her bike, and a fourth *felled* by fire. Indeed, by drawing our attention to these injuries, Webster illustrates, in her choice of clinical examples, an essential feature of the accident, namely its downward movement. The word "accident" is descended from the Latin *cadere*, which means *to be driven or carried by one's weight from a higher to a lower point, to fall down, be precipitated, sink down, go down, sink, fall* (Lewis and Short). This is why, one might say, accidents are not simply what befall us; they are also what affect our upright stance.[4] They cause us to fall headlong to the earth or into the fire . . . or (back) onto the analyst's couch.

But neither are these accidents—and here Webster simply abandons the question of the *Zufall*—chance events, that is, events occurring out the blue. On the contrary, they have a very discernible cause or culprit: *Analysis* is the rainmaker. Unlike my analyst, for whom there were no accidents, Webster allows for lots of accidents, lots and lots of *meaningful* accidents. In a word, she wants to have it both ways. She wants to have her accident and interpret it too. On the one hand, she wants the "physical accidents," the "mishaps" that have "befallen" her patients, to have the power of what happens unintentionally and unexpectedly, by chance, *zufällig*—hence the significance of the word "accident" in her title and throughout her essay. On the other hand, she wants her patients' falls to be interpretable, analyzable, that is to say, motivated by unconscious desire and attributable to the work of analysis (they are the "accidents *of psychoanalysis*").

Indeed, from her opening line—"I found myself reflecting on a series of physical accidents that befell too many of my patients"—it is clear that the sheer number of falls, the *incidence of coincidence*, has led Webster to see the bungled actions of her patients as something other than "purely accidental miscarriages of motor actions" (SE 6:174/GW 4:193). When bad things happen to good patients, when August becomes the cruelest month, an analyst must take note. For the accident itself has become symptomatic; it has become the sign or symptom of analytic work at work, of analytic work in action:

> Analysis stirs the pot, brings things to the surface and, to follow this thought to its limit, makes accidents happen. As analysis gathers momentum, something powerful and strange, something uncanny, seems to be at work, which Freud likened to "summoning the demons from below." . . . How, I wonder to myself, can patient and analyst endure such a perilous affair? The alarming thought is that I act as a dark conduit, providing a place for a demonic contingency to rear its fateful head. As consolation, I remind myself that our biggest problem as therapists is simply that nothing happens.

Although it is true that "we shrinks" might do well to post a warning sign on our consulting-room doors (perhaps something like "Danger: analysis at work!" or "Danger: hazardous area!" or perhaps simply "Proceed with caution!"), there is no need for us to take out any supplementary insurance. No, as Webster's essay demonstrates, all is well that ends well. In the final analysis, both the concept of "accident" and the patient who suffered "third-degree burns all over her body" are doing fine, following their rehabilitation. What was bad has been made therapeutic. In fact, it is precisely through—and presumably only through—the accident that the patient comes to a newfound understanding about herself and her body. The patient's "severe burns" have allowed her to recognize her separation from her mother and to "*feel* this insight on her body" *for the first time*:

> [The patient] said that with her injury, she finally felt that she could know something about the difference between her pain and her mother's. . . . The accident differentiated their pain for the first time. . . . Now, you might say that . . . the burns were unnecessary to [the] treatment. But that's precisely what I've found *isn't* the case in therapy. . . . Change often happens through a chance event that connects and rewrites the meaning of an earlier one.

Thus, Webster moves effortlessly from third-degree burns to a narrative of therapeutic change through the rewriting of the accident. This is *the good news*, I suppose. And we might even speak of the patient's *fortunate* fall. And it is not just a fortunate fall; it is also a literal falling that—assuming it does not kill you or maim you—is psychoanalytically fortunate. Though Webster simply hints at the paradox here, it is clear that the patient's third-degree burns have had a healing effect. They fall in very well (and convincingly) with Webster's interpretation of skin as the "demarcating line between me and you," and they have a transformative effect to the extent that they give another truth, an analytic truth about separation/individuation, its chance. What is a little third-degree burn if it allows you to gain insight about your body? And in the end, to make matters worse—that is, better—Webster subsumes the very concept of "accident" to the "wondrous accident" that is life. Waxing beatific, she concludes: "Accidents, not heredity or biology, are destiny. Every case is a story of the accidental."

Now don't get me wrong. I am all for life, and I think psychoanalysis is a *good thing*, a thing that ought to be loved, supported, even practiced. For this reason, in fact, I think we must remain vigilant when it comes to the accident and the question of accidentality in psychoanalysis. To recuperate the accident (*Unfall*) too quickly, to reduce it (and, with it, the *Zufall*) to a universalizable structure—either by ontologizing it, as Catherine Malabou does in her *Ontology of the Accident*, or by idealizing it, as Webster does here—is not only to put one's actual (as opposed to psychical) life at risk. It is also to miss what is most radical when it comes to Freud's thinking about the accident. For to speak of the "ontology of the accident" is, as we saw in Chapter 1, to contain the accident within "cerebral laws"; it is to recognize, identify, describe, and thus determine the accident as a "constant virtuality of being."[5] It is to forget that, from the very beginning, psychoanalysis always advanced another thinking of the accident beyond the accident to which we are all vulnerable (biologically, neurologically, etc.). As we saw in Chapter 2, Freud singles out the accident in his early work on trauma and points to another order of accidentality, an accidentality to the second degree, according to which it always remains an accident whether or not any particular "accident" becomes traumatizing. In this way, even neurological accidents could not be reduced to mere "cerebral laws"; every neurological trauma was traumatic in its own way.

In her article, Webster considers the accident not in ontological but in hermeneutic terms. There may always be an unconscious intention behind the accident: "Physically, [my patient] took the brunt of the injuries, and in her telling of the accident, there was . . . an element of intentionality to [it].

Why might [she] want to bear these burns (or think she might want to)?" Indeed, in this context, it is hard not to think of Freud and of his interpretations of bungled actions (and Freud is the only authority Webster cites in her article). And yet for Freud—or for my analyst, for that matter—the bungled action that results from the repression of an unconscious intention is precisely *not* an accident (although it may certainly *appear* to be one). That is, Freud never tried to have it both ways. In his discussion of "apparently accidental injuries [*scheinbar zufällige Schädigungen*]" (SE 6:178/GW 4:198) in his chapter on "Bungled Actions" in *The Psychopathology of Everyday Life* (1901), Freud puts it very simply:

> The outsider [or nonanalyst] will find no occasion to see in the accident [*Unfall*] anything other than a chance occurrence [*Zufall*], while someone [e.g., the analyst] who is closely connected with the victim and is familiar with intimate details has reason to suspect the unconscious intention behind the chance occurrence [*Zufall*]. (SE 6:186n1/GW 4:206n1)

The accident is thus no accident for the analyst, who is able to recognize and interpret the unconscious purpose behind the chance occurrence. The analyst sees the bungled action for what it is: the result of an *"unconscious yet operative"* intention (SE 6:272n1/GW 4:302n1). In other words, where Webster claims that analysis "makes accidents happen," Freud says just the opposite. He says that analysis, the work of interpretation, makes accidents *unhappen*.

But let us entertain Webster's theory for just a little while longer. If bungled actions *do* occur more frequently in analysis, if analytic work *does* increase the incidence of faulty acts or faulty functions (and I have no statistical evidence to the contrary), must we conclude, then, that this relation is one of cause and effect? Might we not argue, on the contrary—much as Freud did in Chapter 3 of *The Psychopathology of Everyday Life* or again in Lecture 3 of his *Introductory Lectures*—that it is one thing to claim that bungled actions occur more frequently under certain conditions and quite another to claim that these conditions are their cause: "That would be to confuse the *mechanism* of a process, which is the same in all cases, with the factors *favoring* the process, which are variable and not necessarily essential" (SE 6:21/GW 4:27, my emphasis)? Indeed, in this case, I think it is clear that the mechanism of a bungled action is the same whether or not a person is in analysis (unless, that is, one wanted to argue that the unanalyzed population is free of bungled actions or that the bungled actions of the unanalyzed are qualitatively different from those of the analyzed). The most one could say, therefore, is that—by stirring the pot, by "summoning the demons from below"—analysis serves to *facilitate or favor* the occurrence of bungled actions. What this means of course is that we would have to think facilitation *with* analysis's hermeneutic drive, that is, with its compulsion to make the accident unhappen. Ultimately, though, we would still be left with an undoing of the accident as accident, since these accidents would then be overdetermined events produced for the sake of interpretation.

In what follows, I would like to suggest that we Freudianize Webster's question (or what I take to be her question) by shifting our attention from the accident to the chance occurrence. What if we asked not about the accident, not about the *Unfall*, but about the *Zufall*? What if we asked about random chance and its relation to the unconscious? And what if we did so precisely in the text—*The Psychopathology of Everyday Life*—where psychoanalysis makes the accident unhappen? What is the role of chance in a bungled action? Must we concede that an unconscious intention always arrives at its destination?

Chance and/in the Unconscious

To frame this question, I would like to fast-forward fifteen years to the *Introductory Lectures* (1916–1917), where Freud begins by recapitulating his views on the parapraxes (*Fehlleistungen*). Now what is striking in this recapitulation, it seems to me, is Freud's insistence on their harmless and inconspicuous nature: "All of these occurrences," he tells his audience—and he has just mentioned slips of the tongue (*Versprechen*), slips of the pen (*Verschreiben*), misreadings (*Verlesen*), mishearings (*Verhören*), the temporary forgetting of names or intentions (*Vergessen*), the mislaying or losing of objects (*Verlegen, Verlieren*), errors of a temporary nature (*Irrtümer*)—"they are almost all of an unimportant kind ... and they are without much significance in human life. Only rarely does one of them, such as losing an object, attain some degree of practical importance. For that reason, too, they attract little attention, give rise to no more than feeble emotions, and so on" (SE 15:26/ GW 11:19).

On the one hand, of course, Freud underscores the inconspicuous and harmless nature of the parapraxes for strategic reasons. Where all the other sciences have set aside the parapraxes as being "too unimportant—the dregs ... of the world of phenomena [*der Abhub der Erscheinungswelt*]" (SE 15:27/ GW 11:20), psychoanalysis has recognized their importance. It has not made the mistake of confusing the "vastness" of the problem with the "conspicuousness" of what points to it (SE 15:27/GW 11:20). The result of this has been that psychoanalysis has boldly gone where no science has gone before: It has shown that everything down to the smallest slip of the pen is meaningful and can be interpreted.

On the other hand, however, I would note the following: Freud's insistence on the inconsequential nature of the parapraxes is *significant* in another way. It is significant because it involves the forgetting or omission of a whole category of faulty acts. It is significant, that is, *as parapraxis*. In his rather long list of parapraxes (*Versprechen, Verschreiben, Verlesen, Verhören, Vergessen, Verlegen, Verlieren, Irrtümer*), Freud fails to include *Vergreifen* (bungled actions), which, it so happens, are among the *least* harmless and *most* conspicuous of the parapraxes. To put it in clinical terms: The word "*Vergreifen*" has fallen prey to a repression. So how is it, one may ask, that Freud has forgotten an entire chapter of *The Psychopathology of Everyday Life*? Or, more importantly, given the theory he is expounding here, what is the nature of this forgetting? What is the unconscious motivation behind this apparent accident? Indeed, when it becomes apparent that Freud not only omits to mention bungled actions in his long list of parapraxes (at the beginning of Lecture 2) but also restricts his discussion of them (at the end of Lecture 4) to cases in which an unconscious intention "disguises itself [*maskiert sich*]" as a fortunate or "a *lucky* accident [glücklicher *Zufall*]" (SE 15:77/GW 11:73, my emphasis),[6] it is hard not to suspect a disavowal at work. So what about the cases, so prominent in *The Psychopathology of Everyday Life*, where people injure themselves and risk their own safety? Why have the *Introductory Lectures* pointedly avoided all discussion of the more "serious parapraxes" (SE 6:125/GW 4:138)? Might there be a danger, a chance of danger (for psychoanalysis)—or the danger of chance—in returning to them?

Early on in *The Psychopathology of Everyday Life*, Freud claims that "serious parapraxes . . . are brought about in exactly the same way as . . . innocent ones" (SE 6:125/GW 4:138). Yet even in this text where he will devote a chapter to bungled actions, the question of serious harm seems difficult to confront head on. Twice Freud broaches the subject of a serious bungled action of a medical nature (on the assumption that "a slip of the pen on the part of a doctor who is writing a prescription possesses a significance which goes far beyond the practical importance of ordinary parapraxes" [SE 6:122/GW 4:135]), and twice he conjures it away. "Here again," he concludes at the end of his second example,[7] "the bungled action was a harmless one. . . . This still leaves open the question of whether we may admit the possibility of an unconscious intention in mistakes that can cause serious harm" (SE 6:178/GW 4:197–98).

Having raised the question for a third time, however, Freud stops short. Like an analytic patient whose resistance has been stimulated, Freud is able to go no further: "Here . . . my material leaves me in the lurch . . . and I have to fall back on conjectures and inferences" (SE 6:178/GW 4:198). What follows in his text is speculation, speculation about the use of external events by the unconscious for purposes of self-injury and self-destruction. Now, in the 1901 version of *The Psychopathology of Everyday Life*, Freud can produce no examples from his own practice. Instead he will fall back on the examples of others (Ferenczi, Van Emden, Stärcke). Only in 1907 is he able to provide an example of his own, but when he does, as we will see in a moment, it is the perfect example.

Notwithstanding his many starts and stops or the many editions of *The Psychopathology of Everyday Life*, Freud's chapter on "Bungled Actions" is wonderfully consistent. In all of the examples of bungled actions that end in self-injury (and many involve falling: falling out of a carriage, falling off a horse, stumbling on a heap of stones and falling against the wall of a house, etc.), Freud's conclusion will be the same. Acts that appear to be the "result of chance [*Zufall*] or of unintentional clumsiness [*absichtslosen Ungeschicklichkeit*]" (SE 6:169/GW 4:187) end up serving "unavowed purposes in a very clever way [*in sehr geschickter Weise*]" (SE 6:168/GW 4:186, modified). In short, we must never underestimate the cleverness of the unconscious. Where unconscious intentions are concerned (and concealed), acts that appear clumsy are in fact "exceedingly adroit and well-directed [*höchst geschickt und zielbewußt*]" (SE 6:167/GW 4:185), "unerring" (SE 6:168/GW 4:186) in their aim, "ingenious [*geschickt*]" (SE 6:179/GW 4:198) in their contrivances. They are carried out "with the dexterity [*Geschicklichkeit*] of a conjurer" (SE 6:176/GW 4:195), and they achieve their goals with a certainty that is positively "somnambulistic" (SE 6:140, 142, 168, 250/GW 4:156, 157, 186, 279).[8]

But nowhere is the cleverness of the unconscious more apparent and more striking than in its dealings with chance. Indeed, it would seem that chance doesn't stand a chance when it comes to the unconscious. And this is especially true in cases of self-injury or self-destruction:

> What happens is that an impulse to self-punishment, which is constantly on the watch . . . takes ingenious [*geschickt*] advantage of an external situation that chance happens to offer [*eine zufällig gebotene*

äußere Situation], or lends assistance to that situation until the desired injurious effect is brought about. (SE 6:179 / GW 4:198)

[Self-destruction with an unconscious intention is] capable of making skillful [*geschickt*] use of a threat to life and of disguising [*maskieren*] it as a chance mishap [*zufällige Verunglückung*]. (SE 6:180–81 / GW 4:200)

Even a *conscious* intention of committing suicide chooses its time, means and opportunity; and it is quite in keeping with this that an *unconscious* intention should wait for a precipitating occasion which can take over a part of the causation and, by engaging the subject's defensive forces, can liberate the intention from their pressure. (SE 6:181 / GW 4:201)

These are far from idle thoughts. And the consequences are extremely disturbing. Not only can an unconscious intention take advantage of whatever terrible thing chance happens to throw out, not only can it use, exploit (*ausnützen*), and force (*nötigen*) chance to do its bidding, but it can also pass itself off *as* "chance."[9] And if all of this were not bad enough, Freud adds a footnote in which sexual assault becomes an example of self-injury. Like other "precipitating occasions" that weaken a subject's defenses, sexual assault can result from a "portion of [the woman's] unconscious impulses meet[ing] the attack with encouragement" (SE 6:181n1 / GW 4:201n1).[10] In other words, there is no random chance event that cannot be used (self-)destructively by the unconscious.

But, I would ask: Is it not also the case that the unconscious needs chance? For we must not overlook the fact that "repressed thoughts and impulses . . . do not achieve expression in symptomatic acts and parapraxes by their own unaided [*nicht selbständig*] efforts" (SE 6:270 / GW 4:300). On the contrary, Freud tells us, "the technical possibility" of a bungled action must be examined "independently" of this action and of the repressed intention (SE 6:270 / GW 4:300). Without chance, that is, the unconscious intention to self-injury or self-destruction would have no chance of defeating the subject's defensive forces and crossing the repression barrier. For there is always more than one intention at work in what is called a parapraxis. "Parapraxes," Freud reminds us, "are the outcome of a compromise: they constitute a half-success and a half-failure for each of the two intentions at work" (SE 15:66 / GW 11:61). Self-injuries are no different in this respect: "Self-injuries are as a rule a compromise between the self-destructive drive and the forces that are . . . working against it" (SE 6:181 / GW 4:200, modified). Would it not be the case, then, that there remains something undecidable and uninterpretable about the role of chance in a compromise? After all, chance may have provided an occasion for self-injury, but it may just as well have provided an alternative to self-destruction. Who can say, finally, if this compromise is a triumph or a fall? Would it not be more accurate to say that there is something inherently *chancy* about such a compromise?

As we have seen, then, it is by taking the *Zufall* as *Unfall*, it is by reducing chance to an interpretable category, that Webster ends up rehabilitating the physical accidents of her patients: "Now, you might say that . . . the burns were unnecessary. . . . But that's precisely what I've found *isn't* the case." Her concretization of chance leads to its interpretability but also to an idealization of the accident (the idealization of an interpretable act or event). Freud, too, always suspected an unconscious intention behind a chance occurrence (*Zufall*), and he always assumed that the "severe parapraxes" were interpretable "in exactly the same way as the innocent ones" (SE 6:125 / GW 4:138). Yet it is he who—by not reducing the *Zufall* to the *Unfall*—unwittingly opens the *Unfall* to an uninterpretable *Zufall*. Though I will do no more than suggest a few historical connections here, I think this resistance to interpretation would take us both back and forward in Freud's work: It would take us back to *das akzidentelle Moment* (the accidental aspect, the accidental factor) that determines the structure of trauma in *Studies on Hysteria* (1895), and it would take us forward to *Beyond the Pleasure Principle* (1920), where Freud defines the structure of trauma—and ultimately of the drive—as an accident-like event whose "meaning" lies precisely in its insistent resistance to interpretation, that is, in the repetition of an untimely occurrence.

The Language of Chance

To conclude this discussion of "'self-punishment by means of parapraxes'" (SE 6:185n1 / GW 4:205n1), I would like to return for a moment to Freud's 1907 example of a bungled action that causes serious harm. The case is that of a young woman who breaks her leg in a carriage accident. Here is how Freud describes the accident and the events preceding it:

> The young woman was staying with her jealous husband on the estate of a married sister, in company with her numerous other sisters and brothers with their husbands and wives. One evening in this intimate circle she showed off one of her accomplishments: she gave an accurate performance of the can-can, which was received with hearty applause by her relatives but with scanty satisfaction by her husband, who afterwards whispered to her: "Carrying on like a tart again!" The remark struck home—we will not inquire whether it was only on account of

Is There Such a Thing as a Psychical Accident? 45

the dancing display. She spent a restless night. Next morning she felt a desire to go for a ride.... During the drive she showed signs of nerves; she warned the coachman that the horses were growing skittish, and when the restless animals were really causing a moment's difficulty she jumped out in a fright and broke her leg, while the others who stayed in the carriage were unharmed. Although after learning these details we can hardly remain in doubt that this accident [*Unfall*] was really contrived, we cannot fail to admire the skill [*Geschicklichkeit*] which forced chance [*den Zufall nötigte*] to mete out a punishment that fitted the crime so well. For it had now been made impossible for her to dance the can-can for quite a long time. (SE 6:179–80/GW 4:199)

The example, it would seem, is Freud's speculation come true. The young woman's impulse to self-punishment has taken "ingenious advantage" of the carriage ride in order to bring about a punishment that fits her crime.[11] No more can-can, no more carrying on like a tart, no more showing off or performing in public for *this* young woman. It is the perfect punishment: "It had now been made impossible for her to dance the can-can for quite a long time." But it is also the perfect *example* of punishment insofar as the apparent effects of randomness can be placed wholly in the service of an unconscious truth.

And, in a way, it is also the perfect crime. Freud tells us that the young woman's performance of the can-can is accurate—skillful even, *kunstgerecht*—and that it is received "with hearty applause [*unter großen Beifall*]" by her relatives. And even if we cannot trust the relatives, we can take the husband's spiteful comment as proof of the quality of his wife's performance. This is where the accident comes in. When the young woman jumps from the carriage, she breaks her leg. But if it is no accident that the woman breaks her leg jumping from a carriage, then it can also be no accident that she does so following a very successful performance. After all, "break a leg!" is an idiom used in theater to wish a performer good luck (in German *Hals- und Beinbruch*! Break a neck and a leg!). To break a leg is to perform well, and that is exactly what the young woman has done. Indeed, we might imagine another interpretation of the accident and another unconscious intention, one in which the young woman not only countersigns her performance but also issues a *tart* reply to her husband: "I broke a leg," the accident would be saying, "I performed well!"

Here, one might say, it is the idiom itself that introduces another order of accidentality, for it is *by chance* that "break a leg" has come to mean what it means. Perhaps I could put it this way: If the young woman jumps out of the carriage to break her leg, then what she exemplifies is Freud's theory of interpretable accidents. But if she jumps from the carriage to act out the idiom "break a leg!"—if she is "follow[ing] willy-nilly the signifier's train,"[12] to quote Lacan—then what she exemplifies is the accidental way in which "break a leg!" has come to signify a successful performance.[13]

Now despite the fact that the possibility of this *accidental determination* may be a kind of traumatic accident at the heart of meaning, such a possibility is also a chance because it is inseparable from the ingenious (*geschickt*) way in which meaning is posited.

Fat chance, though, that such a linguistic accident would satisfy my analyst.

CHAPTER 4

What Are the Chances? Psychoanalysis and Telepathy

(Foreign Bodies II)

Telepathy or the Communist Manifesto

To set us on our way, I would like to begin with two lines by George Eliot that describe to a T Freud's attitude toward occultism (so T is for Telepathy; T is for Thought Transference). Here are the lines:

> In such states of mind the most incredulous person has a private leaning towards miracle.[1]

> Who supposes that it is an impossible contradiction to be superstitious and rationalizing at the same time?[2]

The first quotation is from *Middlemarch* (1871–1872), and I quote it not only because it resonates with what, in the "Occultism" chapter of his three-volume biography, Ernest Jones calls Freud's "exquisite oscillation between skepticism and credulity,"[3] his "ambivalent attitude" (J3 390) toward the world of mysticism, his being "in two minds" (J3 392) about whether to make public his views on telepathy. I also quote it because it foreshadows, uncannily, almost to the letter, Freud's own statement, in "Dreams and Occultism" (1933 [1932]), about "the secret inclination towards the miraculous [*die*

47

geheime Neigung zum Wunderbaren]" of someone who regards himself "as a sceptic" (SE 22:53/GW 15:57). As Eliot writes: "The most incredulous person [i.e., the skeptic] has a private leaning [Freud: *geheime Neigung*] towards miracle [Freud: *zum Wunderbaren*]." The second quotation comes from *Daniel Deronda* (1876), and it is posed as a rhetorical question, a question asked in order to make a statement rather than to elicit a response: "Who supposes that it is an impossible contradiction to be superstitious and rationalizing at the same time?"

Now if you read the "Occultism" chapter in *The Life and Work of Sigmund Freud*, you will see that what was simply a rhetorical question for the great English novelist becomes, for Freud's biographer, a remarkable but also a lamentable fact. For analysts who, like Jones, "have undergone a biological, and particularly a neurological, training" (J3 376), the fact that "highly developed critical powers may coexist in the same person with an unexpected fund of credulity" (J3 375) is a hard fact to swallow. And Jones makes no bones about it. In anecdote after anecdote, letter after letter, Jones will bellyache about Freud's primitive thinking and prescientific attitude. Here is just one example from the opening pages of "Occultism":

> In the years before the Great War, I had several talks with Freud on occultism and kindred topics. He was fond, especially after midnight, of regaling me with strange or uncanny experiences with patients, characteristically about misfortunes or deaths supervening many years after a wish or prediction. He had a particular relish for such stories and was evidently impressed by their more mysterious aspects. When I would protest at some of the taller stories Freud was wont to reply with his favorite quotation: "There are more things in heaven and earth than are dreamed of in your philosophy."[4] Some of the incidents sounded like mere coincidences, others like the obscure workings of unconscious motives. When they were concerned with clairvoyant visions of episodes at a distance, or visitations from departed spirits, I ventured to reprove him for his inclination to accept occult beliefs on flimsy evidence. His reply was: "I don't like it at all myself [*Ich mag das alles nicht*], but there is some truth in it," both sides of his nature coming to expression in a short sentence. I then asked him where such beliefs could halt: if one could believe in mental processes floating in the air, one could hold on to a belief in angels. He closed the discussion at this point (about three in the morning!) with the remark: "Quite so, even *der liebe Gott*." This was said in a jocular tone as if agreeing with my *reductio ad absurdum* and with a quizzical look as if

he were pleased at shocking me. But there was something searching also in the glance, and I went away not entirely happy lest there be some more serious undertone as well. (J3 381)

Jones is not amused. He is not amused by Freud's "jocular tone" or "quizzical look." Making light of occult topics is no joke for Jones. It's no joke because he suspects that behind Freud's levity lies a more serious, and therefore a more dangerous, undertone. Were the father of psychoanalysis truly to believe in ghosts, were he to take seriously the existence of telepathy and thought transference,[5] it would be a terrible setback for psychoanalysis. An association with "hocus-pocus and palmistry" (J3 395), as Jones puts it, "could only add to the odium that already invest[s] the 'unscientific' subject of psychoanalysis" (J3 386). In other words, it's a double whammy for Jones: Not only does telepathy call attention to the already shaky marriage between science and psychoanalysis ("the 'unscientific' subject of psychoanalysis"), but it also risks exposing psychoanalysis to further condemnation (the odium, the odium!). Indeed, it is clear from Jones's letters and the tone of his "Occultism" chapter (a chapter in which he also famously disparages Ferenczi: "Ferenczi believed he was being successfully psychoanalyzed by messages transmitted telepathically across the Atlantic from an ex-patient of his" [J3 407])[6] that the censorious spirit conjured up by Freud at the end of his "Dreams and Occultism" lecture[7] is none other than that of Jones: "'Here's another case,' laments the spirit, 'of a man who has done honest work as a scientist all through his life and has grown feeble-minded, pious and credulous in his old age'" (SE 22:54/GW 15:58).

For Jones, then, psychoanalysis must be defended. The prejudice against telepathy is so strong that any association with it could only have the effect "of delaying the assimilation of psychoanalysis" (J3 393) and giving strength to its opponents. Thus, when Freud publishes the short text entitled "The Occult Significance of Dreams" (1925),[8] a text in which, Jones tells us, Freud "pretty plainly indicated his acceptance of telepathy" (J3 394) and then, only a few months later, sends out his circular letter of February 18, 1926, in which he not only avows his "conversion to telepathy" but also declares that he is no longer interested in shielding the body (the institution, the state, or "superstate")[9] of psychoanalysis from the "scandal" of its association with occultism, Jones goes ballistic. It is as if Freud has thrown a "bomb into the psychoanalytic house" (J3 394). Indeed, this breach of homeland security seems to have provoked in Jones something like an anticathexis on a grand scale. Jones must scramble to master and bind the large amounts of stimulus that have broken in and threaten psychoanalysis at the very core of its rationality. In his letter of February 25, 1926, Jones tells Freud to cut it out, to keep his seditious speech to himself: "In your private political opinions you might be a Bolshevist, but you would not help the spread of psychoanalysis by announcing it. So when 'considerations of external policy' [this was Freud's phrase in his letter of February 18] kept you silent before I do not know how the situation should have changed in this respect" (J3 395). Because the personal is political—because, as Jones insists, "psychoanalysis is Freud" (J3 395)—Freud must keep his commie pinko telepathic leanings to himself.

Now if I mention this exchange of letters it is because Freud's response to Jones exemplifies something rather remarkable about his treatment of telepathy and thought transference more generally. As he later writes in "Dreams and Occultism": "We are once again left with a *non liquet*; but I must confess that I have a feeling that here too the scales weigh in favor of thought-transference" (SE 22:54/GW 15:58). I declare the area of thought transference unclear, unproven, undecidable, *but* at the same time I decide. In his response to Jones, this *ambitendency* is even more pronounced: Freud accepts *and* simultaneously rejects telepathy.[10] On the one hand, he assimilates telepathy to his person, that is, to his bodily person (to the Jewish smoker that he is). On the other hand, he eliminates telepathy from the body or being (*Wesen*) of psychoanalysis. That is, he eats his cake and he vomits it too:

> I am extremely sorry that my utterance about telepathy should have plunged you into fresh difficulties. But it is really hard not to offend English sensibilities. . . . When anyone brings up my Fall into Sin, just answer calmly that my conversion to telepathy is my own private affair, like my Jewishness, my passion for smoking . . . and that the theme of telepathy is in essence alien [*wesensfremd*] to psychoanalysis. (J3 395, modified)[11]

That is, Freud responds to Jones by splitting his (Jewish) body from the body of psychoanalysis. It's true, says Freud, that I believe in telepathy, but long live (the science of) psychoanalysis.

Freud splits the ticket: "yes" to telepathy when it comes to himself, "no" to telepathy when it comes to psychoanalysis (or at least this is what he tells Jones to say to those who bring up his "Fall into Sin"). But isn't this dissociation between the body natural and the body politic a rather abrupt way of gathering things up and marking limits? When we know that Freud took a public position on the topic of telepathy,[12] when we know that he struggled for years with its "theorization" ("Tel" 256/266), can we be satisfied with a distinction or opposition of this kind? And then, of course, there are the testimonies. We know from Anna Freud that telepathy "fascinated as well as repelled"[13] her father; we know from Max Eitingon that it "perplexed [Freud] to the point of making him lose his head" ("Tel" 258/268).[14] And, finally, we know from Freud that the subject of telepathy was a never-ending source of resistance for him: "Nothing can be done," he tells us in "Psychoanalysis and Telepathy," "against such . . . clear resistance" (SE 18:190/GW 17:41). All of which would suggest that there is something about Freud's resistance that makes it more cryptic—and more interesting—than Jones's.

Certainly there is resistance, one might say, "but resistance to what? To whom? Dictated by whom, to whom, how, according to what routes [*voies*]?" ("Tel" 423n1/237n2).[15] We begin with this paradox: If Freud returns again and again to telepathy, if he struggles with its theorization, it is not, as Jones would have it, in order to thwart "the relentlessness and monotony of the laws of thought . . . and the demands of reality-testing" (SE 22:33/GW 15:34–35). On the contrary, as we see in all of Freud's telepathy texts, it is in order to drive science beyond science, beyond the state or system of contemporary science. Psychoanalysis, Freud writes as early as "Psychoanalysis and Telepathy" (1941 [1921]), is driven by "a sense of shame that science has . . . refused to take cognizance of what are indisputable problems" (SE 18:178/GW 17:28). Psychoanalysis does not renounce its "descent from exact science" (SE 18:178/GW 17:29). On the contrary, it is "ready to believe what is shown . . . to deserve belief" (SE 22:31/GW 15:32). Thus, in all of his essays on occultism[16] and especially the last, Freud appeals to telepathy because it "seems actually to favor the extension of the scientific" (SE 22:55/GW 15:59). What is more, Freud will remind his audience quite pointedly that the history of science abounds with examples in which new hypotheses were prematurely (and erroneously) condemned. "For a long time," he tells us, "it was regarded as a senseless hypothesis to suppose that the stones, which we now call meteorites, could have reached the earth from outer space or that the rocks forming mountains, in which the remains of shells are embedded, could have once formed the bed of the sea" (SE 22:33/GW 15:34). The best example, though, is that of psychoanalysis itself, which was met with nothing but contemptuous rejection when it argued for the existence of an unconscious.

So, in a way, Jones is too *earnest*. And too *literal*. He misses the *spirit* of Freud's engagement with telepathy. By fearing that Freud may have abandoned or betrayed psychoanalysis by turning to telepathy, it is—ironically—he, Jones, who ends up being not scientific enough. For Freud's interest in telepathy reflects an understanding of science and scientific revolution according to which the challenge to orthodoxy may actually advance the cause of science (and here one might quote Freud's favorite Charcot line: "*La théorie, c'est bon, mais ça n'empêche pas d'exister*" [SE 3:13/ GW 1:24]). In other words, Freud's intention in his telepathy texts is precisely to extend the scientific through the psychoanalytic.

And there's method to his madness. If Freud wants to extend the scientific, if he wants to argue for the existence of telepathy, it is for a special and very particular reason: It is in order to incorporate into psychoanalysis (into a psychoanalytic hermeneutics of interpretation), to bring into the deterministic fold, those psychical events that appear to defy analytic interpretation. That is, as we will see, Freud introduces the question of occultism (whether he is *for* thought transference in "Dreams and Occultism" or *against* superstition in *The Psychopathology of Everyday Life*) precisely in order to exclude the uninterpretable accident (to rule it out, to expel it, *ihn auszuschließen*) from the internal, psychical domain. In other words, when psychoanalysis finally decides to swallow or stomach so-called occult phenomena ("I must confess that I have the feeling that . . . the scales weigh in favor of thought-transference" [SE 22:54/GW 15:58]), when "Freud proposes occultism as a solution,"[17] it is as a means of expelling something else—the accident. Hence psychoanalysis takes in the strange (and seemingly unscientific)—telepathy—in order to rid itself of what is stranger still: the accident. The accident must be evacuated. For it is only by isolating a domain "into which external randomness no longer penetrates" that psychoanalysis gives itself a "chance as a science" ("MC" 375). To put it more bluntly: Freud uses telepathy as a purgative.

But how, then, are we to read Freud's resistance? If telepathy does not represent a "threat against [his] scientific *Weltanschauung*" (SE 22:54/GW 15:58), if, on the contrary, it has a cleansing effect, why this ongoing resistance? Could it be that the telepathic tonic is unpalatable in some other way? Could it be that T (telepathy, thought transference) is the X that brings psychoanalytic theory to a halt precisely because it marks the spot of some indigestible idea? In which case, of course, we have our work *cut out* for us. We must *follow the resistance*.

Freud's Resistance to Telepathy

I would like therefore to point to the many parapraxes that seem to plague Freud's texts on telepathy, beginning with "Psychoanalysis and Telepathy" (1941 [1921]).[18] In this text, which was written in August 1921 for a gathering of the inner circle (Abraham, Eitingon, Ferenczi, Jones, Rank, and Sachs) in the Harz mountains, Freud tells us that he had intended to give reports of three cases of telepathy but that when he sat down to write his presentation, the material for the third case was missing. The first two cases are examples of what Freud calls "unfulfilled prophecies" (SE 18:190/GW 17:40–41), cases in which the content of a prophecy coincides not with an actual future event but with the fulfillment of a wish. In such cases, Freud muses, analysis "may actually be said to have created the occult fact" (SE 18:189/GW 17:40). For, although the prophecies have not come true, they nonetheless offer "conclusive evidence of its being possible to transfer an unconscious wish and the thoughts and knowledge relating to it" (SE 18:189/GW 17:40). They prove, as it were, the possibility of thought transference/telepathy. Presumably, the third case would have clinched the matter. But it is precisely at this point that Freud's unconscious intervenes. Here is Freud's account of his parapraxis:

> I had also intended to bring you [a third] example. . . . But I can now give you visible proof of the fact that I discuss the subject of occultism under the pressure of the greatest resistance. When . . . I looked over the notes which I had put together and brought with me [from Vienna] for the purpose of this paper, the sheet on which I had noted down this last observation was not there, but in its place I found another sheet of indifferent memoranda on quite another topic, which I had brought with me by mistake. Nothing can be done against such a clear resistance. I must ask you to excuse me for omitting this case, for I cannot make the loss good from memory. (SE 18:190/GW 17:41)

One can only imagine that Freud was saving the best for last, and now the last goes missing—for twelve years. The original third case, Strachey tells us, did survive as a separate manuscript to which Freud later appended the following: "*Postscript*. Here is the report, omitted owing to resistance, on a case of thought transference during analytic practice" (SE 18:175). Nowhere in the Standard Edition, however, does the original manuscript of the "*Postscript*" ever appear. This is because, as Strachey's writes in another note, this time to the 1932 essay "Dreams and Occultism," where the third case does finally appear, the original draft was never published: "It resembled the version given here [in 'Dreams and Occultism'] so closely that it was doubtful whether it was necessary to print it separately" (SE 22:48). At which point Strachey adds the following detail: "It should be added, however, that since that volume of the Standard Edition was published, in 1955, the manuscript has once again unaccountably disappeared" (SE 22:48). So we might say that what the editorial history makes "visible" is not only a resistance but also a *surprising* resistance to this case, which might well be called "The Case of the Disappearing Case."

And it gets better. For this vanishing act seems to have been passed on to the text itself. The manuscript of "Psychoanalysis and Telepathy" is the next thing to disappear: "Toward the end of [1925] Freud asked Eitingon for the manuscript of the 'Harz' essay, perhaps with an idea of publishing it at last. Eitingon assured him he had brought it back personally, but apparently it got mislaid. It was found among Freud's papers after his death" (J3 396). From parapraxis to parapraxis: as if there were something about telepathy that needed to be avoided.

In order not to get too bogged down in editorial history, I will add just one final detail. This time it's about the short text entitled "The Occult Significance of Dreams," the 1925 text that, as we saw earlier, was a trauma for Jones. Now there seems to have been great difficulty in getting "Some Additional Notes on Dream-Interpretation as a Whole" (the chapter of which "The Occult Significance of Dreams" is the *third* part) to see the light of day. As Strachey explains in a complicated editorial note, Freud had intended to include "Some Additional Notes on Dream-Interpretation as a Whole" (otherwise known as Supplementary Chapter C [*Zusatzkapitel C*]) to all editions of *The Interpretation of Dreams* starting in 1925. But this "Supplementary Chapter C" (and, even more so, the third section, section C, of this Supplemental Chapter C, as we will see) "seemed dogged by misfortunes" (SE 19:126). Not only was it completely left out of the eighth edition of *Die Traumdeutung* (1930) and thus omitted from the revised (Brill) translation of 1932 and the double volume of Freud's *Gesammelte Werke* in 1942, not only was it "accidentally overlooked" and not included "at the correct chronological point in *G.W.*, 14 (published in 1948)" (SE 19:126), but even when the chapter ("Some Additional Notes on Dream-Interpretation as a Whole") was included in a collective volume of Freud's shorter writings on dreams, it was not reprinted *as a whole*. For what was cut out of Supplementary Chapter C was . . . yes . . . its C section, "The Occult Significance of Dreams." What are the chances, you may ask?

What are the chances that these occurrences are accidents without any further meaning? What are the chances that Freud's resistance to telepathy should raise the question of chance in a way that is so literal ... and literally cut out for us?

The "Accident" in Psychoanalysis

As we know from *The Psychopathology of Everyday Life* (1901) and the first four of Freud's *Introductory Lectures* (1916 [1915]), "nothing in the mind is arbitrary or undetermined" (SE 6:242 / GW 4:270–71). As Freud demonstrates again and again in hundreds of examples of parapraxes, the accident (*Unfall*) is no accident for the analyst, who is able to recognize and interpret an unconscious purpose behind an apparently random event. Unlike the layperson, the analyst understands the random event to be the result of an "*unconscious yet operative*" intention (SE 6:272n1 / GW 4:302n1). As Derrida puts it both succinctly and provocatively in his 1982 lecture "My Chances / *Mes chances*": "There is no random chance in the unconscious [*Pas de hazard dans l'inconscient*]" ("MC" 369/377). There is no random chance in the unconscious because psychoanalysis symptomatizes contingency; it puts the apparent facts of randomness "in the service of an ineluctable necessity" ("MC" 369/377).[19]

So how does chance (*Zufall, Zufälligkeit*) operate in an economy of psychical determinism? If Freud leaves no room for the accident, if, on the contrary, he argues for "the strict determination of apparently arbitrary psychical acts" (SE 6:254n1 / GW 4:283n1), how are we to understand chance occurrences in psychoanalysis? How are we to think chance together with analysis's hermeneutic drive, that is, with its compulsion to make the accident unhappen? And here it seems to me that there is no better place from which to ask these questions than the final chapter of *The Psychopathology of Everyday Life*, where Freud attempts to do both things at once, virtually simultaneously. On the one hand, he claims that "determination in the psychical sphere is ... carried out without a gap [*lückenlos durchgeführt*]" (SE 6:254 / GW 4:283), assuming one takes into account unconscious as well as conscious motivations. On the other hand, and in wake of this claim—immediately following the blank, gap, or space that separates this assertion from the beginning of the next section, which is of course a "(C)" section—Freud suddenly finds room for chance. Suddenly, as it were, the difference that makes all the difference when it comes to distinguishing science from superstition, a *scientific* belief from a *superstitious* belief, hinges on, is contingent on, is determined by, *chance*. In the (C) section of the final chapter of *The Psychopathology of Everyday Life*, Freud decides to turn his attention to chance in order to prove that he is not superstitious person.

Freud believes in chance, so he tells us, but it is a chance that lies safely outside of his mental life; chance is in essence alien (*wesensfremd*) to psychical life. With the superstitious person, it is the other way around; psychical life is full of accidents, and external reality is full of unknown, secret (and futural) meaning. Here is what Freud says:

> I am therefore different from a superstitious person in the following way:
> I do not believe that an event in whose occurrence my mental life plays no part can teach me any hidden thing about the future shape of reality; but I believe that an unintentional manifestation of my own mental activity *does* on the other hand disclose something hidden, though again it is something that belongs only to my mental life [not to external reality]. I believe in external (real) chance [*an äußeren (realen) Zufall*], it is true, but not in internal accidental events [*an innere (psychische) Zufälligkeit*]. (SE 6:257/GW 4:286)

For Freud accidents are limited to those events that take place outside of psychical life. For the superstitious person, it is the other way around: Not only does the superstitious person believe that there are psychical accidents (*psychische Zufälligkeiten*), but s/he also has a tendency to attribute to what are merely random external events a meaning that will become manifest in real—that is, future—events. Unlike Freud, the superstitious person interprets and gives meaning to "external chance happenings [*Zufall*]" (SE 6:257/GW 4:286) by projecting outward, into the outer world, what are really repressed thoughts, fears, and wishes: The superstitious person, says Freud, "projects outwards a motivation which I look for within" (SE 6:257/GW 4:286). Thus, it is by appealing to an opposition between inside and outside, science and projection, truth and fiction, that Freud is able to maintain a distinction between the hermeneutic drive of psychoanalysis, on the one hand, and the hermeneutic drive of superstition, on the other. What the analyst believes and what the superstitious person believes are not the same even if "the compulsion not to let chance count as chance but to interpret it" (SE 6:258/GW 4:287) is common to both. There is belief and there is belief, one might say, "il y a fagots et fagots" (SE 16:281/GW 11:290). Indeed, one might say of belief exactly what Freud says of knowledge in his *Introductory Lectures*: "Belief is not always the same as belief:

there are different sorts of belief, which are far from equivalent psychologically" (SE 16:281/GW 11:290, modified). In the field of a scientific psychoanalysis, that is, there is belief and there is credulity.[20]

And just to prove his point, just to prove that a psychoanalytic belief in chance is not superstitious (that is, unscientific), Freud will—suddenly, out of the blue, for the very first time in *The Psychopathology of Everyday Life*—produce a chance event, an uninterpretable accident.[21] I think you will recognize the anecdote. Having just returned from holiday, Freud is thinking of the many patients he has to visit. One of them is a ninety-year-old woman. On this particular day, however, Freud is running late, so he hails a cab to take him to his patient's house. The cabman knows the old woman's address perfectly well, yet on this particular day he makes a mistake and draws up in front of the wrong house. Now what does this mean? "Is it of any significance," Freud asks, "that I was driven to a house where the old lady was not to be found?" (SE 6:257/GW 4:285–86). What is the meaning of this error? Does it reveal some kind of truth? "Certainly not to me," says Freud, "but if I were *superstitious* I should see an omen in the incident, the finger of fate announcing that this year would be the old lady's last. . . . *I* of course explain the occurrence as an accident without any further meaning [*eine Zufälligkeit ohne weiteren Sinn*]" (SE 6:257/GW 4:286).

The accident is an accident, end of story. Though it would have been a different story if Freud had been the source of the error. In that case, the occurrence would not have been an accident but an action with an unconscious aim requiring interpretation. In that case, the interpretation might have been that Freud did not expect to see the old lady for much longer. In that case, "there would have been *Vergehen*—misconduct and mistaken path" ("MC" 366/375). But that is not the case, and the accident can teach Freud nothing: neither about "the future shape of reality" (SE 6:257/GW 4:286) nor about his own mental activity. The accident is an accident, pure and simple.

"Not so fast," I still hear the voice of my analyst saying, "reality is always the best excuse." Indeed, how not to be reminded, in this analytic context, of Lacan, who opens "Tuché and Automaton" by recalling that, as analysts, on principle, we never allow ourselves to be taken in by what occurs "*as if by chance* [*comme au hazard*]"?[22] As good analysts, that is, we must wonder whether what has occurred *as if by chance* is not precisely the *occurrence of chance* itself. For in this case it would seem that Freud had simply repressed—from within the very text of *The Psychopathology of Everyday Life*—his chapter on "Bungled Actions," where we find not one but two "prequels" to this story. On (at least) two other occasions, as it turns out, this old woman was implicated in a very similar—and all-too-interpretable—bungled action.[23]

The first prequel takes us back to Freud's discussion of bungled actions of a medical nature and to one of his own medical blunders. Freud tells us he has been in the habit of visiting the old woman twice a day for some years and that his routine consists in putting a few drops of eye lotion into her eye and giving her a morphine injection. On this particular day, he puts the morphine into her eye instead of the eye lotion. He is very much alarmed by his mistake, but his fright seems exaggerated given the harmlessness of his action: "A few drops of a two per cent solution of morphine could not do any harm even in the conjunctival sac" (SE 6:177/GW 4:197). Concluding that his fright must have come from another source, he analyzes his mistake and discovers that his first association is to the phrase "sich an der Alten vergreifen" (to do violence to the old woman). As Strachey explains in a footnote: "The German word *'vergreifen'* means both 'to make a blunder' and 'to commit an assault'" (SE 6:178n1). And it is this phrase—"sich an der Alten vergreifen"—Freud tells us, that provides him with "a short cut to the solution" (SE 6:178/GW 4:197). It is a phrase that gets straight to the point: No mistaken path, no misstep here; "it puts [Freud] on the trail of Oedipus and Jocasta" ("MC" 368/376). That is, Freud's association to *vergreifen* leads directly to *begreifen*, to understanding; his *Vergreifen* exemplifies the *Begreifen* or the *Begriff* that will be so central to psychoanalysis, namely the Oedipus complex:

> I was under the influence of a dream which had been told me by a young man the previous evening and the content of which could only point to sexual intercourse with his own mother. . . . While absorbed in thoughts of this kind I came to my patient, who is over ninety, and I must have been on the way [*auf dem Wege*] to grasping the universal human application of the Oedipus myth as correlated with the Fate which is revealed in the oracles; for at that point I did violence to or committed a blunder on "the old woman." (SE 6:177–78/GW 4:285)

A funny thing happens on the way to the old woman's house: Freud and the future of psychoanalysis come together in a parapraxis. Freud is "on the way to grasping the universal human application of the Oedipus myth" when he arrives at the old woman's house. Instead of putting the eye lotion into her eye, he puts the morphine: "At that point I did violence to or committed a blunder on 'the old woman.'" At that point, what was a harmless parapraxis, a bungled action of no consequence, turns into an Oedipal scene. Freud's bungled action, that is, tells us not only about Freud's unconscious psychology. It also tells us about the *"psychology of the unconscious"* (SE 6:259/GW 4:288), about the transformation of *"metaphysics* into *metapsychology"* (SE 6:259/GW 4:288), about the transition from Oedipus myth to Oedipus complex. So it is not just any old parapraxis.

Which brings me to the second prequel (which is in fact the first: it occurs right at the beginning of the chapter on "Bungled Actions"). Again Freud is on his way to visit the old woman, and again there is a hitch:

> There is a house where twice every day for six years . . . I used to wait to be let in outside a door on the second floor. During this long period it has happened to me on two occasions . . . I have gone a floor too high— i.e., I have *"climbed too high* [versteigen]." On the first occasion I was enjoying an ambitious day-dream in which I was "climbing ever higher and higher." On this occasion I even failed to hear that the door in question had opened as I put my foot on the first step of the third flight. On another occasion, I again went too far while I was deep in thought; when I realized it, I turned back and tried to catch hold of the phantasy in which I had been absorbed. I found that I was irritated by a (phantasied) criticism of my writings in which I was reproached with always "going too far." This I had now replaced by the not very respectful expression "climbing too high [*versteigen*]." (SE 6:164–65/GW 4:182)

Twice more, then, something happens to Freud on his way to the old woman's house. Twice more, there is a bungled action because Freud is thinking and dreaming about his future/the future of psychoanalysis. This gives us no fewer than three parapraxes (2 × *versteigen* + 1 × *vergreifen*), all involving the same patient. Together these parapraxes epitomize what Freud calls "combined parapraxes." "Accumulated and combined parapraxes," Freud writes, are the essence of the parapraxes. They are "the finest flower of their kind [*die höchste Blüte ihrer Gattung*]" (SE 15:56/GW 11:50). This is because they contradict "in a far more energetic way [*in ungleich energischerer Weise*]" (SE 6:238/GW 4:265) the notion that a parapraxis is a matter of chance and needs no interpretation. With no other patient in all of *The Psychopathology of Everyday Life* is Freud as *parapraxis-prone* as he is with this old woman. Yet . . . it is precisely with this patient, on his way to her house, that Freud claims to find *an accident without any further meaning*. What are the chances? Is this not an extravagant (*verstiegen*) claim?

But what if we inflected these questions in a slightly more analytic vein? What does Freud mean by singling out a particular "accident" and insisting that it is in itself full confirmation of the difference between psychoanalytic belief and superstitious belief, science and fiction? In short, how should we *read* this "accident"? Is one not led to suspect that Freud's unconscious intention here is to throw a "bomb into the psychoanalytic house" (J3 394)? Indeed, what if the *reality* of this "accident" lay precisely in its resistance to a certain (scientific) psychoanalysis? For if the accident is no accident, if it fails to be an accident, if it succeeds, that is, in being a symptom (thus confirming the analytic premise that everything is overdetermined) . . . then it precisely fails to secure the boundaries between psychoanalysis and superstition. In this way, Freud's "accident without any further meaning" leads to a questioning that is both psychoanalytic and eccentric, ex-centering in relation to psychoanalysis.

Freud's Conversion to Telepathy

Psy-Fi

And this brings us back to telepathy and thought transference, which is where we started out from. That is, it brings us back to the theoretical fiction according to which the unconscious mental processes in one person ("ideas, emotional states, conative impulses") are transferred to another person "through empty space without employing the familiar methods of communication by means of words and signs" (SE 22:39/GW 15:42). And here one might say that Freud's debt to *fiction*, to a kind of science fiction—which we might call *psy-fi*—brings with it a strange *theoretical* foresight. For when Freud *calls up* the analogy between the tele- of tele-pathy and the tele- of the tele-phone, when he *makes the connection* between an "original, archaic method of communication" and other forms of telecommunication, he is, very literally, *ringing in* the future, that is to say, a certain thinking of originary technicity. Here is what he says at the end of "Dreams and Occultism":

> The telepathic process is supposed to consist in a mental act in one person instigating the same mental act in another person. . . . The analogy with other transformations, such as occur in speaking and hearing by the telephone, would then be unmistakable. . . . It would seem to me that psychoanalysis, by inserting the unconscious between what is physical and what was previously called "psychical," has paved the way for the assumption of such processes as telepathy. . . . One is [also] led to a suspicion that this is the original, archaic method of communication between individuals and that in the course of phylogenetic evolution it has been replaced by the better method of giving

information with the help of signals which are picked up by the sense organs. (SE 22:55 / GW 15:59)

Thus, the telepathic process begins to resemble nothing so much as a wireless, routerless, networkless communication. As "the original, archaic method of communication between individuals,"[24] telepathy is the *Ur-Wi-Fi*; it is the *prototype* of all (future) tele-communication devices including but not limited to the telephone. Freud's first analogy is in fact to the tele-graph; telepathy, he says, would be "a kind of psychical counterpart to wireless telegraphy" (SE 22:36 / GW 15:38).

But how not to recall, in this tele-technological context, another instance of tele-communication, in this case one that grounds the very practice of psychoanalysis? For Freud's most elaborate description of psychoanalytic technique—in the *third* of his six papers that make up "The Papers on Technique" (1911–1915 [1914])—begins with an extended simile involving, once again, the telephone.[25] In other words, right from the start, at the heart of the analytic situation, there is, and always was, a "technical interposition" ("LL" 58/76)[26]:

> To put it in a formula: he [the analyst] must turn his own unconscious like a receptive organ towards the transmitting unconscious of the patient. He must adjust himself to the patient as a telephone receiver is adjusted to the transmitting microphone. Just as the receiver converts back into soundwaves the electric oscillations in the telephone line which were set up by sound waves, so the [analyst's] unconscious is able, from the derivatives of the unconscious which are communicated to him, to reconstruct the unconscious, which has determined the patient's free associations. (SE 12:115–16 / GW 8:381–82)

"Can you hear me?" says the patient's transmitting unconscious to the analyst's converting receiver. And though we may find Freud's telephonic simile rather amusing, it is precisely the quality of the analyst's "reception" that allows her/him to bring forth, to render present, what has remained hidden or concealed, namely the patient's repressed raw material (unconscious ideas, representations, facts). Still, one may wonder whether this game of tele-phone, prefiguring as it does the mechanism of transmission of tele-pathy, does not already tell us something about the tele-system (of which tele-pathy would be both the first and final chapter in Freud's work).[27] Does it not tell us that tele-pathy can never guarantee the destination of a communication? Does it not tell us that a transmitting unconscious, much like an outgoing call, can always be tapped, bugged, interfered with, recorded? Does it not put before us the possibility that, through the transference, the analyst—like an *écouteur*—taps into, that is to say, exploits, a difference within the patient's own unconscious? Such that one may wonder whether it is not the unconscious that telephones itself to itself?[28] Indeed, would this not be the most accurate description of what Freud is calling "telepathy" or "thought-transference": Is thought transference not a call (on) which the other happens to pick up?[29]

A Rendezvous with Literature

This is where the missing third case, the "Case of the Disappearing Case," comes in. Not only does this case pick up where Freud left off in 1921, but it also exemplifies a case in which the other (here a patient) miraculously picks up on the thoughts of his analyst. Among all the cases of telepathy or thought transference, Freud tells us, this is one that leaves the "strongest impression" (SE 22:47/GW 15:50) on him; it is also the only case in which the question of thought transference (*Gedankenübertragung*) merges with the transference/countertransference (*Übertragung/ Gegenübertragung*) relation between analyst and analysand. In every other example, the telepathic communication takes place outside of analysis. In other words, this is the only case—or call—in which we have (at least) two transferences on the line.[30]

The case is that of Herr P., an "intelligent and agreeable" (SE 22:48/GW 15:51) man, whom Freud has continued to see, for free, even though the case offers no chance of therapeutic success. One day Herr P.—who may or may not be Sergei Pankeiev, the Wolf Man[31]—comes to his session just minutes after the London analyst Dr. Forsyth has left Freud's office ("an occurrence," Freud assures us, "of which [P.] was unaware" [SE 22:49/GW 15:52]) and brings up a startling series of jealous thoughts and associations beginning with the revelation that the young woman he is dating and with whom he is afraid to have sex calls him "Herr von Vorsicht [Mr. Foresight]" (SE 22:48/GW 15:52), or, as Maria Torok puts it, "Mr. P., Prudence" ("A" 98).

What is so astonishing about P.'s associations is that P. seems to know things he could not possibly know: "Could P. have known that Dr. Forsyth had just paid me his first visit? Could he have known the name of the person [Dr. Freund] I had visited in his house? Did he know that Dr. Jones had written a monograph on the nightmare?[32] Or was it only *my* knowledge about these things that was revealed in his associations?" (SE 22:52/GW 15:55). What did P. know, and when did he know it?

Though the evidence for the occult nature of P.'s associations to Dr. Freund and Dr. Jones remains inconclusive, Freud notes that the miraculous emergence of the name "Herr von Vorsicht"—"even taken by itself [*auch isoliert*]"—would be enough to support "the apparent fact of thought-transference" (SE 22:53/GW 15:56). What allows the scales to "weigh in favor of thought-transference" (SE 22:54/GW 15:58) is an event that both *says Vorsicht* (foresight) and *brings* foresight.

Concretely, what Herr von Vorsicht foresees is the end of his own analysis: "He had been warned that his analysis . . . would come to an end as soon as foreign pupils and patients returned to Vienna; and that was in fact what happened shortly afterwards" (SE 22:51/GW 15:55). So if P. brings the name *Vorsicht* into his analysis "unheralded" (SE 22:50/GW 15:54), right after it has become significant to Freud as a result of Dr. Forsyth's arrival, it is because P.'s unconscious sees the writing on the wall. Watch out!—*Vorsicht!*—says his unconscious, the end is near. But because he also wishes to continue his analysis ("evidently because he felt comfortable in a well-tempered father-transference" [SE 22:48/GW 15:51]), this name out of nowhere is also an unconscious attempt to keep Freud on the line: "'I'm a Forsyth too: that's what the girl calls me. . . . Do come back to me; after all I'm a Forsyth too'" (SE 22:51/GW 15:54). Forsyth, here . . . hello, hello.

But there is also another (English) name that Freud's converting receiver is able to reconstruct from the name "Vorsicht": not "Forsyth" but "Forsyte." Indeed, he reminds us that, for a German speaker, the two names "can scarcely be distinguished" (SE 22:49/GW 15:52). What is more, the name "Forsyte" has become a kind of cipher between analyst and patient:

> [P.] possessed a rich English library and used to bring me books from it. I owe to him an acquaintance with such authors as Bennett and Galsworthy.[33] . . . One day he lent me a novel of Galsworthy's with the title *The Man of Property*, whose scene is laid in the bosom of a family . . . bearing the name of "Forsyte." . . . Only a few days before the occurrence I am speaking of, he had brought me a fresh volume from this series. The name "Forsyte," and everything typical that the author had sought to embody [*verkörpern*] in it, had played a part, too, in my conversations with P. and it had become part of the secret language which so easily grows up between people who see a lot of each other. (SE 22:49/GW 15:52)

Thus, Freud tells us, "Forsyte" means the same to P. as it does to him. And it is to this name "Forsyte" that Freud first calls our attention when he considers P.'s association. What Freud deems so remarkable is not only the name itself ("Herr von Vorsicht") but also the manner (*Art*) in which this name has managed to weave itself into P.'s own experiences. P. does not say, for example, "'The name "Forsyte," out of the novels you are familiar with, has just occurred to me.'" No—and here Freud shifts names—"what he *did* say now was: 'I'm a Forsyth too: that's what the girl calls me'" (SE 22:51/GW 15:54).

In other words, P.'s message is clear. Unlike the linguistic accident that creates static on the line in the case of P.'s association to Dr. Freund—"the evidential value of this case is totally destroyed by a chance circumstance [*durch eine Zufälligkeit*]. The man whom I had visited . . . was not only called 'Freund'; he was a true friend [*Freund*] to us all" (SE 22:52/GW 15:56)—in the case of P.'s association to Dr. Forsyth, there is no such indetermination:

> How is it to be explained that [Herr P.] became receptive to [Dr. Forsyth's] presence on the very day of his arrival and immediately after his first visit? One might say it was chance [*Zufall*]—that is, leave it unexplained. But it was precisely in order to exclude chance [*um den Zufall auszuschließen*] that I discussed P.'s . . . associations [to Dr. Freund and Dr. Jones], in order to show you that he was really occupied with jealous thoughts about people who visited me. (SE 22:53/GW 15:57).

Three associations all occupied with jealous thoughts about foreign doctors visiting one's analyst: This can be no accident, *as we all know*. And for Freud the meaning is clear: "Come back to me [Doctor] . . . I'm a Forsyth too" (SE 22:51/GW 15:54). But, for this to be the case, for *Vorsicht* to constitute foresight about Forsyth, something else must also be true: "P. had in fact selected from his personal concerns *the very name* with which I was occupied at the same time as a result of an occurrence of which he was unaware" (SE 22:49/GW 15:52, my emphasis). No "chance circumstance" has come, in this case, to destroy the possibility of a telepathic communication. In other words, Freud has found it necessary to deny chance in order to make room for telepathy. And this, one may conclude, was the whole point of telepathy in the first place.

Yet, *on the way there*, on the way to his confession of faith, there is that other name, that other name which is really the same, since, as Freud says, one can speak interchangeably of the "name 'Forsyte' or 'Forsyth'" (SE 22:50/GW 15:54). "'Forsyte' or 'Forsyth,'" says Freud, same difference. Yet, as we have also heard, the name "Forsyte" and "everything typical that [Galsworthy] had sought to embody in it" has also become part of the "secret language" between Freud and P. So how are we to understand this embodiment? What if P. were saying "I'm a Forsyte too"?[34] After all, as we are reminded by this endlessly proliferating chain—*Vorsicht*-Forsyte-Forsyth-foresight-*Voraussicht*[35]—"psychical acts and structures are invariably overdetermined" (SE 13:100/ GW 9:122) . . . that is, *every call* is a conference call (and we didn't need the NSA to tell us this).

As it happens, *The Forsyte Saga* gives us a very precise definition of a "Forsyte" in the volume to which Freud refers.[36] As one Forsyte explains it: "A 'Forsyte' is a man who is decidedly more than less a slave of property. He knows a good thing, he knows a safe thing, and his grip on property—it doesn't matter whether it be wives, houses, money, or reputation—is his hall-mark" (FS 194). He is, as the title of the first volume makes clear, "a man of property," his most distinctive feature his "possessive instinct" (FS 349, 552, 723, 832, 833, 848, 849). To be a "Forsyte," as the 850-page saga makes abundantly clear, is to act in accordance with the "possessive principle" (FS 807), a principle that consists in "avoiding the unexpected" (FS 237).

And yet *The Forsyte Saga* is nothing if not the disturbing encounter of this "possessive instinct" with "something strange and foreign" (FS 80), the unfathomable "enigma" (FS 111) that exceeds calculation, "a sort of visitation" that impinges on, and "brings destruction" (FS 549) to, a possessive world. In the course of the saga, the "possessive principle" is unsettled by what the "man of property" calls "infernal mischance" (FS 823). "Chance," as the narrator declares ironically at the end of the trilogy, "visits the lives of even the best invested Forsytes" (FS 723). Though this visitation may take the rather predictable form of Beauty and Passion in Galsworthy's novels, by the end of the saga one thing is clear: The name "Forsyte" will never again be separated from the disruptive possibilities of chance.

Perhaps, then, one might say that what returns with Freud's remarkable third case is not only the resistance to chance but also a very Forsytean impasse. For something rather remarkable happens in the wake of telepathy's *Vorsicht*-Forsyte-Forsyth saga. It is a little as if the psychoanalytic saga of "telepathy" had encountered its own dispossessive principle at the very end of "Dreams and Occultism." On the very last page of this text, psychoanalysis runs into something it can neither assimilate nor eliminate, neither interiorize nor foreclose ("Geo" 321/330), in the form of a gold coin.

It is a very well-known example: A mother speaks during her analytic session of a gold coin from her childhood and then—"immediately afterwards" (SE 22:56/ GW 15:60), only the briefest time after it has become significant to her—her ten-year-old son (also in analysis) brings her a gold coin for her to put aside for him. At which point Freud confesses that psychoanalysis can make neither heads nor tails of the occurrence:

> The mother reported the occurrence to the child's analyst and asked her to find out from the child the reason for his action. *But the child's analysis threw no light on the matter*; the action had forced its way that day into the child's life like a foreign body [*wie ein Fremdkörper . . . eingedrängt*]. A few weeks later the mother was sitting at her writing desk to write down, as she had been told to do, an account of the experience, when in came the boy and asked for the gold coin back, as he had wanted to take it with him to show in his analytic session. *Once again the child's analysis could discover no explanation of his wish*. (SE 22:56 / GW 15:60–61, my emphasis).

"Failure, then," writes Derrida, "in the face of the foreign body" ("Tel" 257/266). But I think we must also read this failure as a kind of chance, for psychoanalysis's failure to discover an explanation for what forces itself into the psychical life of the child is also a chance (to) return to the *Fremdkörper*,[37] that is, to a figure that, from the earliest days of psychoanalysis, testified to what was both inside and outside the psyche—as a result of "accidental factors [*das akzidentelle Moment*]" (SE 2:4 / GW 1:82).

In the final analysis, then, the name "Forsyte" and the child's gold coin return us to what was "alien to psychoanalysis [*wesensfremd*]." And yet they do so with a twist. For not only do they suggest that "telepathy" marks the necessity of suspending our naïve confidence in distinctions or oppositions such as inside/outside, science/superstition, self/other. They also recall to us the importance of the "foreign body" for psychoanalysis. And they do so through telepathy, through Freud's discussion of telepathy. What connects the "foreign body" of *Studies on Hysteria* to the "foreign body" of "Dreams and Occultism" is *telepathy*. Now what is miraculous, if I can put it this way, is that this "telepathic" *connection* occurs in or as a *break* in analytic understanding: "analysis threw no light on the matter," "again . . . analysis could discover no explanation." As a result, the "foreign body" has a curious *ring* to it. For it has, in fact, *cut in* on the line between patient and analyst (and here one must also hear the foreign body as a foreign agent, perhaps a Russian who not only hacks computers but also bugs phones); it cuts in and in so doing establishes a *chance connection*, a connection made possible by disconnection, by a failure or breakdown in the communication system. That is, the "foreign body" disturbs the very systematicity of the telecommunication system by *dialing up*, as it were, both the reserves of chance and the powers of overdetermination. In other words, Freud's "foreign body" strikes gold: It allows for determinism but only by reintroducing the chance that telepathy set out to exclude.

But how, then, are we to read the end of "Dreams and Occultism" and, in particular, its final line: "And this brings us back to psychoanalysis, which was what we started out from" (SE 22:56/GW 15:61)? Was telepathy a departure from psychoanalysis? Was it a mistaken path? Or has the "foreign body" returned us to the kind of "chance observation [*zufällige Beobachtung*]" (SE 2:3/GW 1:81) with which psychoanalysis began? Could it be that this *Vergehen* leads not to Freud's theory of meaningful accidents but to what George Eliot calls "air-blown chances, incalculable as the descent of thistle-down"?[38]

CHAPTER 5

The Speculative Turn
Plato's Place in the Theory of the Drives

> Was there not a "demon" of repetition in our lives, and must it not stem from our human instincts being profoundly conservative? Might it not therefore be that all living things are in mourning for the inorganic state, the original condition from which they have by accident emerged?
>
> —D. M. THOMAS, The White Hotel

Philosophy, Psychoanalysis, and the Pleasure Principle

This chapter began as a paper written for the second annual meeting of the International Society of Psychoanalysis and Philosophy, otherwise known as ISPP, or SIPP in French (Société Internationale de Psychanalyse et Philosophie). Now, if I mention the name of the society, it is because, when I sat down to write my paper for this conference, I got confused. I couldn't remember which came first, "philosophy" or "psychoanalysis." And in my uncertainty, I put philosophy before psychoanalysis—that is, until I checked the website. At first I attributed my hesitation to forgetfulness and to the reversibility of the letters in the acronym (IS*PP*). I then blamed my idiosyncratic ordering on a compulsive tendency to alphabetize (philosophy comes before psychoanalysis, after all). Finally, I assumed that my chosen order must signal some sort of unacknowledged theoretical prejudice or politico-institutional narcissism. In other words, I interpreted "philosophy and psychoanalysis" as my own neurotic symptom. That is, until I received a series of emails from Jeffrey Bloechl, who was the organizer of the conference. I quote from the first of these:

The Speculative Turn 69

> I am writing you ... to invite you to an international conference on *psychoanalysis and philosophy*, to take place at Boston College. ... This will be the second annual meeting of the International Society for *Philosophy and Psychoanalysis* (ISPP), a group founded in Leuven and Paris about one year ago. (my emphasis)

As Jeff's email makes clear, the conference in question is one that will treat the topic of "psychoanalysis and philosophy," but the society (ISPP), indeed the very society that will host this conference on "psychoanalysis and philosophy," is called the International Society for Philosophy and Psychoanalysis. And just to confirm that this was neither a mistake nor a typo on Jeff's part, here is the second email I received from him when I (and others) agreed to participate in this conference:

> First a word of gratitude to all of you for accepting our invitation to gather at Boston College. ... On behalf of both the steering committee of the International Society for *Philosophy and Psychoanalysis* and the Boston College program in Psychoanalytic Studies, and indeed the Philosophy Department here, thank you. (my emphasis)

So, for me but for also for Jeff, the PP in ISPP stood for "philosophy and psychoanalysis." Jeff, like me, teaches in a philosophy department, and, like me, he may be guilty of a certain unconscious or not-so-unconscious prioritizing of philosophy over psychoanalysis. That is, in both of our cases, one might suspect that the reversal was motivated by self-interest or institutional affiliation. Indeed, how not to suspect the workings of the pleasure principle (PP) when the (French) website plainly states—it maintains unequivocally—that the two relationships ("psychoanalysis and philosophy," "philosophy and psychoanalysis") are *not* equivalent?

From the French website we learn that SIPP grew out of a desire to cultivate the relationship between analysts and philosophers, its goal being to advance those currents of contemporary thought that explore the relationship "between psychoanalysis and philosophy or—and this is not equivalent—between philosophy and psychoanalysis [*entre psychanalyse et philosophie, ou—ce qui n'est pas équivalent—entre philosophie et psychanalyse*]."[1] Now I wouldn't want to belabor this point, since I don't know the history of the creation of the website (and whether, for example, one language came first: Was it a French-English website or an English-French website, or were the website pages composed simultaneously in truly bilingual fashion?), but the English version of this relationship is not the same. In fact, it is not at all equivalent. Instead of merely distinguishing between "psychoanalysis and philosophy," on the one hand, and "philosophy and psychoanalysis," on the other, the English website brings out what is, historically, the problematic proximity between the two disciplines. Like the French website, it refers to currents of contemporary thought, but in this case these currents have "brought psychoanalysis to bear on philosophy, and—from another angle—brought philosophy into psychoanalysis."[2] That is, as the English-language version of the website suggests, what was an ordinal question (what comes first: philosophy or psychoanalysis?) also has a dynamic, even a coercive, dimension. Either psychoanalysis will be *brought to bear* on philosophy, it will *bear down* on philosophy, in which case, presumably, psychoanalysis will have an effect on philosophy, it will change philosophy. Or else philosophy will be *brought into* psychoanalysis, in which case, one can only assume, philosophy will be taken up by psychoanalysis, it will be taken into psychoanalysis, in such a way as to extend psychoanalysis's scope and influence. Either way, it would seem, psychoanalysis comes out on top. In fact, one might say that by giving psychoanalysis the first but also the last word, whether in terms of the "relationship between *psychoanalysis* and philosophy or—and this is not equivalent— between philosophy and *psychoanalysis*" or by "br[inging] *psychoanalysis* to bear on philosophy, and—from another angle–br[inging] philosophy into *psychoanalysis*," the ISPP/SIPP website becomes something of a *psychoanalytic phantasy*. And in the end, who knows? It may be that by reversing the terms of the relationship, by putting "philosophy" before "psychoanalysis," by challenging the PP of ISPP/SIPP, Jeff and I were also, implicitly, carrying out an analytic function. We were playing, however unintentionally, the role of the reality principle. In our own unconscious way, we were trying to address, or perhaps even redress, the symptomatic asymmetry proposed by ISPP/SIPP.

For we must not forget that Freud never claimed pride of place for psychoanalysis. On the very first page of *Beyond the Pleasure Principle*, he tells us plainly that "priority and originality [*Priorität und Originalität*] are not among the aims that psychoanalytic work sets itself" (SE 18:7/GW 13:3). In fact, he will insist on the belatedness of psychoanalysis in "On the History of the Psychoanalytic Movement" (1914) and "An Autobiographical Study" (1925 [1924]). *From the first*, that is, Freud tells us that psychoanalysis will have come *second*. And he repeats this claim—so many times, in fact, that his insistence on secondariness becomes a kind of originality: one that precisely puts into question the need for originality. But if coming first is not the point (as it was for me, Jeff, or the analysts of ISPP/SIPP), how are we to understand Freud's relationship to philosophy? On what might such a relationship turn?

A Discovery in Two Times:
The Sexual Etiology of Hysteria

Even the idea for which Freud is best known was not first expressed by him. Freud is very clear about this: He was not the first to recognize a sexual meaning behind hysterical symptoms. "The idea," Freud writes, "for which I was being made responsible had by no means originated with me" (SE 14:13/GW 10:50). On the contrary, the "scandalous idea" (SE 14:15/GW 10:52) of the sexual etiology of hysteria had been imparted to him by three illustrious men: the physiologist Josef Breuer, the neurologist Jean-Martin Charcot, and the gynecologist Rudolf Chrobak. Three times, on three separate occasions, the idea of a sexual etiology had been divulged to Freud.

The problem is that the idea had been communicated to him in the form of a witty remark. That is, when Breuer tells Freud in his friendly and instructive way that "these things are always *secrets d'alcôve*!" (SE 14:13/GW 10:51); or when Charcot suddenly breaks out with great animation ("hugging himself and jumping up and down on his toes several times in his own characteristically lively way"): "*Mais, dans des cas pareils c'est toujours la chose génitale, toujous . . . toujours . . . toujours*" (SE 14:14/GW 10:51); or when Chrobak describes the sole, reliable prescription for hysteria as

"'Rx Penis normalis

dosim

repetatur!'" (SE 14:15/GW 10:52)

the message is "*in a particular way* hollow or void"[3] (though its sexism is loud and clear). All three men (the physiologist, the neurologist, the gynecologist)—like "the butcher, the baker, the candlestick maker" in the old nursery rhyme—intimate a sexual scene but do so in language that is "in special ways—intelligibly—used not seriously" (HTDT 22).

Years before the publication of *Jokes and Their Relation to the Unconscious*, in other words, we find a Freud who is already taking the *Witz* seriously. He takes his mentors' off-the-cuff remarks literally, word for word (*wörtlich*). The result is that he is able to hear in their words "more than they knew themselves or were prepared to defend" (SE 20:24/GW 14:48). Thus, although Freud cannot claim priority for this "new and original idea" (SE 14:13/GW 10:50), he can and does take responsibility for *espousing* it:

> I am well aware that it is one thing to give utterance to an idea once or twice in the form of a passing *aperçu*, and quite another to mean it seriously [*ernst mit ihr zu machen*]—to take it literally [*wörtlich*] and pursue it in the face of every contradictory detail, and to win it a place among accepted truths. It is the difference between a casual flirtation and a legal marriage with all its duties and difficulties. "*Épouser les idées de* . . ." is no uncommon figure of speech, at any rate in French. (SE 14:15/GW 10:52–53)

What is "scandalous" is not the passing *aperçu*, the affair or casual flirtation, but the legal marriage "with all its duties and difficulties." The scandal is Freud's decision to take the joke—this nineteenth-century "locker room banter"—seriously.

Yet as any reader of these passages knows, there is something very funny about the seriousness with which Freud receives these statements from his mentors. Freud plays up his own naïveté, his lack of experience, his unsophistication, and surprise in the face of these scandalous declarations. He assumes the role of straight man who is by turns "astonished" (SE 14:13/GW 10:51), "paralyzed with amazement" (SE 14:14/GW 10:51), and mystified by the words of his teachers—"I had never heard of such a prescription, and felt inclined to shake my head over my kind friend's cynicism" (SE 14:15/GW 10:52). It is as though Freud were staging his own literal-mindedness in order precisely to turn the tables on the joke. The joke is on the joke, one might say. By becoming a serious psychoanalytic truth, the laugh is on the joke.

For Freud, then, and here I return to my original point, it was never a matter of being first or of putting psychoanalysis first. On the contrary, his discovery of the sexual etiology in hysteria only emerged for him some years later.[4] And here Freud's language leaves no room for doubt. This discovery only occurs belatedly, *nachträglich, après coup*:

> But these three identical opinions [those of Breuer, Charcot, Chrobak], which I had heard without understanding, had lain dormant [*geschlummert*] in my mind for years, until one day they awoke in the form of an apparently original discovery [*bis sie eines Tages als eine scheinbar originelle Erkenntnis erwachten*]. (SE 14:13/GW 10:50)

> What I heard from [Breuer, Charcot, Chrobak] lay dormant and inactive within me [*schlummerte unwirksam in mir*], until the chance of my

cathartic experiments brought it out as an apparently original discovery [*als anscheinend originelle Erkenntnis hervorbrach*]. (SE 20:24 / GW 14:48–49)

Indeed, if Freud speaks of his discovery as being "apparently [*scheinbar/anscheinend*] original," it is because this discovery is *not* original in any traditional sense. It is not original in that it does not come first or earliest. Freud has absorbed the idea of the sexual etiology of the neuroses "in a cryptomnesic way,"[5] as he readily and repeatedly acknowledges. But, ironically, one might say that this discovery *is* original in its very secondariness. For if the discovery occurs twice—the first time as farce, the second time as breakthrough—it is only in its repetition that it becomes what it is and can be recognized as such. That is, only in its repetition do we have an important or *serious* "discovery." And what is more, it is worth noting that this discovery repeats, in its very belatedness or secondariness, the delay that structures the "thing itself," namely, the psychical or sexual trauma that leads to hysteria (as we saw in Chapter 2). In other words, by registering and repeating the inscription of sexual trauma as *theoretical* delay, Freud's "apparently original discovery" repeats *as theory*, on the level of theory, not one but *two* scenes of an earlier missing.

Seriously though, it is no joke when one is the only one to take the joke seriously. Freud reminds us of this:

> The silence which my communications met with, the void which formed itself about me, the hints that were conveyed to me, gradually made me realize that assertions on the part played by sexuality in the etiology of the neuroses cannot count upon meeting with the same kind of treatment as other communications. I understood that ... I was one of those who have "disturbed the sleep of the world." (SE 14:21 / GW 10:59–60)

To take the joke seriously is no laughing matter. And yet there is something about this rude awakening that attests to the force and originality of psychoanalysis's discovery.

The Labors of Psychoanalysis

Again and again Freud will tell us that an idea, so essential to psychoanalysis as to be indissociable from it, did not originate with him. He was not the first to recognize the incomparable significance of sexual motive forces in unconscious life.[6] He was not the first to bear witness to the importance of the Oedipus complex.[7] He was not the first to acknowledge the id or to recognize sublimation or to speak of the preexistence of feelings of guilt. Even when it comes to the theory of repression, that is, to "the cornerstone [or foundation: *Grundpfeiler*] on which the whole structure of psychoanalysis rests" (SE 14:16/GW 10:54), Freud cannot claim priority for psychoanalysis. Others had gotten there before him, in particular "the great thinker Schopenhauer" (SE 17:143–44/GW 12:11–12). Not only did Schopenhauer "assert the dominance of the emotions and the supreme importance of sexuality but he was even aware of the mechanism of repression" (SE 20:59–60/GW 14:86). Once again, in other words, psychoanalysis comes second:

> Probably very few people can have realized the momentous significance for science and life of the recognition of unconscious mental processes. It was not psychoanalysis, however, let us hasten to add, which first took this step. There are famous philosophers who may be cited as forerunners—above all the great thinker Schopenhauer, whose unconscious "Will" is equivalent to the psychical drives of psychoanalysis. It was this same thinker, moreover, who in words of unforgettable impressiveness admonished mankind of the importance, still so greatly underestimated by it, of its sexual craving. (SE 17:143–44/GW 12:11–12)[8]

> I imagined [the theory of repression] to be entirely original, until Otto Rank showed us a passage in Schopenhauer's *World as Will and Representation*. . . . What [Schopenhauer] says there about the struggle against accepting a distressing piece of reality coincides with my concept of repression so completely that once again I owe the chance of making a discovery to my not being well-read. . . . I had therefore to be prepared—and I am so, gladly—to forgo all claims to priority. (SE 14:15–16/GW 10:53)

> Following a verbal usage of Nietzsche's . . . we will in the future call [the mental region that is foreign to the ego] the "id [*das Es*]." (SE 22:72/GW 15:79)

> A friend . . . called my attention to the fact that the "criminal from a sense of guilt" was known to Nietzsche too. The pre-existence of the feeling of guilt, and the utilization of a deed in order to rationalize this feeling, glimmer before us in Zarathustra's sayings "On a Pale Criminal." (SE 14:333/GW 10:391)

Once again Freud is the first to say that he is not the first.

And once again, as he did in the case of the three illustrious men, Freud draws our attention to knowledges that are not equivalent psychologically.

The difference between knowledges is of course well known from the practice of analysis: If an analyst transfers her knowledge to a patient "as a piece of information" (SE 16:281/GW 11:291), this knowledge is not the same—it does not have the same effect or force—as the knowledge that comes from an internal change in the patient as a result of analysis.[9] In other words, what was true of Breuer, Charcot, and Chrobak is also true of Schopenhauer and Nietzsche.[10] Like the scientists who communicated to Freud "a piece of knowledge which, strictly speaking, they themselves did not possess" (SE 14:13/GW 10:50), the philosophers who put forward "speculations about the unconscious" (SE 14:16/GW 10:54) both "know" and *do not* "know" the unconscious. They know the unconscious in that they have formed certain judgments about it, and they do not know it in that they have "formed their judgment on the unconscious without being acquainted with the phenomena of unconscious mental activity [*ohne die Phänomene der unbewußten Seelentätigkeit zu kennen*]" (SE 13:178/GW 8:406).

Analytic theories, on the other hand, are based on clinical practice. What this means is that, unlike philosophical theories, they can be taken seriously: "Our theories are ... not just fabricated out of thin air or thought up over the writing desk."[11] Freud's claim—and it is a dogmatic one—is that philosophers cannot give an account of "the facts of transference and of resistance" (SE 14:16/GW 10:54)[12] because they have "no kind of observation other than self-observation" (SE 19:217/GW 14:104). They can only speculate or conjecture about the unconscious. They can only put forward the unconscious as a *premise* (*Voraussetzung*), whereas psychoanalysis puts it forward as a *product* or a *finding* (*Ergebnis, Erwerb*), as a theoretical inference "legitimately drawn from innumerable observations" (SE 14:17/GW 10:55). This is why Freud will often associate philosophy with abstractions, guesses, intuitions—and speculation. Speculation is no substitute for "a patient and tireless elaboration of facts from the world of perception" (SE 19:217/GW 14:104).[13]

In other words, the "laborious approaches" (SE 18:180/GW 17:30)[14] of psychoanalysis are the gold standard for research when it comes to questions of sexuality, repression, and the unconscious. Or as Derrida puts it in the opening pages of "To Speculate—on 'Freud'": "Schopenhauer's and Nietzsche's words and 'notions' resemble psychoanalytic discourse to the point of being mistaken for it. But they are lacking the equivalent of a content proper to psychoanalysis, which alone can guarantee value, usage, and exchange" ("SoF" 266/284). Philosophical abstractions issue only the "simulacra of concepts" ("SoF" 266/284). To have content or value, a philosophical concept must *first* be *seconded* by psychoanalysis:

> There are famous philosophers who may be cited as forerunners. . . . Psychoanalysis has this advantage only, that it has not affirmed . . . the psychical importance of sexuality and the unconsciousness of mental life . . . on an *abstract* basis, but has demonstrated them in matters that touch every individual personally and force him to take up some attitude towards these problems. (SE 17:143–44/GW 12:12)

> Nietzsche [is] another philosopher whose guesses and intuitions often agree in the most astonishing way with the laborious findings of psychoanalysis [*mit den mühsamen Ergebnissen der Psychoanalyse*]. (SE 20:59–60/GW 14:86)

> What [Schopenhauer] says about the struggle against accepting a distressing piece of reality coincides with my concept of repression so completely . . . I had therefore to be prepared . . . to forgo all claims to priority in the many instances in which laborious psychoanalytic investigation [*die mühselige psychoanalytische Forschung*] can merely confirm the truths which the philosopher recognized by intuition. (SE 14:15–16/GW 10:53)

Only the laborious, painstaking findings of psychoanalysis can give value to the philosopher's guesses and intuitions. Thus, even if there is something disagreeable and "painful [*pénible*]" ("SoF" 263/281) about the ease with which the philosopher intuitively arrives at the truths of psychoanalysis,[15] Freud remains unflappable. He has no need for originality: "I am very ready to give up [*opfere*] the prestige of originality . . . especially as I can never be certain, in view of the wide extent of my reading in early years, whether what I took for a new creation might not be an effect of cryptomnesia [*eine Leistung der Kryptomnesie*]" (SE 23:245/GW 16:90–91). Or as he writes to Georg Groddeck in 1917: "If you are so sure of the autonomy of your acquisitions, why do you still need originality?" (GG 37/B 333).

The Icarus Complex: Georg Groddeck and Alfred Adler

For Freud, on contrary, there seems to be something symptomatic and dangerous about this need for originality.[16] Following the secessions of Adler and Jung, he will even caution his would-be followers against the danger of such a need or desire. In his very first letter to Groddeck (June 5, 1917)—in response to Groddeck's envy and anguish at not being himself the author of *The Psychopathology of Everyday Life* and *The Interpretation of Dreams*—Freud expresses his misgivings with some brutality:

The Speculative Turn 77

Thus, while I would like to hold out both my hands to you to receive you as a colleague, there is only one disturbing circumstance, the fact that you have not managed to overcome the trivial ambition of claiming originality and priority. If you are so sure of the autonomy of your acquisitions why do you still need originality? Anyway, can you be sure in this respect? You must be 10 or 15 or perhaps 20 years younger than I am (1856). Could you have absorbed the main ideas of psychoanalysis in a cryptomnesic way [*auf kryptomnestischem Wege aufgenommen haben*]? In a way similar to my discoveries relating to my own originality? What's the use of struggling for priority against an older generation?

I regret this point of your information particularly since experience has shown that an untamed ambitious individual [*ein ungebändigter Ehrgeiziger*] sooner or later jumps up and turns into an eccentric [*Eigenbrötler*] to the detriment of science and of his own career [*zum Schaden der Wissenschaft wie seiner eigenen Entwicklung*]. (GG 37/B 333)

Given the necessary possibility of cryptomnesic absorption, why struggle for priority? Why risk it? We know from experience what happens to people when they let their ambitions get the best of them. Too much ambition and you can kiss your career goodbye. Instead of being original in a good sense, in the sense of being innovative, creative, imaginative, inventive, you become "an eccentric or unusual person" (*OED*), *an original* (*Eigenbrötler*), to the detriment of science and your own development.

Now it is worth noting that Freud immediately connects this danger to Groddeck's commitment to "philosophical theories": "Why do you jump from your solid basis into mysticism, cancel out the distinction between mental and somatic, commit yourself to philosophical theories, which are not called for" (GG 37–38/B 33)? By canceling out the distinction between mental and somatic (and Freud uses the verb *aufheben*), that is, by sublating the somatic, by assimilating and reducing it to the psychical, Groddeck commits himself, Freud laments, to "philosophical theories" that are pernicious here. Indeed, what is lost in this sublation, what Groddeck's "monistic inclination [*monistische Neigung*]" (GG 38/B 334) ends up discarding or disregarding (*geringschätzen*), is precisely difference. Groddeck is too much at home with the "temptation offered by unity": "I am afraid you are a philosopher whose monistic inclination causes you to discard . . . differences . . . in the face of the temptation offered by unity [*die Lockung der Einheit*]. Can we get rid of differences like that? [*Werden wir damit die Differenzen los?*]" (GG 38/B 334). In other words, the lure of unity, the desire for "a flawless and complete theory [*lückenlose und abgerundete Theorie*]" (SE 11:20/GW 8:16)—the philosophical phantasm (PP) par excellence, according to Freud—is the siren song that lulls vulnerable analytic minds to sleep. In contrast, true analytic work proceeds "step by step, without the inner need for completion, continually under the pressure of the problem immediately at hand and taking infinite pains not to be diverted from the path."[17]

But perhaps no example is quite as revealing of the perils of unbridled ambition and system building[18] as that of Alfred Adler: "The Adlerian theory was from the very beginning a 'system'—which psychoanalysis was careful to avoid becoming" (SE 14:52/GW 10:96).[19] Not only does Freud speak of Adler's "uncontrolled craving for priority [*unbändige Prioritätssucht*]" (SE 14:51/GW 10:95);[20] he also speaks of his "particularly speculative disposition" (SE 14:50/GW 10:94), his tendency to provide only "sweeping synthesis [*weitumfassende Synthese*]" and "misleading generalization [*irreführende Verallgemeinerung*]" (SE 10:140/GW 7:371).

Although Freud considered Adler's ideas about the primacy of feelings of inferiority to be "radically false," they were consistent and coherent enough, and, in spite of everything, they were "founded upon a theory of the drives" (SE 14:60/GW 10:105). Or rather they took the theory of the *drives* (plural) and reduced it to a theory of *the* drive (singular), to a theory of *one* drive—the aggressive drive: "The view of life which is reflected in the Adlerian system," writes Freud, "is founded exclusively on the aggressive drive" (SE 14:58/GW 10:102). Everything is pressed into the service of power and domination ("masculine protest, self-assertion and the aggrandizement of the personality" [SE 14:57/GW 10:102]). Adler reduces both the formation of character and the neuroses to the desire for power and to the need to compensate for self-perceived and constitutional inferiorities. And in so doing, he repudiates sexuality. Or rather sexuality becomes nothing more than another expression of aggression, as Freud remarks with some consternation: "[Adler] positively considers that the strongest motive force in the sexual act is the man's intention of showing himself master of the woman—of being 'on top.' I do not know if he has expressed these monstrous notions [*diese Ungeheuerlichkeiten*] in his writings" (SE 14:53/GW 10:97). In other words, for Adler just as for Groddeck, an uncontrolled craving for priority leads to a theoretical regression—namely, to a solution (*Lösung*) that presents itself as a deliverance (*Erlösung*) from "the revolutionary and inconvenient advances of psychoanalysis" (SE 17:53/GW 12:82).

But in the case of Adler, it also leads to a bit of confusion, which I will call, for reasons that will become clear in a moment, "priority confusion" (which, like "nipple confusion," is also bound up with early, humanizing processes). Freud tells us that, on one occasion at the Vienna Society, Adler made fun of what he took to be a psychoanalytic impasse: "If you ask where repression comes from, you are told 'from civilization'; but if you go on to ask where civilization comes from, you are told 'from repression.' So you see it is all simply playing with words" (SE 14:56/GW 10:101).

For Freud, of course, there is no cause for confusion, since both thesis and antithesis are true: Civilization comes from the repression of prior generations, and present-day repression comes from the need to maintain this civilization. What so addles Adler, it would seem, or at least this is Freud's reading of his confusion, is a logic such that it becomes impossible to say for sure which comes first: the chicken or the egg. Freud concludes the anecdote as follows:

> I once heard of a child who thought people were laughing at him, and began to cry, because when he asked where eggs came from he was told "from hens," and when he asked where hens came from he was told "from eggs." But they were not playing with words; on the contrary, they were telling him the truth. (SE 14:57/GW 10:101)

Like the child in Freud's story, Adler wants a single, simple, founding principle or origin. And it is here that Adler's "striving ... for a place in the sun [*Streben ... nach einem Platz an der Sonne*]" (SE 14:51/GW 10:95) must throw shade on psychoanalysis. In order to preserve his system intact, Adler must turn away "from observation and from the technique of psychoanalysis," just as he must "re-interpret, distort or jettison the factual findings of analysis" (SE 14:62–63/GW 10:108). Only that which does not require one to plumb the depths of sexuality is acceptable, even desirable. In the end, Freud tells us, Adler is nothing but a sunseeker, a creature of the light who has found his "stay in the underworld of psychoanalysis [*Aufenthalt in der Unterwelt der Psychoanalyse*] too uncomfortable" (SE 14:66/GW 10:113).

And here we may perhaps read the Adlerian *system* as a narcissistic extension of the man. Here is Freud's description of Adler in "On the History of the Psychoanalytic Movement":

> I may even speak publicly of the personal motive for his work, since he himself announced it in the presence of a small circle of members of the Vienna group:—"Do you think it gives me such great pleasure [*ein so großes Vergnügen*] to stand in your shadow [*Schatten*] my whole long life?" To be sure, I see nothing reprehensible in a younger man freely admitting his ambition. ... But even though a man is dominated by a motive of this kind he should avoid being ... "unfair." ... How little Adler has succeeded in this is shown by the profusion of petty outbursts

of malice which disfigure his writings and by the indications they contain of an uncontrolled craving for priority. (SE 14:51/GW 10:94)

In other words, as Adler reportedly tells Freud, it gives him no pleasure to follow in Freud's footsteps or to stand in his shadow. What gives him pleasure, on the other hand—we must assume—is his system building, his *erection* of a system (and if we take his notion of "organ inferiority" seriously, if we understand it as what, in a literal sense, acts as a spur and calls for compensatory activity, we might even venture to read in this erection a sign of *phallic narcissism*).[21] Thus, the system, by means of which Adler takes leave of psychoanalysis on his "agreeable upward journey [*bequeme Auffahrt*]" (SE 14:66/GW 10:113), is a way of giving himself pleasure, of pleasuring himself.

And if there is anything Freud warns us against, it this kind of system-pleasure (which would be not a sublimation of thinking but a pathology, a permanent priapism, a literal and literalizing phallogocentrism). Science, of course, is Freud's antidote to this kind of pleasure-seeking activity. Not only can psychoanalysis not repudiate its descent from the exact sciences, but the exact sciences are *exacting*. As scientists, Freud reminds us, psychoanalysts remain distrustful "of the power of human wishes and of the temptations of the pleasure principle" (SE 18:178–79/GW 17:29). So much so, in fact, that they are willing to "sacrifice everything [*alles zu opfern*]" if it means attaining "some fragment of objective certainty" (SE 18:179/GW 17:29). Thus, everything associated with systematic unity must be sacrificed: "the dazzling brilliance of a flawless theory, the exalted consciousness of having achieved a comprehensive view of the universe, and the mental calm brought about by the possession of extensive grounds for expedient and ethical action" (SE 18:178–79/GW 17:29). Only in this way can analysis be sure to exclude (*auszuschließen*) "the wishes of mankind from material reality" (SE 18:179/GW 17:29). As Lacan reminds us, analysis "in no way allows us to accept some such aphorism as *life is a dream*."[22]

Rather, psychoanalysis labors in the underworld. It labors "in the depths" (SE 14:66/GW 10:113). And this is what distinguishes it from other disciplines or forms of knowledge. Freud will insist that what sets psychoanalysis apart—from philosophy but also, as we saw in Chapter 4, from any kind of "successful speculation" that abandons the "habits of patient humdrum work" (SE 18:180/GW 17:30)—is its shadowy, subterranean world and painstaking research.[23] There is no gratifying upward journey. There is only the "long, patient and unbiased work" (SE 20:50/GW 14:76) of psychoanalysis.[24]

Seduction, Speculation, and the Death Drive

And this brings us back to philosophy and psychoanalysis. As we know from the letters[25] and from Ernest Jones's biography, Freud was both fascinated and repelled by philosophy. There was always something dangerously seductive about its speculative tendencies. In response to Jones's question as to how much philosophy he had read in his youth, Freud's answer was: "Very little. As a young man I felt a strong attraction toward speculation and ruthlessly checked it."[26] Or, as we read in Freud's account of the history of the psychoanalytic movement: "I learnt to restrain speculative tendencies [*Ich erlernte es, speculative Neigungen zu bändigen*] and to follow the unforgotten advice of my master, Charcot: to look at the same things again and again until they themselves beg[a]n to speak" (SE 14:22/GW 10:60).

Psychoanalytic theory is not a theory that falls ready-made from the sky. It is the fruit of an "unprejudiced examination of the facts" (SE 11:20/GW 8:16), and it holds fast to the habit of "always studying things themselves" (SE 14:19/GW 10:58). In other words, Freud's impulse to speculate is something that must be inhibited, repressed—and ruthlessly so. Curb your (speculative) enthusiasm, one can hear Freud's scientific superego saying. Do not let psychoanalysis become a "speculative system" (SE 16:244/GW 11:250) or a "speculative theory" (SE 14:77/GW 10:142).[27] Avoid "any contact with philosophy proper" (SE 20:59/GW 14:86). Do not erase or reduce—in the name of the system, a flawless and complete theory—the observed facts, that is to say, "what [is] accidental and personal" (SE 14:63/GW 10:109) in psychoanalysis. Do not take flight from reality.[28] You *may not be* like this (like philosophy). Remember: The foundation of psychoanalysis lies in "observation alone" (SE 14:77/GW 10:142).

So speaks the (scientific) superego. And yet, as we also know, the superego has a double aspect, for its task is to repress the ego's earliest identifications. Thus, the superego's relation to the ego is not exhausted by its prohibition: You *may not be* like this (like philosophy). It also comprises the precept: You *ought to be* like this (like philosophy). In other words, Freud's striking gesture of denegation, his quasi-phobic avoidance of philosophy, cannot help but reflect the force of his attraction to philosophy. As Derrida remarks: "The avoidance (of Schopenhauer, of Nietzsche, of philosophy), such avoidance must not, it seems to me, be interpreted too simplistically. On the one hand, if there is such a persistent avoidance of both philosophy and what Freud calls . . . 'speculation,' if there is such a persistent avoidance, it is, of course, because there is temptation, tendency, inclination"

(LVLM 283).²⁹ And what is avoided is pleasure, a pleasure that would be incompatible with psychoanalysis and would inhibit its aims:

> I have denied myself the very great pleasure [*den hohen Genuß*] of reading the works of Nietzsche, with the deliberate object of not being hampered [*behindert*] in working out the impressions received in psychoanalysis by any sort of anticipatory ideas. (SE 14:15–16/GW 10:53).

> Nietzsche ... was for a long time avoided [*gemieden*] by me. ... I was less concerned with the question of priority than with keeping my mind unembarrassed [*an der Priorität lag mir ja weniger als an der Erhaltung meiner Unbefangenheit*]. (SE 20:60/GW 14:86)

Freud must deny himself the pleasure, the very great pleasure, of reading Nietzsche. Unlike Adler and Groddeck, who overindulged their speculative tendencies, Freud must abstain from reading philosophy. He must not yield to his "lust for speculation"; for to give in to philosophy, to take too great a pleasure in philosophy, would be to lose his head and, with it, his (open) mind.³⁰

And yet in his later years, as we well know, Freud lets himself go. He no longer holds back: "In the works of my later years (*Beyond the Pleasure Principle* [1920], *Group Psychology and the Analysis of the Ego* [1921], and *The Ego and the Id* [1923]), I have given free rein to the inclination, which I kept down for so long, to speculation" (SE 20:57/GW 14:84). Although there is still more work to be done, although Freud still expresses some anxiety about his proximity to philosophy—"I should not like to create an impression that during this last period of my work I have turned my back upon patient observation and have abandoned myself entirely to speculation. I have ... always remained in the closest touch with analytic material. ... Even when I have moved away from observation, I have carefully avoided any contact with philosophy proper" (SE 20:59/GW 14:85–86)—it is clear that the success of psychoanalysis, or perhaps the success of his self-analysis, has had a therapeutic (an anxiolytic) effect on his speculative impulses. Freud has become less neurotic, less inhibited in his ability and his willingness to speculate.

It is here that Freud's 1920 text *Beyond the Pleasure Principle* marks a watershed in the history of psychoanalysis. Not only is Freud able to speculate in this text, but he is also able to do so in a way that is *weitausholend*. His speculation, when it comes, is far-reaching and far-ranging: It takes us back to the origin of consciousness and to the beginning of life, as we saw in Chapter 2. And yet even in this text, the buildup to what will be Freud's

The Speculative Turn

weitausholende Spekulation takes time—and the back-and-forth movement of his examples (of traumatic dreams, children's play, and the transference neuroses). Thus, in the opening paragraphs of *Beyond the Pleasure Principle*, Freud begins not with speculation but only with "speculative assumptions," which he carefully distinguishes from philosophy:[31] "It is of no concern to us in this connection to enquire how far, with this hypothesis of the pleasure principle, we have approached or adopted any particular, historically established philosophical system. We have arrived at these speculative assumptions [*zu solchen spekulativen Annahmen*] in an attempt to describe and to account for the facts of daily observation in our field of study" (SE 18:7/GW 13:3).

And then nothing. No further speculation in *Beyond*. For three whole chapters, Freud hems and haws, he pussyfoots around, he beats around the bush. Until, finally, we get the payoff. After some heavy *fort/da* play in which Freud maintains and then loses his direction ("This does not seem to necessitate any far-reaching limitation of the pleasure principle" [SE 18:11/GW 13:8]; "No certain decision can be reached from the analysis of a single case like this" [SE 18:16/GW 13:13]; "The consideration of these cases and situations . . . are of no use for *our* purposes . . . they give no evidence of the operation of tendencies beyond the pleasure principle" [SE 18:17/GW 13:15]),[32] we get the money shot: "What follows is speculation, often far-reaching speculation [*Was nun folgt, ist Spekulation, oft weitausholende Spekulation*], which the reader will consider or dismiss according to his individual predilection" (SE 18:24/GW 13:23, modified). Of course, when Freud finally goes all the way, when he gives in to his long-suppressed (*niedergehalten*) inclination, his speculation is not easy to contain; it is unrestrained, expansive, far-reaching (*de grande envergure*). Or as Strachey suggests by translating *weitausholend* as "far-fetched": It is hard to swallow.

When speculation returns, you might say, it returns *with a vengeance*. A vengeance that is both figurative and literal. For not only does Freud's speculation go full throttle in Chapter 4 of *Beyond*, it also culminates in the hypothesis of "a *death* or *destructive drive* [*Todes- oder Destruktionstrieb*]" (SE 20:57/GW 14:84, modified). When Freud finally speculates, he speculates that "'*the aim of all life is death*'" (SE 18:38/GW 13:40) and that "the organism wishes to die only in its own fashion" (SE 18: 39/GW 13: 41). In short, Freud's speculation is a speculation "unleashed . . . as unleashing" (LVLM 324)—the unleashing of death and (self-) destruction.

Paradoxically, however, Freud's speculative hypothesis of the repetition compulsion and of the death drive breathes new life into psychoanalytic theory. Indeed, dissolution (*Auflösung*) and disintegration (*Zerfall*) provide Freud with a new solution (*Lösung*) to the problem of the drives:[33]

> I have given free rein to the inclination ... to speculation, and I have also contemplated a new solution to the problem of the drives. (SE 20:57/GW 14:84)

> Starting from speculations [*Ausgehend von Spekulationen*] on the beginning of life and from biological parallels, I drew the conclusion that, besides the drive to preserve living substance and to join it into ever larger units, there must exist another, contrary drive to dissolve those units [*aufzulösen*] and to bring them back to their primeval, inorganic state. That is to say, as well as Eros there was a death drive. (SE 21:118/GW 14:477–78, modified)

> As a result of a little speculation [*Mit etwas Aufwand von Spekulation*], we have come to suppose that this [destructive] drive is at work in every living creature and is striving to bring it to ruin [*zum Zerfall zu bringen*] and to reduce life to its original condition of inanimate matter. (SE 22:211/GW 16:22, modified)

Freud's speculative hypothesis of death and destruction brings new life to the theory of the drives; it brings new life to what is "the most important ... portion of psychoanalytic theory" (SE 7:168n2/GW 5:67n1, modified).[34] This is because the hypothesis of a death drive is, ultimately, a rethinking of "life," of the phenomena of life. To say that the organism follows "its own path to death" is, for Freud, to give us "the picture of the phenomena of life" (SE 18:39/GW 13:41).[35] In short, the organism's attempt *not to die* is an attempt *to die* (but only in its own way)—and that's life!

Thus, if life is neither simply opposed to nor identified with death, if life is already "life death" (two words, no hyphen, as Derrida writes it in the title of his 1975–1976 seminar *Life Death* and on the first page of "To Speculate—on 'Freud'"), must the same not be said of the "life" of psychoanalysis? Does psychoanalysis not also, inevitably, speak "about" the very concepts that implicate its own life as theory, practice, and technique whenever it speculates on the drives? What would it mean to speak of the "life death" of psychoanalysis? Or another way of asking this question: What would it mean to take Freud's speculative play seriously?

For starters, it would mean resisting any fixed position or side. We would have to take our distance from those who take seriously the so-called theses of *Beyond*—theses that, as Derrida says, "one would be hard pressed ... to find there" (LVLM 341); we would have to resist siding with

The Speculative Turn

those who structure their entire discourse "upon the *seriousness* of *Beyond* (the most spectacular case in this respect being Lacan)" (LVLM 341, my emphasis). Likewise, we would have to resist taking sides with those who take *Beyond lightly*, that is, with those who shrug off the text as a "very *unserious* game on the part of the master" (LVLM 341, my emphasis) and who say "the master was [just] playing, he wasn't being serious ("SoF" 377/402, modified). To take Freud's speculation seriously, we would have to take seriously the *play*, the back-and-forth, the "game-like character of his speculation" (LVLM 343). For it is the serious play of speculation in *Beyond* that *seriously* challenges the foundations of psychoanalytic theory. In a more analytic vein one might say that, by changing his (psychoanalysis's) relation to his (its) own repressed element (that is, speculation), Freud succeeds in *bringing* the initial findings of psychoanalysis *into play* (beginning with the dominance of the pleasure principle and the theory of dreams as wish fulfillment). And this success is bound up with the hypothesis of the repetition compulsion and the death drive.

Now Freud himself will wonder just how seriously to take his own speculative hypotheses: "It may be asked whether and how far I am myself convinced of the truth of the hypotheses that have been set out in these pages" (SE 18:59/GW 13:63–64). If Freud suddenly reflects on how seriously he takes his own speculation at the end of Chapter 6, it is not only because he has finally learned how to speculate at long last (and we can only imagine the pleasure).[39] It is also because his speculation has just landed him in a very strange place (*Stelle*) indeed. At the end of Chapter 6, immediately preceding this back-and-forth with himself, Freud has unwittingly steered his course into the harbor of Plato's philosophy. His speculation had led him to take seriously an incredibly far-fetched hypothesis—"a myth rather than a scientific explanation" (SE 18:57/GW 13:62). This hypothesis, he declares, is of "so fantastic a kind" (SE 18:57/GW 13:62) that he would never have ventured to produce it had it not fulfilled the one thing he desired most of all, namely, a theory in which the origin of the (sexual) drive can be traced to back to a "*need to restore an earlier state of things*" (SE 18:57–58/GW 13:62–63). Out of the blue, like a flare illuminating the horizon or a hallucinated breast, "the theory which Plato put into the mouth of Aristophanes in the *Symposium*" (SE 18:57/GW 13:62) comes as the culmination of all of Freud's speculative desires.[40] At the end of Chapter 6, then, it is the philosopher and not the scientist, the "poet-philosopher [*Dichterphilosoph*]" (SE 18:58/GW 13:63) and not the wise Weismann, who is able to bring Freud's speculative hypothesis to its climax. Science has failed to throw any light on the "obscurity [*Dunkel*] that reigns ... in the theory of the drives" (SE 18:53/GW 13:57). It has led only to a dead end, an impasse, "an equation with two unknown quantities" (SE 18:57/GW 13:62). Instead it is Plato's fantastic hypothesis that leads Freud's speculation to its paroxysmal moment and pleasurable release: "But this is, I think, the place [*Stelle*] for breaking off" (SE 18:58/GW 13:62, modified).

Thus, Plato plays a crucial—and paradoxically analytic—role, I will suggest, in Freud's ability to speculate with pleasure in *Beyond the Pleasure Principle*. Plato helps bring Freud's speculation-envy[41] to an end. After *Beyond*, as we know, Freud is able to give free rein to his inclination to speculate, and, in one of his very last references to "speculation," in "Analysis Terminable and Interminable" (1937), he even claims that, without speculation, there can be no movement, no forward step for psychoanalysis: "Without ... speculation ... —I had almost said 'phantasying [*Phantasieren*]'—[psychoanalysis] shall not get another step forward" (SE 23:225/GW 16:69). Psychoanalysis needs speculation, as it were, if it is not to remain inhibited, clenched, *verklemmt*.

And not only is Freud able to accept his speculative tendencies in the wake of *Beyond*, he is also able to embrace the "mythological" nature of the drives. In 1933, in his letter to Albert Einstein "Why War?" (1933 [1932]) or in his *New Introductory Lectures* (1933 [1932]), Freud speaks of "our mythological theory of the drives" (SE 22:212/GW 16:23, modified); he explains that "the theory of the drives is ... our mythology [*Die Trieblehre ist ... unsere Mythologie*]" (SE 22:95/GW 15:101, modified).[42]

But it is here that we must pause and recall that Freud's relation to Plato is not a simple one. It is not that psychoanalysis has embraced philosophy or become philosophical, for example. For if Aristophanes's myth marks the climax of Freud's speculative turn in *Beyond*, the same myth occupies a very different place in the *Three Essays*. As we will see, what is valorized here (*da*) in *Beyond* (1920) is precisely what is devalorized there (*fort*) in the *Three Essays* (1905) or in "An Outline of Psychoanalysis" (1938). Though it may be obvious, it is an obscure obviousness that one must begin by recalling: Over the course of thirty years, from the first edition of the *Three Essays* in 1905 to "An Outline of Psychoanalysis" in 1938, by way of *Beyond*, Freud treats Plato like a yo-yo, a wooden reel, a plaything, a *Spielzeug*—or an analyst. Indeed, what I am suggesting here is that we take this game, this game of *fort/da*,[43] seriously. For Plato, more than any other philosopher in Freud's work (be it Aristotle, Augustine, Berkeley, Brentano, Cicero, Democritus, Descartes, Diderot, Empedocles, Fichte, Hegel, Heraclitus, Herder, Hobbes, Kant, Lucretius, Maine de Biran, Nietzsche,

Plotinus, Rousseau, Schelling, Schiller, Schleiermacher, Schopenhauer, Smith, Vaihinger, or Voltaire), plays a *vital*—literally a life-and-death—role in Freud's "mythology."

Playing with Plato

THREE ESSAYS ON THE THEORY OF SEXUALITY

As one might expect, there is no simple beginning or origin when it comes to claims about the *Symposium* in Freud's work.[44] Chronologically, we find Freud's first reference to the dialogue in 1905, in the first edition of the *Three Essays on the Theory of Sexuality*. Editorially, however, Freud's first reference to the *Symposium* is to be found in the fourth Preface to the *Three Essays*, a preface that is completed in 1920, just months before the publication of *Beyond the Pleasure Principle*. Although it is chronologically second, as "front matter," this Preface immediately precedes the first reference to the *Symposium* in the *Three Essays*. And this is important because, as we will see, what Freud says in the Preface contradicts[45] what he says in the body of the text. From the first, that is, Plato is both *fort* and *da*.

I will begin with the first reference, that is, with the reference that is chronologically second. In his 1920 Preface, Freud draws up a postwar balance sheet of the state of psychoanalysis. On the positive side, he notes, with pleasure, that "interest in psychoanalytic research remains unimpaired in the world at large" (SE 7:133/GW 5:31). Not only has interest in psychoanalysis in general survived "the flood-waters of war," but certain, purely psychological theses and findings of psychoanalysis "have come to enjoy increasing recognition and have won notice even from those who are in general opposed to [its] theories" (SE 7:133/GW 5:31). Even the opponents of psychoanalysis have been won over by the findings of psychoanalysis. These findings include: "the unconscious, repression, conflict as a cause of illness, the advantage accruing from illness, the mechanisms of symptom formation" (SE 7:133/GW 5:31).

But not all parts of Freud's theory have shared the same fate. On the contrary, "that part of the theory which lies on the frontiers of biology . . . is still faced with undiminished opposition" (SE 7:133/GW 5:31, modified). Freud attributes this opposition to his continued insistence on the importance of sexuality in all human achievements and to his attempt to enlarge the concept of sexuality. As Freud says, that part of the theory of psychoanalysis that insists upon the primacy of sexuality has "even led some who for a time took a very active interest in psychoanalysis to abandon it and to adopt fresh views which were intended to restrict once more the factor of sexuality in normal and pathological mental life" (SE 7:133/GW 5:31). While the purely psychological theses and findings of psychoanalysis were met with general acceptance and approval by those who were in principle opponents, the theory of sexuality, on the other hand, elicited great resistance even among friends. In the words of French analyst Jean Laplanche: *"What is accepted is repression but what is repressed is the repressed, and the repressed is sexuality."*[46] Or in the words of Molière: "Que diable allait-il faire dans cette galère [Why on earth did he have to get involved in that business]?"

It is the business of sexuality that, as Freud complains, leads people to raise the "senseless charge" of pansexualism against psychoanalysis, according to which psychoanalysis would explain "'everything' by sex [*'alles' aus der Sexualität*]" (SE 7:134/GW 5:32).[47] To dispel this accusation (baseless, according to him),[48] Freud will now claim a respectable, philosophical heritage. Here, then, in this 1920 Preface, Freud makes an appeal—first to Schopenhauer and then to Plato (just as he does in Chapter 6 of *Beyond*)—in order to legitimate the psychoanalytic theory and concept of sexuality:

> People have gone so far in their search for high-sounding catchwords as to talk of the "pansexualism" of psychoanalysis and to raise the senseless charge against it of explaining "everything" by sex. We might be astonished at this, if we ourselves could forget the way in which emotional factors make people confused and forgetful. For it is some time since Arthur Schopenhauer, the philosopher, showed mankind the extent to which their activities are determined by sexual impulses—in the ordinary sense of the word. . . . And as for the "stretching [*Ausdehnung*]" of the concept of sexuality . . . anyone who looks down with contempt upon psychoanalysis from a superior vantage point should remember how closely [*wie nahe*] the enlarged sexuality of psychoanalysis coincides [*zusammentrifft*] with the Eros of the divine Plato. (SE 7:134/GW 5:32)

From Schopenhauer the world has received a theory of sexuality "in the ordinary sense of the word." But from Plato, "the divine Plato," it has received a broad and extended concept of sexuality under the name of "Eros," a concept that coincides so closely with the "expanded sexuality of psychoanalysis [*die erwiderte Sexualität der Psychoanalyse*]" (SE 7:134/GW 5:32, modified) that it has become synonymous with it. In other words, the psychoanalytic theory of sexuality finds its precursor and greatest support in "the Eros of the divine Plato." In 1920, that is, we have a downright positive (albeit self-serving) identification with Plato.[49]

But it is a little difficult to take this identificatory bromance seriously. This is because in the original edition of the *Three Essays*—and this is the very first reference to the *Symposium* in all of Freud's published work[50]—Plato is associated with the very thing from which psychoanalytic theory wishes to *depart*, namely, the popular view of the sexual drive. It is this popular view, naïve and unscientific, which sees the sexual object as fixed and forming part of the drive, that psychoanalysis sets out to challenge. In 1905, in other words, it is this popular view of sexuality that Plato's "poetic fable" so beautifully reflects: "The popular view of the sexual drive is beautifully reflected in the poetic fable which tells how the original human beings were cut into two halves—man and woman—and how these are always striving to unite again in love" (SE 7:136/GW 5:34).

Again, it is hard to take Freud seriously here. As anyone who has taught the *Symposium* to undergraduates at an American university will tell you, this is not the whole story. In fact, one might say that Freud has literally cut *two halves* out of the story told by Aristophanes, for the two halves that he mentions—"man and woman"—represent the two halves of only one kind of human being, the androgynous kind, the kind that combines both genders. In the beginning, according to Aristophanes, there were three kinds of human beings and, more importantly, *four other halves*. Here is what Aristophanes says:

> There were three kinds [*genē*] of human beings, that's my first point. Each of us, then, is a "matching" half [*symbolon*] of a human whole. Because each was sliced like a flatfish, two out of one, and each is always seeking the half that matches him. That's why a man who is split from the double sort (which used to be called "androgynous") runs after women. Many lecherous men have come from this class, and so do lecherous women who run after men. Women who are split from a woman, however, pay no attention at all to men; they are oriented more towards women, and lesbians come from this class. People who are split from a male are male-oriented. While they are boys, because they are chips off the male block, they love men and enjoy lying with men and being embraced by men; those are the best boys and lads, because they are the most manly in their nature. (191d–192a)[51]

This is hardly, let us just say, a reflection of the popular view of the sexual drive. By cutting out two halves of the story told by Aristophanes, Freud becomes something of a puppeteer who feigns surprise at the sudden arrival of the very puppets he has cleverly hidden offstage. In the line immediately following the one in which he equates the popular view of sexuality with this poetic fable, Freud writes: "It comes as a great surprise [*eine große Überraschung*] therefore to learn that there are men whose sexual object is a man and not a woman, and women whose sexual object is a woman and not a man." No student of Plato's poetic fable would be at all surprised by this discovery.

But we must remember that Freud's appeal to Plato's poetic fable comes under the heading "Deviations in Respect of the Sexual Object," and if Freud turns to homosexuality or "inversion" to exemplify one possible deviation with respect to the sexual object (his other examples being pedophilia and zoophilia), he does so not in order to explain homosexual object choice but rather to show that object choice does not follow necessarily or directly from the sexual drive. In other words, Plato's poetic fable would indeed, much like the popular view of the sexual drive, still derive sexual object choice from sexual drive. In this way, Aristophanes's speech would remain a classic story of origins, a poetic fable that eulogizes the intimacy of the connection between drive and object.

In his conclusion to the section, Freud gives us what is, therefore, a very non-Platonic account of the nature of the connection between drive and object:

> It has been brought to our notice that we have been in the habit of regarding the connection between the sexual drive and the sexual object as more intimate than it in fact is. Experience of the cases that are considered abnormal has shown us that in them the sexual drive and the sexual object are merely soldered together [*Die Erfahrung . . . lehrt uns, daß hier zwischen Sexualtrieb und Sexualobjekt eine Verlötung vorliegt*]—a fact which we have been in danger of overlooking in consequence of the uniformity of the normal picture, where the drive appears to bring with it the object [*wo der Trieb das Objekt mitzubringen scheint*]. We are thus warned to loosen the bond that exists in our thoughts between drive and object. It seems probable that the sexual drive is in the first instance independent [*unabhängig*] of its object. (SE 7:147–48 / GW 5:46–47, modified)

Experience teaches us that there exists here a *soldering* between the sexual drive and the sexual object. The sexual drive is *soldered* to the sexual object. What does this mean? On the one hand, it means something very simple: Between the sexual drive and the sexual object there exists a connection about which one can say *neither* that it is innate (one is not born with one's sexual drive attached to any particular sexual object) *nor* that it is acquired (the fact that one's sexual drive should cathect an object is not a matter of sheer contingency from without).

On the other hand, however, there is something strange and surprising about this connection. "Soldering" is a trope, a figural or metaphorical expression for a connection that cannot be reduced to a given alternative (innate/acquired, somatic/psychical).[52] It is a trope that suggests an unnatural or non-natural connection, an artificial joining that is in no way assured by nature (though it may have a naturalizing effect). This is why, as we saw in Chapter 2, sexuality remains a "weak point [*schwacher Punkt*]" (SE 7:149/GW 5:48, modified) or breaking point or turning point in the constitution of the human.

Before returning to *Beyond the Pleasure Principle*, however, I would like to turn for just a moment to Plato's poetic fable, for soldering appears in Aristophanes's story too, though in a somewhat different form. For psychoanalytic theory, as we have seen, human sexuality is characterized by a figure, a "soldering." For Aristophanes, on the other hand, Eros becomes something more literal—and more serious. Toward the end of Aristophanes's speech, Hephaestus, the lame god, the god of metals and metallurgy, the god of binding and unbinding, asks the lovers what it is they want from each other:

> Suppose that, as they lay together, Hephaestus should come and stand over them, and showing his implements should ask: "What is it, good mortals, that you would have of one another?"—and suppose that in their perplexity he asked them again: "Do you desire to be joined in the closest possible union, so that you shall not be divided by night or by day? If that is what you are craving, I am ready to fuse and weld you together in a single piece [*syntēxai kai sumphusēsai eis to auto*], that from being two you may be made one."[53]

The lovers are perplexed by Hephaestus's questions. They do not seize upon the "dream of unity with the primal object"[54] that is being offered them. They cannot say what it is they want from one another. They never answer Hephaestus.[55] Instead Aristophanes answers for them: "Surely you can see that no one who received such an offer would turn it down . . . namely, to be so joined and fused with his beloved that the two might be made one" (192e, modified). Hephaestus's proposed action would *literally* restore the two lovers to their lost wholeness, to an earlier state of things, to a world before punishment or nostalgia. It would "heal the wound of human nature" (191d). Paradoxically, one might say, the Eros of Plato's poetic fable strives to cancel itself out; it longs for a kind of pre-difference or in-difference to sexual difference. That is to say, by literalizing the figure of soldering, by taking Hephaestus's fantasy seriously, Plato's poetic fable suggests something like an "autoimmune" possibility of sexuality, a sexuality that would be undone by fusing (*suntēkō*) and welding (*sumphusaō*).

In a way, then, one might say that, when he appeals to Plato in *Beyond the Pleasure Principle* and gives free rein to his speculative tendencies, Freud returns to this autoimmune possibility—not as the literalizing fantasy of a figure of return to unity but as the very *serious play* between the death of sex (the death drive) and the life of Eros (the life drive). When Freud appeals to Plato, that is, he does so in order to associate "the drive for reuniting [*Trieb zur Wiedervereinigung*]" (SE 18:58 / GW 13:63), the drive to return to sexual predifferentiation, with the drive to return to a "prior, pre-animated"[56] or "inanimate state [*zum Leblosen*]" (SE 18:38 / GW 13:40, modified). In other words, as we will see, the myth of Aristophanes returns in Freud's speculation on the death drive, but it returns with a difference.

Beyond the Pleasure Principle

Let us return now to Chapter 6 of *Beyond*. When Freud appeals to the poet-philosopher, it is not, as it was in the *Three Essays*, in order to take leave of philosophy, to depart from its poetic fable. Rather it is to invoke Plato's fantastic, mythical hypothesis in support of his own:

> Science has so little to tell us about the origin of sexuality that we can liken the problem to a darkness into which not so much as a ray of a hypothesis has penetrated. In a very different place we *do* meet with such a hypothesis, which, however, is of such a fantastic kind—surely more of a myth [*ein Mythus*] than a scientific explanation—that I would not dare to cite it here, were it not that it fulfills just that condition whose fulfillment we desire. For it derives a drive from *the need to restore an earlier state of thing*s . . . I mean of course the theory which Plato put into the mouth of Aristophanes in the *Symposium*, and which deals not only with the *origin* of the sexual drive but also with the most important of its variations in relation to its object. "The original human nature was not like the present, but different. In the first place, the sexes were originally three in number, not two as they are now; there was man, woman, and the union of the two. . . ." Everything about these humans, however, was double, they had four hands and four feet, two faces, double private parts, etc. Thereupon, Zeus was moved to

divide each human in two parts, "like a sorb-apple which is halved for pickling." After the division had been made, "the two parts, each desiring its other half, came together, and threw their arms about one another eager to grow into one." (SE 18:57–58/GW 13:62, modified)

In Freud's quotation of Plato in *Beyond*, the three kinds of human beings described by Aristophanes are all present as are the four halves (namely, man-man and woman-woman) that were missing from Freud's earlier version of the "poetic fable" in the *Three Essays*. And what is more, Plato's "theory" is now being praised for recognizing, among other things, "the most important variations of [the sexual drive] in relation to its object," that is, the very thing it failed to recognize in the *Three Essays* when it so "beautifully reflect[ed]" the popular view of the sexual drive. The Eros of the divine Plato in *Beyond* is no longer *fort* (devalorized) but *da* (valorized). *Here* it is that with which the psychoanalytic theory of sexuality identifies and identifies itself. *Here* it shares a kinship with the psychoanalytic understanding of sexuality. When Freud returns to the Aristophanes myth in *Beyond*, it is with *a difference that brings sameness*. The myth that was made gone with is made nice with.

Now I am not the first to call attention to this reversal. Jean Laplanche has commented on it at length. But his reaction is one of great consternation. He is appalled by the way Freud yo-yoes Plato around. In his 1991 seminar entitled "Le fourvoiement biologisant de la sexualité chez Freud,"[57] Laplanche points with dismay to Freud's changing position on the Aristophanes myth. Where the *Three Essays* constituted an "event"[58] in Freud's thinking—with its insistence on polymorphous perversity, on the partial drives, on the erogenous zones—*Beyond* ushers in an Eros that is nothing but a travesty of infantile sexuality in "mythical guise" (TB 4/10). According to Laplanche, Freud betrays the great insight of the *Three Essays* by turning the sexual drive into the life drive in *Beyond*. The life drive, says Laplanche, is "an extraordinary invention designed to denote sexuality while desexualizing it" (TB 103/116). Reducing sexuality to its binding, unifying, synthesizing, totalizing form, says Laplanche, is to forget the ravages of libido, of *Lucifer amor*. It is to forget the anarchic, unbound, self-destructive functioning of sexuality in the *Three Essays*. Laplanche reminds us that the true opposition lies not between life and death but between two principles, both of which pertain to sexuality: the principle of binding that regulates the *sexual* life drives and the principle of unbinding that regulates the *sexual* death drives.[59] In other words—and there is a very clear diagram of this relation in the volume *Sexual: La sexualité élargie au sens freudien*

(2007)⁶⁰—Freud's "second dualism" (life drive versus death drive) should be subsumed under the term "sexuality." With the introduction of the life drive in *Beyond*, sexuality has become a watered-down version of itself. Sexuality after 1920, one might say, in homage to Blanchot's 1964 text on the apocalypse, "is disappointing."

But what is curious and interesting about Laplanche's attack on *Beyond* is that Aristophanes's myth returns again and again as the symptom of Freud's *fourvoiement*, his mistake, his going astray. Aristophanes's myth is, for Laplanche, the X that marks the spot of a regression:

> In contrast to the foil [*repoussoir*] that it was in the *Three Essays on the Theory of Sexuality*, Aristophanes' myth now emerges, thanks to an extraordinary and magical metamorphosis, as the very paradigm of sexuality. What is in danger of disappearing is the fragmented, perverse and goal-less sexuality [*la sexualité morcelée, perverse et non finalisée*] that was described in the *Three Essays*. (TB 104/117, modified)

Or again in "The So-Called Death Drive: A Sexual Drive":

> But what is troubling for the attentive reader is this: in the *Three Essays on the Theory of Sexuality* Freud had used Aristophanes' myth, specifically the concise expression of "popular opinion" as a foil [*repoussoir*], in order to underscore the value of his own conception of sexual life. And here, in *Beyond the Pleasure Principle*, this very same myth is given as the primordial model, the very prototype of Eros! It is, however, beyond doubt that between the sexual activity described in the *Three Essays* and the life drive understood as Eros in *Beyond the Pleasure Principle*, the discrepancies are not mere details. They are opposed to each other at every point. The first is autoerotic, fragmented and fragmenting [*morcelée et morcelante*], its sole aim being satisfaction by the shortest path; it has no consideration for the independence of the object, which is, to a large extent, exchangeable. Eros, on the contrary, is synthesis and an aspiration to synthesis; it is totally oriented toward the object—the total object. ("SDD" 168/201)

There is something unacceptable—not to say repellent, *repoussant*—for Laplanche in discovering that what was *fort* has come *da*. Either the myth is *fort*, a "repoussoir," a foil, as it was in the *Three Essays*, in which case sexuality preserves all of its original radicality. Or the myth becomes the prototype of sexuality, as Laplanche exclaims with great exasperation, marking *with an exclamation point* what he takes to be a going astray of the drive: "And here, in *Beyond the Pleasure Principle*, this very same myth is given as the primordial model, the very prototype of Eros!" Laplanche will even refer to this understanding of Eros as an "Aristophano-instinctual conception [*une conception instinctuelle-aristophanesque*]" of the drive ("SDD" 163/194, my emphasis), and it is hard not to hear the language of Molière once again. By embracing the myth of Aristophanes in *Beyond*, Freud has forgotten his own theory of sexuality. By using the Aristophanes myth as a *poussoir* rather than a *repoussoir*, Freud has given the push to the very perversity of (infantile) sexuality.

Sexuality must be protected: from this biologizing-instinctualizing gesture but also from a possible consonance or connivance with philosophical concepts. At the end of the first section of "The So-Called Death Drive," Laplanche will make these reservations concerning an all-too-great proximity with philosophy very clear:

> In current cultivated opinion the death drive has become a handy ideological theme [*un thème idéologique commode*]. . . . [Let us] remember the case of philosophy, in which the death drive finds an all too facile echo in Heidegger's "being-toward-death" or in Hegelian dialectics. In this, to be frank, I fail to find any genuine consonance, but a heterogeneity that profits neither psychoanalysis nor philosophy. ("SDD" 171/204–5, modified)

Neither psychoanalysis nor philosophy will benefit from a confusion of tongues. What is called for is not "a handy ideological theme" but "the return of a 'demonic' sexuality" (TB 4/10), that is to say, sexuality as internal attack, as autoattack or autoaggression (TB 106/118). What is needed is a notion of sexuality that threatens the unity, totality, and integrity of the ego.

When we remember that what Laplanche is protecting here is the *perversity* of sexuality, sexuality as a *perversion* of the vital function, sexuality as polymorphous *perversity*, this gesture may seem strangely paradoxical. Sexuality as perversion must be protected from further "perversion"—at the hands of philosophy.[61] On the one hand, sexuality must be protected from the unifying, binding, *life drive*, that is, the totalizing Eros that falls under the aegis of the divine Plato.[62] On the other hand, sexuality must be protected from the *death drive*, whose proximity to Hegel and Heidegger risks turning psychoanalysis into just another philosophy of death. On the third hand, as Molière might say—and here the important name would be Derrida, whom Laplanche never mentions, as far as I know—sexuality must be protected from "the beyond of sexuality silently at work in sexuality" (LVLM 359). In other words, sexuality as polymorphous perversity must have the first but also the last word if psychoanalysis is not to give up the prestige of originality.

Perhaps, though, I could put it this way: Laplanche takes sexuality too seriously.[63] That is to say, he does not take the *gamelike character* of Freud's speculation in *Beyond* seriously enough. He pokes fun at Freud's reversal. As if he sensed behind Freud's play with Plato a scandal to be repudiated: a more originary play between psychoanalysis and philosophy. And he is right. There is something very strange about the myth of Aristophanes when it returns in *Beyond*, beginning with the fact that Freud's language moves back and forth, *fort* and *da*, between the death drive and the life drive (Eros).

In Chapter 6, Freud tells us that the myth of Aristophanes traces the origin of a drive—in this case the origin of the sexual drive (Eros)—to "*a need to restore an earlier state of things [dem Bedürfnis nach Wiederherstellung eines früheren Zustandes]*" (SE 18:57/GW 13:62). But Freud's italicized language is not neutral here. He has just used the same language (also italicized) in Chapter 5 to describe the death drive in its "circuitous paths to death [*Umwege zum Tode*]" (SE 18:39/GW 13:41): "*A drive is an urge inherent in organic life to restore an earlier state of things [Ein Trieb wäre also ein dem belebten Organischen innewohnender Drang zur Wiederherstellung eines früheren Zustandes]*" (SE 18:36/GW 13:38, modified). In the case of the death drive, of course, this "earlier state of things" is death, that is to say, the "inanimate state" (SE 18:38/GW 13:40).

But then, suddenly, surprisingly, with the myth of Aristophanes, there is Eros instead of death. Instead of "the drive to return to the inanimate state [*der [Trieb] zum Leblosen zurückzukehren*]" (SE 18:38/GW 13:40, modified), there is "the drive for reuniting [*de[r] Trieb zur Wiederveinigung*]" (SE 18:58/GW 13:63, modified). Thus, while Freud's language *recalls* the death drive from Chapter 5, it also *reinscribes* it as life drive. In other words, the life drive (Eros)—in Freud's text—*repeats* the death drive (Thanatos) *differently*.[64] Just as Freud's version of the myth of Aristophanes repeats Plato's version with a twist (or rather, as we will see, without the twist). In Freud's account of Aristophanes's myth, Eros is the immediate result of Zeus's intervention:

> "The original human nature was not like the present, but different. In the first place, the sexes were originally three in number, not two as they are now; there was man, woman, and the union of the two . . ." Everything about these primeval humans was double: they had four hands and four feet, two faces, two privy parts, and so on. Eventually

> Zeus decided to cut these humans in two, "like a sorb-apple which is halved for pickling." After the division had been made, "the two parts, each desiring its other half, came together, and threw their arms about one another eager to grow into one." (SE 18:57–58/GW 13:62, modified)

With Zeus's intervention, Freud finds what he was looking for: the origin of a drive as the tendency to restore an earlier state of things.[65] So it is here, following Zeus's initial cut, that Freud finds Eros.

In Aristophanes's story, however, Eros is not mentioned at this point. Instead the desire that Freud takes to be "erotic" is fatal:

> Now, since their natural form had been cut in two, each one longed [*pothoun*] for its own other half, and so they would throw their arms about each other, weaving themselves together, wanting to grow together. In that condition they would die from hunger.... Whenever one of the halves died and one was left, the one that was left still sought another and wove itself together with that. Sometimes the half he met came from a woman, as we'd call her now, sometimes it came from a man; either way, they kept on dying. (191b)

It is only after this first and fatal intervention that Zeus takes pity on human beings and moves their genitals around to the front. Only with Zeus's second intervention, that is, does Eros even enter the picture: "So Zeus brought about this relocation of genitals, and in doing so he invented interior reproduction.... This, then, is the source of our desire to love each other. Eros is born into every human being; it calls back the halves of our original nature together; it tries to make one out of two and heal the wound of human nature" (191b–c). In other words, where Plato distinguishes between the intervention that brings death (Thanatos) and the intervention that brings love (Eros), Freud (mis)takes the first for the second. Or rather, by *insisting* on the second, on Eros, he repeats the sameness of inanimation (death drive) as difference (life drive). Or better yet: He repeats the sameness of inanimation as *différance*.[66] For what emerges from Freud's speculative play in *Beyond*, what emerges from his *fort/da* with Plato, is quite literally a structure of alterity—death drive/life drive—without opposition and without identity.

But we must also read this *différance* on the level of psychoanalytic theory. If what binds psychoanalysis to philosophy is Freud's speculation on the death drive, then this binding would take place beyond the pleasure principle (PP). In which case, psychoanalytic speculation would lead not to the pleasure of self-pleasure, not to the erection of a system. Rather it would lead, and here we must recall the final words of *Beyond*, to *a limp member*. For *Beyond the Pleasure Principle* famously ends with the reference to a limping: "What we cannot reach flying, we must reach limping. . . . Scripture tells us it is no sin to limp" (SE 18:64/GW 13:69, modified).

Conclusion: *After* Beyond

I will mention just one more reference to the *Symposium* in Freud's work, and it is his final reference in "An Outline of Psychoanalysis" (1938). In the chapter entitled "The Theory of the Drives" (*Trieblehre*), the philosophical concept of Eros no longer serves as a hypothetical example of the need to restore an earlier state of things. Instead, psychoanalysis recognizes Eros as a forward-moving, future-oriented drive:

> If we assume that living things [*das Lebende*] came later than lifeless ones [*das Leblose*] and arose from them [*und aus ihm entstanden ist*], then the death drive fits in with the formula we have proposed to the effect that a drive tends towards [*anstrebt*] a return to an earlier state. In the case of Eros . . . we cannot apply this formula. To do so would presuppose that living substance was once a unity [*Einheit*] which had later been torn apart and was now straining towards [*anstrebt*] reunion [*Wiedervereinigung*].* (*Poets [*Dichter*] have imagined [*phantasiert*] something of this sort, but nothing like it is known from the actual history of living substance.) (SE 23:149/GW 17:71, modified)

In the end, there is no unity, no predifferentiation toward which Eros would strive. Which leaves us with these questions: Is Freud not repeating here the possibility of a life drive that returns as the (self-differentiating) origin of the death drive? Is he not repeating such a possibility by putting emphasis on what propels this force of difference—whether we call it "life" or "psychoanalysis"—into the future?

PART II
Freu*derrida*

CHAPTER 6

For the Love of Psychoanalysis
Deconstruction and Psychoanalysis

The "Friend" of Psychoanalysis

"I can no longer consider you as a friend," said the Satyr,
"a fellow who with the same breath blows hot and cold."

—AESOP, "The Satyr and the Peasant"

In the very last section of his 2001 interview with Élisabeth Roudinesco, titled "In Praise of Psychoanalysis," Jacques Derrida assumes the mantle of "friend of psychoanalysis": "I like the expression, 'friend of psychoanalysis' [*J'aime l'expression 'ami de la psychanalyse'*]" (FWT 167/271, modified), he says, as he begins his response. This expression, "friend of psychoanalysis," refers back, most immediately, to Roudinesco's allusion to Sándor Ferenczi's "beautiful idea" of founding a "Society of Friends of Psychoanalysis" that would bring together writers, artists, philosophers, and jurists interested in psychoanalysis (FWT 166/269, modified). But Derrida does not quote her exactly. He does not say "friends of psychoanalysis" (as Jeff Fort's otherwise excellent translation has it). No, when Derrida responds to Roudinesco, he speaks in the singular, as the singular "friend" that he is: "I like the expression 'friend of psychoanalysis.' It evokes the freedom of an alliance, an engagement with no institutional status" (FWT 167/271, modified).

If Derrida modifies and transforms Roudinesco's expression, if he does not refer back to the plural phrase she has used, it is because he is inflecting the phrase otherwise (he is not simply mentioning it; he is also altering it). The quotation marks around the phrase "friend of psychoanalysis" are what are called in English "scare quotes." Used even when they are not required, these quotes immediately elicit our attention and our doubt; they cause uncertainty to be associated with the "friend." Indeed, as I will suggest in this chapter, Derrida's relationship to psychoanalysis *hinges* on our reading these quotation marks as scare quotes. Not only do these quotation marks serve to distance the "friend of psychoanalysis" from a "Society of Friends," but they also provide this "friend" with a particular and quite special proximity to psychoanalysis. Unlike the Satyr in Aesop's fable who cannot "consider . . . as a friend . . . 'a fellow who with the same breath blows hot and cold,'" the "friend of psychoanalysis" is precisely one who is capable of this double gesture.

But this is not all. For in the case of the "friend of psychoanalysis," this gesture is not only double; it is also simultaneous. The "friend" is someone who—with the *same* breath—blows both hot and cold. Hence there is, in Derrida's work, as we will see, not only a contradictory but also a somewhat violent way of treating psychoanalysis. The "friend of psychoanalysis" does not simply accept or receive something called "psychoanalysis." In the first place, there is no such thing. There is no single and unified concept of psychoanalysis. There is not *one* psychoanalysis: "There is not '*la* psychanalyse'—whether one understands it . . . as a system of theoretical norms or as a charter of institutional practices" ("Res" 20/34). Consequently, the one who calls himself a "friend of psychoanalysis," the one who reaffirms "psychoanalysis," always does two things at once. He says "yes" to psychoanalysis, but at the same time he selects, filters, interprets, and thereby transforms what is called "psychoanalysis." That is, the "friend of psychoanalysis" is never neutral. He intervenes. "Simultaneously faithful and violent" ("Imp" 6/15), faithful and unfaithful, "respecting through disrespect" (LLF 36/38), he chooses, prefers, sacrifices, excludes, leaves certain things behind, precisely in order to keep what has been called, for over a century now, "psychoanalysis," *alive*. Though "psychoanalysis is ineradicable [*ineffaçable*]" and its revolution "irreversible"—"it is . . . mortal" ("PSS" 260/52). Were psychoanalysis to remain unchanged, intact, unharmed by its "friend(s)," it would not survive: It would be certain death for psychoanalysis. So, when the "friend of psychoanalysis" treats psychoanalysis with violence, he does so *out of love*.

From "Freud and the Scene of Writing" (1967) to "Psychoanalysis Searches the States of Its Soul" (2000), by way of *The Post Card* (1980) ("To Speculate—on 'Freud,'" "Le facteur de la vérité," "Du tout") and *Resistances of Psychoanalysis* (1996) ("Resistances," "For the Love of Lacan," "'To Do Justice to Freud'"), not to mention "*Fors*: The Anglish Words of Nicolas Abraham and Maria Torok" (1976), "Me—Psychoanalysis" (1979), "Telepathy" (1981), "Geopsychoanalysis" (1981), "My Chances/*Mes chances*: A Rendezvous with Some Epicurean Stereophonies" (1982), "Let Us Not Forget—Psychoanalysis" (1990), *Archive Fever* (1995), and "And Say the Animal Responded?" (1997), that is, from his very first essay on Freud presented in March 1966 at the Société psychanalytique de Paris at the invitation of André Green to his keynote address to the International Psychoanalytic Association (IPA) at the Estates General of Psychoanalysis on July 10, 2000, in the Grand Amphitheater of the Sorbonne, Jacques Derrida will *always* have been such a "friend."

With one breath, then, the "friend of psychoanalysis" says "yes" to psychoanalysis: "yes" to the existence of psychoanalysis, "yes" to the event of psychoanalysis. The "friend of psychoanalysis" loves psychoanalysis and, loving psychoanalysis, wants to keep it alive:

> In a word, this "yes" of friendship assumes the certainty that psychoanalysis remains an ineffaceable historical event, the certainty that it is a *good thing*, and that it ought to be loved, supported. . . . "The friend" salutes a sort of Freudian revolution; he assumes that it has already marked and should continue to mark, always otherwise, the space in which we live, think, work, write, teach, etc. (FWT 167–68/271–72).

The "friend" is one who loves and supports the *necessity* of psychoanalysis. In this way, the "friend" salutes not only the past ("it has already marked") but also the future ("it should continue to mark, always otherwise"), and above all "the future-to-come" (FWT 168/273), of this revolutionary event. Indeed, to ensure the survival of what is most revolutionary in the psychoanalytic revolution, to keep alive its "revolutionary force [*puissance révolutionnaire*]" (FWT 172/280), its absolute originality and secret law, the "friend of psychoanalysis" must give his "irreversible approbation" (FWT 167/271) to the certainty that psychoanalysis is a good thing.

With the same breath, however—and this is why we must read the quotation marks as scare quotes—the "friend of psychoanalysis" remains on his guard. There can be no "friendship" without a certain "problematic proximity"[1]: "The friend maintains the reserve, withdrawal, or distance necessary for critique, for discussion, for reciprocal questioning, sometimes the most radical of all" (FWT 167/271). The "yes" of friendship may, thus, always be followed by the most serious reservations or doubts:

> This "yes" of friendship assumes the certainty that psychoanalysis . . . is a *good thing* . . . even when one cultivates the most serious questions concerning a great number of phenomena referred to as "psychoanalytic," whether it's a question of theory, of institution, of law, of ethics or of politics.[2] (FWT 167/271, modified)

In a word, the "yes" of the "friend of psychoanalysis" remains vigilant when it comes to the project of psychoanalysis, its discourse, its language, its concepts, its institution, and its politics; the "yes" of the "friend" is always a "yes, but" (*oui, mais*). To love psychoanalysis is to submit its texts to an active, deconstructive reading. To love psychoanalysis is to reserve the right, if not the duty, to criticize psychoanalytic concepts whenever these remain problematic and naïve (and therefore deconstructible). Hence this double gesture—both hot and cold—that belongs to the "friend of psychoanalysis": irreversible approbation and endless vigilance.

*An Invincible Force (*Puissance invincible*): A Reason without Alibi*

Perhaps another way of putting this or another way of understanding this gesture is to say that Derrida will always have loved psychoanalysis "in [his] own manner" (EO 87/118).[3] It was never a matter, says Derrida, of "taking . . . seriously" Freud's "unbelievable mythology (be it neurological or metapsychological)" ("FSW" 228/337) or of using Freudian concepts "otherwise than in quotation marks" ("FSW" 197/294). The "friend" of psychoanalysis was always mistrustful of Freud's debt to metaphysics and, from the very beginning, justified his theoretical reticence by appealing to the "metaphysical complicities [*complicités*] of psychoanalysis" ("FSW" 198/294, modified): "All of [Freud's] concepts, without exception, belong to the history of metaphysics, that is, to the system of logocentric repression" ("FSW" 197/294).[4]

For the "friend" of psychoanalysis, psychoanalysis's naïveté, its unquestioned complicity with classical philosophical oppositions and their violent hierarchies (for example, speech/writing), its incantatory or rhapsodic way of repeating old philosophical gestures—and here Derrida singles out Lacan: "Lacan at that time . . . referred habitually, in a frequent, decisive, self-confident, and sometimes incantatory way, to Heideggerian speech, to *logos* as interpreted by Heidegger, to truth" ("LL" 54/73, modified); "Despite many elliptical and rhapsodic variations [in Lacan's work] . . . I have never encountered any rigorous questioning of the value of truth in its most pertinent historical and architectonic site" ("Pos" 108n1/114n33)— betrayed the credulous, sterilizing, and even dogmatic elements of the psychoanalytic project. "Faced with so many metaphysical schemas at work in the Freudian and Lacanian projects" (FWT 171/278), the "friend" of psychoanalysis remained on his guard. It is for this reason that Derrida speaks, early on, of the task that inevitably falls to the "friend" of psychoanalysis: "The necessity of an immense labor [*travail*] of deconstruction of [psychoanalysis's] concepts and of the metaphysical phrases that are condensed and sedimented within them" ("FSW" 198/294, modified).

But why this immense labor if all of Freud's concepts, without exception, belong to the history of metaphysics? If such a labor is warranted, it is because there are resources in psychoanalysis that cannot simply be reduced to, or exhausted by, this conceptual heritage: "The Freudian discourse—in its syntax, or, if you will, its labor [*travail*]—is not to be confused with these necessarily metaphysical and traditional concepts. Certainly it is not exhausted by belonging to them" ("FSW" 198/294). Hence, there was always, from the very beginning, an alliance between the "labor" of deconstruction and the "labor" of psychoanalysis. What seduced Derrida in Freud were "those elements of psychoanalysis that [could] not easily be contained within logocentric closure" ("FSW" 198/296, modified), specifically the "impulse [*impulsion*] coming from psychoanalysis in general . . . to deconstruct the privilege of presence, at least as consciousness and egological consciousness" ("LL" 55/74). What Derrida points to are not Freud's "theses" but the "impetus [*élan*] of the initial Freudian send-off [*coup d'envoi*]" (FWT 176/286, modified), the ways in which Freud's "most venturesome soundings [*coups de sonde*]" (FWT 172/280) exceed the conceptual mastery bequeathed to him by and as "metaphysics." This is why Derrida always describes Freud's historical originality—"that moment of world history, as 'signaled' by the name 'Freud'" ("FSW" 228/337, modified)—as a breaking, a breaching, a rupturing, or an opening ("la percée freudienne [the Freudian breakthrough]" ["FSW" 199/296], "la coupure freudienne [the Freudian break]" ["FSW" 209/310], "la trouée freudienne [the Freudian breach]" ["FSW" 228/337, modified]) of this conceptual heritage.

And yet to give oneself over to Freud's *coup d'envoi*, to his *coups de sonde*, one must also be ready, and be able, to give up the most foundational of psychoanalytic concepts. Thus, in his late interview with Roudinesco, and much to Roudinesco's dismay, Derrida delivers a kind of coup de grâce to Freud's "grand conceptual framework" (FWT 172/279):

> I may be mistaken, but the id, the ego, the superego, the ideal ego, the ego ideal, the secondary process and the primary process of repression, etc.—in a word, the large Freudian machines (including the concept and the word "unconscious"!)—are . . . only provisional weapons, or even rhetorical tools cobbled together [*bricolés*] to be used against a philosophy of consciousness, of transparent and fully responsible intentionality. I have little faith in their future. I do not think that a metapsychology can hold up for long under scrutiny. . . . The "friend of psychoanalysis" in me is mistrustful not of positive knowledge but of positivism and of the substantialization of metaphysical or metapsychological agencies. The grand entities (ego, id, superego, etc.), but also the grand conceptual "oppositions"—which are too solid, and therefore very precarious—that followed those of Freud, such as the real, the imaginary, and the symbolic, etc. or "introjection" and "incorporation"—these seem to me to be carried away . . . by the ineluctable necessity of some "differ*a*nce" that erases or displaces their borders. Which in any case deprives them of all rigor. I am therefore never ready to follow Freud and his followers in the functioning of the grand theoretical machines, in their functionalization. (FWT 172–73/279–80)

Psychoanalysis's machines, its entities, its conceptual oppositions have become too "grand," "too solid." They have ossified and therefore become precarious. Hence, one might hear the *éloge* in this chapter's heading ("Éloge de la psychanalyse") not only as praise ("In Praise of Psychoanalysis," as the English has it) but also as eulogy or elegy (*éloge* comes from the Latin *elogium* "inscription on a tomb" and from the Greek *elegia* "elegy"). Although Freud's "provisional weapons" or "rhetorical tools" may have been necessary "for breaking with psychology within a given context of the history of science" (FWT 172/279), his battles are no longer our own. Like "bayonets and horses,"[5] to quote Barack Obama's now famous phrase, their value and pertinence no longer obtain outside a specific context.

Indeed, when we forget that the id, the ego, and the superego are figural inventions ("rhetorical tools"), when we forget that they were "provisional weapons" cobbled together to be "used against a philosophy of consciousness," when we literalize their "as if" nature and take them for "scientific and scientifically assured concepts" (FWT 174/283), we not only fall prey to ideology or ideological mystification ("What we call ideology is precisely the confusion of linguistic with natural reality"),[6] but we also collude with what threatens to turn psychoanalysis (and sometimes from within psychoanalysis itself) into just another "theological, metaphysical, genetic, physicalist, cognitivist" discourse ("PSS" 240/12).

For if there is anything that marks the specificity of the psychoanalytic revolution for Derrida, it is what he calls the "reaffirmation of a reason 'without alibi'" (FWT 172/280):

> The very aim [*visée*], and I do say *aim*, of the psychoanalytic revolution is the only one not to rest, not to seek refuge, in principle, in what I call a theological or humanist *alibi*. That is why it can appear terrifying, terribly cruel, pitiless.... All the philosophies, the metaphysics, the theologies, the human sciences end up having recourse, in the deployment of their thought or their knowledge, to such an alibi. (FWT 173/281)

When psychoanalysis mistakes its fictional narratives for truths about the world, when it substantializes its metaphysical or metapsychological agencies, it retreats from its own breakthroughs. It forgets itself and betrays itself when it seeks an alibi for its thought, its discourse, or its writing in philosophy, metaphysics, theology, or the human sciences (in neuroscience, for example, as we saw in Chapter 1). As the only revolution whose aim is the unrelenting deployment of its thought and knowledge, psychoanalysis, much like its "friend," "can appear terrifying, terribly cruel, pitiless."

"Too Much at Home": When Psychoanalysis Becomes Too Philosophical

And perhaps nowhere is the pitilessness of the "friend" more on display, or his cruelty more staged, than in the essay provocatively titled "For the Love of Lacan" (1991). In this essay, written for a UNESCO colloquium devoted to the work of Jacques Lacan, Derrida quite spectacularly and unexpectedly declares his love for Lacan: "And if I were to say now: 'You see, I think that we loved each other very much, Lacan and I [*nous nous sommes beaucoup aimés, Lacan et moi*]'" ("LL" 42/60); "and ... if I repeated 'we loved each other very much, Lacan and I'" ("LL" 42/60–61); "Who will ever have the right to say: 'We love each other'?" ("LL" 43/61); "Was this not a way of saying that I loved and admired him a lot [*que je l'aimais et l'admirais beaucoup*]?" ("LL" 56/74).

In fact, much of "For the Love of Lacan" reads like a love letter, one that proclaims the future and promise of "the *name* Lacan" ("LL" 46/64):

> If I said "yes" ... if I was happy to accept the invitation [to speak] ... it is because this colloquium ... constitutes an international homage to Lacan. And it is with this event, this justly deserved and spectacular homage to Lacan, that I was happy to be asked to associate myself. Not only but also because, in our time ... I find a political significance in this homage. I consider it an act of cultural resistance to pay homage publicly to a difficult form of thought, discourse, or writing, one which does not submit easily to normalization by the media, by academics, or by publishers, one which rebels against the ... philosophical or theoretical neo-conformism in general ... that flattens and levels everything around us, in the attempt to make one forget what the Lacan era was, along with the future and the promise of his thought, thereby erasing the *name* of Lacan. ("LL" 45–46/63–64)

Derrida's declarations of love are an act of resistance—a resistance to the erasure of the name Lacan.[7] If Derrida says "yes," if he accepts to speak at an international conference that names Lacan and only Lacan in its title (*Lacan avec les philosophes* [Lacan with the Philosophers]), it is in order to honor, acclaim, applaud, salute, praise, commend, and pay tribute (homage) to Lacan. It is in order to say "yes" to someone whose "being-with" or "coming-to-terms-with" philosophy has attained "a refinement, a scope, an unexpected illumination of the 'searchlight effect' ['*coup de phare*']" ("LL" 46/65). In this, Lacan would be unique in the history of psychoanalysis: "Lacan's refinement and competence, his philosophical originality, have no precedent in the tradition of psychoanalysis" ("LL" 47/65). Like Freud's *coup d'envoi* or *coups de sonde*, the historical originality of Lacan's *coup de phare* is its piercing effect.

And yet, just as spectacularly as the "friend" of psychoanalysis declares his love for Lacan, he declares war on Lacan. We might speculate that by staging such a provocation—"And if I were to say now: 'You see, I think that we loved each other very much, Lacan and I,' I am almost certain that many of you here would not stand for it. Many would not stand for it, which explains many things" ("LL" 42/60)—Derrida is also at the same time staging his politics of friendship: "Can one speak of loving without declaring love, without declaring war, beyond all possible neutrality?" (PoF 228/255, modified). For it is certainly the case that "For the Love of Lacan" rehearses all of Derrida's earlier attacks on Lacan. In his denunciation of Lacan's appropriation of certain motifs in philosophy—"phonocentrism, logocentrism, phallogocentrism, full speech as truth, the transcendentalism of the signifier, the circular return of reappropriation toward what is most proper about the proper place, whose borders are circumscribed by lack, and so forth" ("LL" 54/73), it is impossible not to hear reverberations of *Positions* (1971)[8] or "Le facteur de la vérité" (1975). In fact, the particular topic of the UNESCO conference, "Lacan with the Philosophers," homes in on what Derrida always found most troubling in Lacan, namely, Lacan's being-with philosophy, or being-with the philosophers. For this reason, "For the Love of Lacan" revisits, somewhat compulsively, the scenes of this past history. But it does so, if I can put it this way, with a twist, that is to say, in a way that seems particularly *cruel*.

If the "friend" of psychoanalysis appears especially cruel in this essay, it is, I would argue, because Derrida's declarations of love are being used as the example par excellence of the phenomenon of *destinerrance*. In "For the Love of Lacan," Derrida returns to the problem of the (love) letter and its destination, that is, to the necessary possibility of the letter's nonarrival and its internal drifting. Derrida returns, that is, to the question that always separated him "most closely" ("LL" 62/81) from Lacan.[9] Thus, when Derrida declares "nous nous sommes aimés," his aim is first and foremost to give an example of this internal drifting, this *destinerrance*:

> As for being shocked to hear someone say "we" when speaking all alone after the death of the other, there is no reason for it. This is one of the most common phenomena of what I have called *destinerrance*. It inflicts an internal drift on the destination of the letter, from which it may never return. . . . It is always me who says "we"; it is always an "I" who utters "we," supposing thereby, in effect, in the asymmetrical structure of the utterance, the other to be absent, dead, in any case incompetent, or even arriving too late to object. . . . The asymmetry is even more violent if we're talking about a reflexive, reciprocal, or specular "we." Who will ever have the right to say: "We love each other"? But is there any other origin of love, any other amorous performative than this presumptuousness [*outrecuidance*]? If there is some "we" in being-with, it is because there is always one who speaks all alone in the name of the other; there is always one who lives more, lives longer. . . . When we are with someone, we know *without delay* that one of us will survive the other. So he already does and will be able or will have to speak on his own. ("LL" 42–43/61–62)

For any (love) letter or declaration of love to be what it is, that is, for it to be structurally readable, it must remain readable beyond the death of the addressee. Thus, the presumptuousness or impertinence (*outrecuidance*) of Derrida's declaration of love is not determined by the moment of Lacan's death. The presumptuousness is structural: It is already there *without delay* from the moment an "I" says "we." Hence, the thinking of destination can never be dissociated from a thinking of death or of destination as death. The addressee is dead, already dead, from the moment someone says "we": "We love each other."

But if the presumptuousness of Derrida's "nous nous sommes aimés" has a further effect here—if indeed it is exceptionally shocking or cruel—it is because "For the Love of Lacan" stages Derrida's personal ambivalence toward Lacan in such a way that Lacan's actual death seems *literally* to underscore the *murderous* quality of what is a *structural* predicament. For there is something excessive about "For the Love of Lacan," something ruthless about Derrida's repeated appeal to personal anecdote that lends an aura of cruelty to this essay. The essay begins, for example, by staging an exclamation in both the conditional and future anterior—"What wouldn't Lacan have said! What will he not have said!" ("LL" 39/57)—and then proceeds to tell story after story of Lacan's appropriations but also misappropriations of Derrida's work (even referencing, at one point, the relevant pages of Élisabeth Roudinesco's monumental *History of Psychoanalysis in France*) before concluding with an ironic and self-ironic but also exultant "What will I not have said today!"

It is no coincidence, therefore, that Derrida returns at length, in the final section of "For the Love of Lacan," to one of his "envois [dispatches]" from *The Post Card* in which the issue is precisely love and murder:

> Murder is everywhere, my unique and immense one. We are the worst criminals in history. And right here I kill you . . . the living one over there whom I love. . . . I kill you, I annul you at my fingertips. . . . To do so it suffices only that I be readable—and I become unreadable to you, you are dead. If I say that I write for dead addressees . . . it is not in order to play. ("LL" 65–66/84, modified)

To write a love letter is to kill without delay. This is not a malicious act but an inevitability of structure. What it means, however, is that when a declaration of love becomes the *example* of *destinerrance*, one must distinguish between two things. One must distinguish between what the *declaration* says, on the one hand, and what the *example* says, on the other. In this case, what the declaration says is "We loved each other very much," but what the example says is "I kill you, I annul you." That is, when a declaration of love becomes the example of *destinerrance*, the "friend" of psychoanalysis *literally* and *simultaneously* blows hot and cold.

Now what elicits this exemplary cruelty from the "friend" of psychoanalysis is, paradoxically, Lacan's proximity to philosophy. It is Lacan's excessive confidence or trust (*confiance*) in philosophy. Lacan is too unguarded—too friendly!—with the philosophers. Paradoxically and perversely, Lacan's discourse will be "too philosophical" for Derrida, "too much at home [*trop en confiance*] with the philosophers" ("LL" 56/74):

> *too much at home* with a Sartrian neo-existentialism ... *too much at home* with Hegel/Kojève the "master" (and Hegel/Kojève is also Heidegger, for Kojève does not anthropologize only the phenomenology of spirit; he also Heideggerianizes it ...) ... *too much at home* with the philosophers and with Heidegger. ("LL" 56/74–75, my emphasis)

To be too confident or "too much at home," as Peggy Kamuf beautifully translates "trop en confiance," is to be too *heimlich*, too comfortable with, too wedded to, not "eccentric" or "ex-centering" ("LL" 54/72) enough, in relation to philosophy and to the philosophical as such. It is to remain embedded in a certain dominant state of the history of philosophy, namely that dominant state which Derrida has called "phallogocentrism." It is to cozy up to a certain discourse of mastery. Hence Derrida's warning: Do not get too cozy with the philosophers.

Thus, if the "philosopher" *cruelly* deprives the psychoanalyst of a home in philosophy, if he *cruelly* situates the self-wounding possibilities of psychoanalysis in its "rather somnambulistic submission to a history of metaphysics" (FWT 6–7/19, modified), it is not only to expose the residue of credulity in (Lacanian) psychoanalysis. It is also, and above all, to reawaken psychoanalysis to its own most radical possibilities. It is to keep "something like revolution ... revolution as psychoanalytic reason" (DP2 159/216) alive. Speaking daggers to the one he loves, the "philosopher" "must be cruel only to be kind."[10] For it is only by causing psychoanalysis great discomfort (it is only by analyzing its resistances, its "5 + or −1 concepts or places of 'resistance'" ["PSS" 246/23]) that the "friend" is able to give psychoanalysis back its revolutionary force, a force that "always involves the reaffirmation of a reason 'without alibi'" (FWT 172/280).[11]

Could one not say, then, that there was love in being cruel and that the "friend" of psychoanalysis was simply betraying his love for psychoanalysis by treating it cruelly? And that, by being cruel, the "friend" was *exemplifying* the cruelty at the heart of the psychoanalytic revolution? What if cruelty was, in the end, an essential part of the revolutionary and irreversible legacy of psychoanalysis? Would it not mean that the cruel questioning of the "friend" was a way of remaining "simultaneously faithful and violent" ("Imp" 6/15), faithful and unfaithful, not only to psychoanalysis but also, in another way, to the "philosophical as such" ("LL" 54/72)?

Cruelty and Psychoanalysis

And here we must return to the phrase "without alibi" (*sans alibi*), a phrase that can be heard in (at least) two ways. As we have seen, the phrase "without alibi" translates a certain psychoanalytic imperative: Do not seek refuge for your discourse in ontological or transcendental structures; do not get too comfortable with the history of metaphysics. In this sense, psychoanalysis would remain "without alibi" just as it would remain "without peer"—unequaled, unrivaled in its ability to claim psychical suffering as its own affair ("The only discourse that can today claim the thing of psychical suffering as its own affair would indeed be what has been called, for about a century, psychoanalysis" ["PSS" 240/13]). But we can also hear "without alibi" in a second, more privative sense, as when we say of someone that "s/he has no alibi." According to this second sense, to "have no alibi" or to be "without alibi" is to be, if not implicated in, at least associated with, a crime and by extension a cruelty: "One rarely speaks of alibis . . . without some presumption of a crime. Nor of crime without a suspicion of cruelty" ("PSS" 279/88).

Thus, whether we read "without alibi" as the distinctive feature of the psychoanalytic revolution or as the legal reference to a criminal defense, it is clear that to be *without* alibi is *not to be without* cruelty. On the contrary, one might say that psychoanalysis comes into its own (*proprius*), that it becomes *properly* psychoanalytic, when it becomes "terrifying, terribly cruel, pitiless . . . even to psychoanalysis, even to those who, on both sides of the couch, more or less pretend to put their trust in psychoanalysis" (FWT 173/281). No psychoanalysis without cruelty. In short, no psychoanalysis that does not end up lending both its ear and its name to cruelty: "No other discourse of knowledge stands ready to take an interest in something like cruelty—except what is called psychoanalysis, whose name . . . would become in turn more indecipherable than ever" ("PSS" 240/13). Unlike other discourses of knowledge (that of religion or metaphysics, for example), psychoanalysis would thus be in a unique position to address this irreducible thing in the life of the living being that is the possibility of cruelty.

And here again the "friend" twists the knife. Just as we saw a decade earlier in "For the Love of Lacan" (1990), in "Psychoanalysis Searches the States of Its Soul" (2000) the "friend" blows both hot and cold. On the one hand, he puts the question of cruelty at the heart of the psychoanalytic project: "Only a psychoanalytic revolution would be, in its very project, up to the task of taking account of the grammatical syntax, conjugations, reflexivities, and persons" ("PSS" 240/13) that are implicated in "this strange and familiar word 'cruelty'" ("PSS" 239/11): "making oneself or letting oneself suffer, oneself, the other as other, the other and others in oneself, me, you, he, she, you plural, we, they, and so forth" ("PSS" 240/13). On the other hand, the "friend" puts the question of cruelty *to* the psychoanalytic project. Psychoanalysis has yet to think the problem of cruelty *properly* (for example, as distinct from the economic problem of sadism or masochism).[12] To do so, psychoanalysis would have to take into account history, in particular the history of law. It would have to call into question the metaphysical axioms of ethics, law, and politics:

> As I see it, psychoanalysis has not yet undertaken and thus still less succeeded in thinking, penetrating, and changing the axioms of the ethical, the juridical, and the political, notably in those seismic places where the theological phantasm of sovereignty quakes and where the most traumatic, let us say in a still confused manner the most cruel events of our day are being produced. ("PSS" 244/21)

> What remains to be thought *more psychoanalytico* would thus be a mutation of cruelty itself—or at least new historical figures of an ageless cruelty, as old and no doubt older than man. ("PSS" 270/70)

Regarding the most unprecedented and inventive examples of cruelty in the contemporary world—not to mention the "ongoing performative mutations" ("PSS" 274/78) that have followed from them (for example, "the new Declaration of Human Rights . . . the condemnation of genocide, the concept of crime against humanity . . . the growing struggle against the vestiges of forms of punishment called 'cruel' . . . namely . . . the death penalty" ["PSS" 244–45/21])—psychoanalysis has not said or done enough. And here the "friend" shows no mercy: "These are things about which . . . psychoanalysis as such, in its statutory and authorized discourse, or even in the quasi totality of its productions, has so far said next to nothing, has had next to nothing original to say" ("PSS" 245/22). In other words, in the very place where we might expect the most precise, the most nuanced, "the only appropriate response" ("PSS" 245/22), that is, a *proper* response from psychoanalysis, psychoanalysis says nothing.[13]

It offers us nothing (or "next to nothing") when it should have "something indispensable and essential not just to *say* but also to *do* on this subject. Without alibi" ("PSS" 245/23). According to the "friend," the psychoanalytic revolution has not even scratched the surface, let alone tackled and analyzed, the (onto-theological) metaphysics of sovereignty that still dominates our ethical, juridical, and political practice. It is as if psychoanalysis were resisting its own revolutionary force and potential, resisting itself but also its future by not reckoning with, and measuring up to, those "events that constitute a cruel mutation of cruelty, a technical, scientific, juridical, economic, ethical and political, ethical and military, and terrorist and policing mutation in our age" ("PSS" 270/70). For this reason, the "friend" pulls no punches. If psychoanalysis does not revolutionize itself, if it does not transform itself and its thinking at the rhythm of these cruelties, it will not survive: It will be "deported, overwhelmed, left on the side of the road, exposed to all the drifts of the currents, to all appropriations . . . or else, inversely, it will remain rooted in the conditions of a period that saw its birth, still aphasic in the Central European cradle of its birth" ("PSS" 245/22). It will either be swept up and blown away or rot and wither on the vine.

As we have seen, the question of cruelty is a question for psychoanalysis, addressed to psychoanalysis, as its privileged addressee—"What does 'cruel' mean?" ("PSS" 262/56); "What is this, cruelty? Where does it begin? Where does it end?" ("PSS" 280/89). But it is also a question used to interrogate or cross-examine psychoanalysis: "What would psychoanalysis have to tell us on this subject?" ("PSS" 263/56); "And what if there were, sometimes, cruelty in *not* putting to death? And what if there were love in *wanting* to give death . . . one to the other, one for the other, simultaneously or not? And what if there were some 'it is suffering cruelly in me, in some me' without it being possible to suspect anyone of *exercising* cruelty? Or of *wanting* it? . . . Is the alibi still avoidable? Is it not already too late?" ("PSS" 280/89).[14] It thus becomes impossible not to hear the question of cruelty in "Psychoanalysis Searches the States of Its Soul"—"Where does cruelty begin and end?" ("PSS" 263/56)—as the reprise of another question, this time from *The Death Penalty, Volume I*: "Where does the cruelty of the questioning of a question begin and where does it end?" (DP1 167/237).

So we must also speak, as I will in Chapter 8, of Derrida's *question about the question*, about the authority of the question and the questioning form. How do the possibility and reality of cruelty, how does the *question* of cruelty force us to ask a question not only about what comes before the question but also about the future of the question, that is, about the future of philosophy, the future of reason and what is proper to deconstruction?

Which brings me to Derrida's question, his deconstructive question in "Psychoanalysis Searches the States of Its Soul." A question that begins, cryptically, by telling us what it is not:

> [My] question will not be: Is there some death drive (*Todestrieb*) that is, and Freud regularly associates them, a cruel drive of destruction or annihilation? Or again: Is there also a cruelty inherent in the drive for power or for sovereign mastery (*Bemächtigungstrieb*) . . . ? My question will be, rather . . . Is there, for thought, for psychoanalytic thought to come, another beyond, if I can say that, a beyond that would stand beyond these *possibles* that are still *both* the pleasure and reality principles *and* the death or sovereign mastery drives, which seem to be at work wherever cruelty is on the horizon? In other words, altogether other words, can one think this apparently impossible, but otherwise impossible thing, namely, a beyond the death drive or the drive for sovereign mastery, thus the beyond of a cruelty, a beyond that would have nothing to do with either drives or principles? ("PSS" 240–41/14)

The deconstructive question is not—properly speaking—psychoanalysis's question ("Is there some death drive . . . a cruel drive of destruction or annihilation?" "Is there a cruelty inherent in the drive . . . for mastery?"). Rather, it is a question addressed to a "psychoanalytic thought to come," to a thought that would no longer be properly psychoanalytic, a thought that would no longer have anything to do with the Freudian discourse that orders itself, "its economy, its topography, its metapsychology" ("PSS" 241/14), around the principles (the pleasure principle and the reality principle) or the drives (the death drive and the drive for mastery). In this text addressed to analysts, the "friend" calls on psychoanalysis to think a beyond that would be beyond the death drive (*Todestrieb*) and the drive for mastery (*Bemächtigungstrieb*), a beyond that would be beyond (the beyond of) *Beyond the Pleasure Principle*.[15] A beyond that would perhaps be "a beyond of cruelty." What the "friend" of psychoanalysis pushes psychoanalysis to think— and the difficulty of the question is perhaps not without its own cruelty—is "an unconditional without sovereignty, *and thus without cruelty*, which is no doubt a very difficult thing to think" ("PSS" 276/82, my emphasis).

How is psychoanalysis to think such a thing? How is psychoanalysis to think something that would stand beyond "all pleasure or reality principle, beyond all drive for power and perhaps all death drive" ("PSS" 254/40), that is, beyond all the "possibles" of its economy, its topography, its metapsychology? In the closing pages of "Psychoanalysis Searches the States of Its Soul," Derrida suggests that this beyond of the beyond comes to us as an "originary affirmation": "the originary affirmation *from which*, and thus *beyond which*, the death drive and the power, cruelty, and sovereign drives determine themselves as 'beyond' the principles" ("PSS" 276/82–83). What Derrida is suggesting here is that the economic and symbolic conditionality of the drives—their possibility and their theorization[16]—does not and cannot constitute itself without some reference to the unconditional. No death drive, one might say, without the "inflexible unconditionality of the unconditional" ("PSS" 277/84). No death drive, translating this time from Freu*derrida* to *Freu*derrida, without the attributes of life having been at some time awakened in inanimate matter by an *event*, "the action of a force of whose nature we can form no conception [*durch eine noch ganz unvorstellbare Krafteinwirkung*]" (SE 18:38/GW 13:40). The origin of life, *as the origin of the death drive*, is inconceivable (*unvorstellbar*). We cannot imagine an event of this kind, says Freud. And yet the action of such a force is *inseparable from*—indeed it is *inscribed in*—the origin of the death drive. What this means is that there is always something in the death drive, and thus something in (its) cruelty, that cannot be limited to operations within a psychical, economic, or symbolic system. In fact, one might say that there is always an incalculable "event" repeating itself in and through the cruelty of the death drive (in the repetition compulsion, for example), an event whose future is not *necessarily* predetermined.

It is perhaps no coincidence, therefore, that the "originary affirmation of beyond the beyond" ("PSS" 276/83) is associated with the particular figure of the event in "Psychoanalysis Searches the States of Its Soul."[17] It is associated, that is, with Derrida's thinking of what can no longer be determined by metaphysical interpretations of possibility or virtuality. Indeed, in many of his late interventions ("The University without Condition," "Psychoanalysis Searches the States of Its Soul," "Autoimmunity: Real and Symbolic Suicides," *Rogues*), Derrida takes up the figure of the event. But in "Psychoanalysis Searches the States of Its Soul," this figure is also associated with his thinking of cruelty, or, rather, with what resists thought and therefore remains to be thought "perhaps beyond any cruelty" ("PSS" 278/87).

The event, Derrida tells us, belongs not to the possible but to the impossible. As long as I can produce and determine an event, what happens remains "within a horizon of anticipation or precomprehension" ("UWC" 234/73): "It is the unfolding of what is already possible" ("UWC" 234/73). Although Derrida will not say that *nothing* happens, what happens still belongs to the order of the possible. For an event to be an event, it must puncture this horizon of possibility: "If what arrives belongs to the horizon of the possible . . . it does not arrive, it does not happen, in the full sense of the word" ("UWC" 234/73).

In other words, for an event to be an event "in the full sense of the word," for an event to be an event "worthy of the name" ("PSS" 254/40), it must surprise, overwhelm, put to rout the orders "of power and of the possible" ("PSS" 278/86–87). It must exceed not only the order of theoretical knowledge or of science, what Derrida here calls "the *constative*" ("PSS" 277/84); it must also exceed—and here Derrida insists—the order of "the *performative*," "which covers, along with the power or the possibility of the 'I can,' 'I may' . . . institutionality in general, ethical, juridical, political . . . responsibility" ("PSS" 277/84):

> Even where they register or produce some event, the orders of the constative or performative remain orders of power and the possible. . . . But an event, the coming of an event worthy of this name, its unpredictable alterity, the arrivance of the arrivant, all of this is what exceeds even any power. . . . The unconditional coming of the other, its event without possible anticipation and without horizon . . . are irruptions that can and must put to rout the two orders of the constative and performative, of knowledge and the symbolic. Perhaps beyond any cruelty. ("PSS" 278/87)

Exceeding the orders of power and the possible, the event is *perhaps* beyond any cruelty. But let there be no mistake: The "perhaps" of the event does not leave us with a *decidable* answer as to the beyond of the beyond. It does not allow us to posit a space of noncruelty beyond cruelty or to speak of a transcendence of cruelty. For the simple reason that—like the death drive—cruelty is originary: "There is and will be cruelty, among living beings" (FWT 76/126); "Cruelty there is [*Cruauté il y a*]. Cruelty there will have been [*Cruauté il y aura eu*], before any personal figure, before 'cruel' will have become an attribute, still less anyone's fault" ("PSS" 280/89). Instead, the "perhaps" of the event gives us to think the beyond of the beyond from a place that is no longer simply outside cruelty.

And it is here, in this form—in the form of *le pas au-delà*, the step-(not)-beyond—that the status of the cross-examination of the "friend" acquires special significance. For Derrida's provocative "Address to the [E]states General of Psychoanalysis,"[18] his cruel questioning of psychoanalysis, demands that we think simultaneously *both* the question of "the beyond of the beyond" ("PSS 241/15) *and* the cruelty of the question. That is, it requires that we think the beyond of the beyond from a place that is neither cruel nor noncruel. Getting to the beyond of the beyond is not simply a matter of getting beyond. Rather, it is about reading the trace of this cruelty; it is about reading the history or historicity of Derrida's "love" for psychoanalysis, as I have tried to do in this chapter.

To conclude, then, I would like to turn to Derrida's apostrophe in "Psychoanalysis Searches the States of Its Soul."[19] At the very end of his "Address to the [E]states General of Psychoanalysis" the "friend" speaks directly, in the vocative, to the psychoanalysts present in the Grand Amphitheater of the Sorbonne on July 10, 2000: "Along with a few others, *you* psychoanalysts know this. *You* could or *you* should know it better than anyone" ("PSS" 278/87, my emphasis). "Better than anyone," psychoanalysts know how to "make the leap toward the im-possible" ("PSS" 279/87). Psychoanalysts could or should know how to remain hospitable to the unpredictability of the event, to the coming of the other in general. One may hear this as a general statement about psychoanalysis; after all, Derrida says that psychoanalysis can claim "some privilege in the experience of the unpredictable coming of the other" ("PSS" 276/83). But Derrida's apostrophe here also addresses his "friends"[20]—it stages his address—in a very specific and localized way. He is addressing his "friends," and he is thanking them for inviting him to speak at their Estates General at their own risk and peril: "You knew how to make the leap toward the im-possible, by exposing yourself . . . to the visit of the stranger" ("PSS" 279/87). He is the stranger, the "philosopher," who has come to salute his psychoanalyst "friends" but also to cross-examine them "without assurance of salvation" ("PSS" 279/87).

Could one not say that this apostrophe comes from a place that is neither cruel nor noncruel? And that it does so exemplarily, both in theory and in practice? Indeed, when the "friend" calls for a "new psychoanalytic reason," when he calls for a "new psychoanalytic Enlightenment," a "revolution in psychoanalytic reason" that would "come to terms with the impossible, negotiate with the non-negotiable . . . calculate with the unconditional as such" ("PSS" 276–77/83–84), he is not simply indicting psychoanalysis for having failed to measure up to the "new historical figures of an ageless cruelty" ("PSS" 270/70). He is also calling for what, in

For the Love of Psychoanalysis

the "ineffaceable *historical* event" that is psychoanalysis (FWT 167/271, my emphasis), carries the future *here and now*.

Thus, if the "friend" blows hot and cold, if Derrida must be cruel in order to be kind *in the same breath*, it is because there remains for deconstructive thought, for the deconstructive thought of cruelty, something revolutionary—something *breathtaking*—about psychoanalysis.

CHAPTER 7

Cruelty and Its Vicissitudes

Les cygnes comprennent les signes.
—VICTOR HUGO, *Les Misérables*

Signs

I would like to take as my point of departure three short epigraphs. On May 2, 2013, Maryland became the eighteenth American state and the sixth state in six years to abolish the death penalty.[1] It thereby became the first US state south of the Mason-Dixon line to take a stand against the death penalty in nearly fifty years, joining only West Virginia. In a brief interview after signing the bill, Democratic governor Martin O'Malley, a Roman Catholic opposed to capital punishment, waxed historical: "I don't know exactly what the timing is, but over the longer arc of history I think you'll see more and more states repeal the death penalty."[2]

My second epigraph is a statement made just one year earlier by Connecticut governor Dannel Malloy on April 25, 2012, when he signed into law a bill that replaced the Connecticut death penalty with life without parole:

> My position on the appropriateness of the death penalty in our criminal justice system evolved over a long period of time. As a young man, I was a death penalty supporter. Then I spent years as a prosecutor and

pursued dangerous felons in court, including murderers. . . . I saw people who were poorly served by their counsel. I saw people wrongly accused or mistakenly identified. I saw discrimination. In bearing witness to those things, I came to believe that doing away with the death penalty was the only way to ensure it would not be unfairly imposed.[3]

My third and final epigraph is a statement from the American television series *Breaking Bad*: "Every life comes with a death sentence."

Since 1999, when Derrida began his two-year seminar on the death penalty, eight more states, eight new states—New York and New Jersey in 2007, New Mexico in 2009, Illinois in 2011, Connecticut in 2012, Maryland in 2013, Delaware in 2016, and Washington in 2018—have eliminated the death penalty. In fact, according to the Death Penalty Information Center website, the number of death sentences per year has "dropped dramatically" since 1999.[4] In 1999, 279 people were given death sentences in the United States as compared to thirty in 2016. The total number of executions in 1999 (and 1999 is the peak year for number of executions since the reinstatement of the death penalty in 1976) was ninety-eight; the total number of executions in 2017 was twenty-three; eighteen people have been executed in the United States in 2018 so far.

A few other notable developments that have taken place since Derrida's *Death Penalty* seminars: (1) In 2002, the Supreme Court held in *Atkins v. Virginia* that it was unconstitutional to execute defendants with "mental retardation." (2) In 2005, the Supreme Court in *Roper v. Simmons* struck down the death penalty for juveniles. (3) Finally, in 2010, a poll by Lake Research Partners found that a clear majority of voters in the United States (61 percent) would choose a punishment *other* than the death penalty for murder, including life with no possibility of parole with restitution to the victim's family (39 percent), life with no possibility of parole (13 percent), or life with the possibility of parole (9 percent).

I think we should take these developments as "signs," much like "signs" to which Derrida alludes in *The Death Penalty, Volume I*: "A number of recent signs . . . which come to us, of course, from the United States . . . this avalanche, this precipitation of signs, seems to confirm—and how not to celebrate this—the diagnosis or prognosis we have been giving here [in this seminar] for months" (DP1 190/265). Such avalanching or precipitating "signs" remind us that "a mutation is under way" (FWT 72/121). They show us that the process of deconstruction, the deconstruction of the death-dealing discourse (*le discours morticole*) that prevails in the majority of American states, is accelerating in a critical and highly significant way.

And yet a deconstructive sign, if we can call it this—the sign that a mutation is under way—is not, *or not exactly*, a historical sign, a *Geschichtszeichen*. For Kant, "a historical sign"[5] (and this is the word he uses to describe the French Revolution in the second part of *The Conflict of the Faculties*) is a sign that recalls, demonstrates, and foretells the tendency toward progress of the entire human race. A historical sign, as Derrida glosses it in *The Death Penalty, Volume II*, would be "a sign . . . that reminds us, recalls to our memory (*rememorativum*), demonstrates (*demonstrativum*) that there is some future [*de l'avenir*]. . . . [It] tells us (*prognostikon*) that there is some future and possible progress to come because we remember (*rememorativum*) that there has already been progress, that there is thus a possibility already attested to as possibility" (DP2 201/270). Indeed, the experience (*Erfahrung*) and event (*Begebenheit*) of the French Revolution must be regarded as a sign of this kind, a sign that "would allow progress toward the better to be concluded as an inevitable consequence [*als unausbleibliche Folge*]" (CoF 301/Ak 7:84). According to Kant, the mode of thinking of the spectators of the French Revolution demonstrates a universal yet disinterested sympathy, that is, "a moral character of humanity . . . which not only permits people to hope for progress toward the better, but is already itself progress" (CoF 302/Ak 7:851). In other words, the French Revolution *will have been the sign*—the reminder and the promise—of the possibility of progress even if, as Kant says, "the revolution . . . should finally miscarry, or . . . everything should switch back to its earlier track [*ins vorige Gleis zurückgebracht würde*]" (CoF 304/Ak 7:88, modified).

Although Derrida gives, as he says, "[his] most convinced sympathy [*ma sympathie la plus convaincue*]" to the abolitionist discourse (FWT 148/241), and although a worldwide abolition of the death penalty would without question constitute extraordinary progress for Derrida, it would be better (it would be progress!) to have no teleo-theological illusions about the possibility of a "pure, simple, and definitive abolition of the death penalty" (Victor Hugo) that would be an end to the death penalty. Hence Derrida will conclude his 1999 seminar with the following rather provocative statement:

> Even when the death penalty will have been abolished, when it will have been purely and simply, absolutely and unconditionally, abolished on earth, it will survive, there will still be some death penalty [*il y en aura encore*]. Other figures will be found for it, other figures will be

invented for it. . . . Let us harbor no illusion on this subject: even when it will have been abolished, the death penalty will survive; it will have other lives in front of it, and other lives to get its teeth into [*d'autres vies à se mettre sous la dent*]. (DP1 282–83/380)

That is, the process of deconstruction *will* and *will not* lead to the end of the death penalty just as it will and will not lead to the end of blood (*le sans sang*) and to the end of cruelty with which the death penalty is always associated. "There will still be some death penalty [*il y en aura encore*]"; there will still be some cruelty: "There is and will be cruelty, among living beings, among men [*de la cruauté il y en a, il y en aura entre les vivants, entre les hommes*]" (FWT 76/126). Thus, one might say that, in this sense, a deconstructive sign is precisely that which registers the mutations that are taking place in our experience of the death penalty *without theological or humanist alibi*, that is to say, in the absence of any "philosophical prophecy [*philosophische Vorhersagung*]" (CoF 304/Ak 7:88).

In this chapter I will suggest that we read Derrida's *Death Penalty* seminars as themselves a sign, a sign not only of the mutative or "propulsive force"[6] of deconstruction but also of the mutative or propulsive force of a deconstructive reading of signs. This chapter will move, in other words, from Derrida's discussion of the death penalty as the literal sign of the onto-theologico-political in *The Death Penalty, Volume I* to a session of *The Death Penalty, Volume I* in which the guillotine becomes a double-edged sign: a "sign of love for mankind" (Dr. Guillotin) and "the special and eternal sign of barbarity" (Victor Hugo). Finally, I will turn to Derrida's repeated appeal to psychoanalysis in his discussions of the death penalty (in "Psychoanalysis Searches the States of Its Soul," in *The Death Penalty, Volume II*, and in *For What Tomorrow . . .*), and I will suggest that we read this appeal (and the particular *Stimmung* that is the Jewish joke) as a sign of a new alliance (without institution), namely, philosophy's alliance with psychoanalysis, that is to say, with "the only discourse that can today claim the thing of psychical suffering as its own affair" ("PSS" 240/13).

Death Penalty as Sign of an Alliance: The Hyphen in the Theologico-Political

What has become urgent in 1999, as Derrida's *Death Penalty* seminars demonstrate, is a deconstruction of the death penalty, that is, a deconstruction of the political theology of the death penalty. As is clear from the Death Penalty Information website, a death-dealing discourse still dominates the political discourse of the United States, "the most Christian democracy in the world" (DP1 192/267). But this death-dealing discourse also dominates the philosophical discourse of the Christian, European West. Again and again, in his many discussions of the death penalty, Derrida will point to this strange and *stupefying* "fact":

> I will set out from what has long been for me the most significant and the most stupefying—also the most stupefied—fact in the history of Western philosophy: never, *to my knowledge*, has any philosopher *as such*, *in his properly philosophical discourse*, never has any philosophy *as such* contested the legitimacy of the death penalty. From Plato to Hegel, from Rousseau to Kant (who was undoubtedly the most rigorous of them all), they all expressly, each in his own way, and sometimes not without much hand-wringing (Rousseau), took a stand *for* the death penalty. (FWT 145–46/235–36, modified)[7]

As Peggy Kamuf amusingly observes, this "stupefaction" comes as a resounding slap: "It is as if Derrida, in the name of philosophers or philosophy as such, were giving (himself) a big smack, delivering a slap to 'the history of Western philosophy.'" Plato, Hegel, Rousseau, Kant—"whack, whack, whack, whack," writes Kamuf (TF 187–88). Derrida continues:

> Those who maintained a public discourse against the death penalty never did so, to my knowledge . . . in a strictly philosophical way. They did so either as writers (Voltaire, Hugo, and Camus in France) or as jurists and men of the law (Beccaria . . . Badinter . . .). . . . If this massive and highly significant "fact" can be proven, we then have to ask ourselves what *welds* [*ce qui* soude], so to speak, philosophy and, more precisely, ontology, in their essence or, what amounts to the same thing, in their hegemonic tradition—what *welds* them, then [*ce qui les soude, donc*], to the political theology of the death penalty. (FWT 147/238–39)

In other words, there is *no philosophy against the death penalty*.[8] No philosophy qua philosophy that has not been seduced by the death penalty. No rigorous, *philosophical* system that has not assumed a death-dealing, death-prone, pro-death discourse. No philosophy *as such* that has not embraced the *principle* of the death penalty. This "fact" is for Derrida "the most significant and stupefying [*la plus signifiante et la plus stupéfiante*]." And also perhaps the most terrifying. Philosophy (ontology) has been soldered (*soudée*), welded, *wedded* to the death penalty and to the principle of sovereignty from which it is inseparable. It is precisely for this reason, Derrida says, that "a 'deconstruction' of what is most hegemonic in philosophy must . . . pass through a deconstruction of the death penalty" (FWT 88/146, modified).

In other words, the deconstruction of the death penalty is not simply "one necessity among others"; it is not simply "a particular point of application" (FWT 148/240). On the contrary, says Derrida, "I would be tempted to say that one cannot begin to think the theologico-political, and even the onto-theologico-political, except from this phenomenon of criminal law that is called the death penalty" (FWT 145/235). This is because the death penalty is what holds everything together: "If one could speak here of an architectonic . . . the death penalty would be the keystone or, if you prefer, the cement, the solder . . . of the onto-theologico-political" (FWT 148/240, modified).

As keystone, cement, or solder, the death penalty is "the prosthetic artifact" (FWT 148/240) that holds up and holds upright what is a non-natural thing, a non-natural alliance, a historical law. In French, this move from keystone to cement to solder is more emphatic still: "La peine de mort serait une clé de voûte ou, si vous préférez, un ciment, la soudure . . . de l'onto-théologico-politique [the death penalty would be a keystone or, if you prefer, a cement of sorts, *the* solder . . . of the onto-theologico-political]." That is, it is the final image, the image of welding or soldering that imposes itself most forcefully—by means of the definite article—on Derrida here.

As figure, "solder" makes explicit a non-natural connection, an artificial or prosthetic joining, a breakable or fallible link: "This *soldering* of ontology to the political theology of the death penalty," says Derrida, is "at once powerful and fragile, historical and non-natural (this is why the image of a technical *alloy* occurs to me here)" (FWT 147/238, modified). In addition to the technical, metallurgical, and perhaps Freudian use of the term "soldering" (as we saw in Chapter 5, Freud uses the term *Verlötung*, soldering, to describe the non-natural connection between the sexual drive and the sexual object)—Derrida offers us yet another image of the death penalty, this time in the form of a linguistic sign. In the very opening session of *The Death Penalty, Volume I*, Derrida describes the history and the horizon of sovereignty of the death penalty as a hyphen, *un trait d'union*, indeed "the hyphen in the theologico-political": "If one wants to ask oneself 'What is the death penalty?" or 'What is the essence and the meaning of the death penalty?' it will indeed be necessary to reconstitute this history and this horizon of sovereignty as the hyphen in the theologico-political [*en tant que trait d'union du théologico-politique*]" (DP1 22–23/49).

Thus, if we read the death penalty (its history and its horizon of sovereignty) as a hyphen, "the hyphen in the theologico-political," we must also read it as a "sign," indeed, the most literal and technical of signs. According to the *OED*, a hyphen is "the *sign* used to join words to indicate that they have a combined meaning or that they are linked in the grammar of a sentence" (my emphasis). One might say, in other words, that the death penalty is a *sign* of hyphenation, that is to say, the *sign* par excellence of the onto-theologico-political, the sign of philosophy's wholly (holy-) unholy alliance with the political theology of the death penalty. I would just add that this hyphen, this trait of union, resembles nothing so much as a bit of solder . . . except perhaps the blade of the guillotine, to which I will now turn.

Reading the Signs

If the death penalty is the "hyphen in the theologico-political," if it is the "cement" or "solder" that upholds the sovereign power of the state, then the *guillotine* would be, paradoxically, the most powerful and intoxicating (heady?) theologico-political bonding agent (a kind of French epoxy) in revolutionary and postrevolutionary France. Indeed, this is why so much of *The Death Penalty, Volume I* is spent tracking the history and the horizon of sovereignty of the guillotine, from the fabled birth of Joseph Ignace Guillotin (a birth precipitated by the screams of a man who was being tortured on the wheel) to his invention of the guillotine, the "humanitarian machine"; to Victor Hugo's tireless campaign against the death penalty; to the glory of decapitation in Jean Genet's *Our Lady of the Flowers* (1943) or *The Miracle of the Rose* (1946); to Albert Camus's atheist, humanist, immanentist *Reflections on the Guillotine* (1957); to the "vile and terrible"[9] and Christ-like appearance of the guillotine in the 1972 executions of Claude Buffet and Roger Bontems in Robert Badinter's *L'Exécution* (1973). But the guillotine is exemplary in another way as well, for it remains the notorious example of a double-edged sign: a sign of love *and* barbarity. And it will be this internal tension, this division, or self-contestation within the sign that tells not only a Christian, European story of death—the death of the death penalty in France—but also another story, an older and far more ancient story, the story of "this irreducible thing" ("PSS" 239/12) that is the possibility of cruelty.

There is no history of the death penalty without blood, says Derrida—*sans sang* (DP1 191/267). That is, there is no history of the death penalty that

Cruelty and Its Vicissitudes

is not bloody, bloodthirsty, sanguinary. And in this history, the guillotine cuts an imposing figure: a figure of cruelty painted red. As Derrida writes:

> This color [red] ... inundates all of Hugo's texts against the death penalty, from the red made to flow by the guillotine, "the blood-swigging crone," "the infernal scarlet machine," up to the posts of red wood that supported the blade ("two long joists painted red, a shelf painted red, a basket painted red, a heavy crossbeam painted red in which a thick, enormous blade of triangular shape seemed to fit together by one of its sides"). (FWT 142/229–30)

But this red machine with its red menace is also red because it, "she"—Hugo insists on the femininity of this cruel machine—is full of blood (Derrida writes, still commenting on Hugo):

> She absorbs blood; she assimilates it and does not splatter, hence the progress people credit her with: she causes blood to flow, to be sure, but she economizes on it by drinking it, by making it disappear right away into herself, by swallowing it, by gulping it down, by no longer letting it appear so much on the outside, by minimizing it, by reducing it, by sparing it. She is hemophilic, but so hemophilic that she keeps the blood for herself, she keeps it to herself. She economizes blood. (DP1 206/285)

Whether Hugo's *la buveuse de sang* ("the blood-swigging crone") refers to *la* guillotine or *la* place de Grève (the site where public executions were performed in Paris), one thing is clear: *She* is bloody with blood, a blood sucker, an old, vampiric witch whose blood lust cannot be satisfied without consuming the lifeblood of others. *She* is no longer a young woman—that is, she is no longer a menstruating woman (no menstrual blood here)[10]—but "an old woman, an old whore who is losing her teeth.... She can no longer eat, she drinks" (DP1 206/284). And what she drinks is blood. She's bloody with the blood of others.

But this bloody history of the guillotine also includes "signs" of love. The guillotine is an old whore in the abolitionist language of Victor Hugo, but it is hailed in the pro–death penalty literature as "a sign of man's love for man [*un signe de l'amour de l'homme pour l'homme*]" (DP1 193/268), "this brilliant sign of love for mankind [*ce génial signe d'amour des hommes*]" (DP1 194/270). The guillotine is a philanthropic, a "humanitarian machine" (DP1 192/268); it is a machine said to be "progressive, individualist, egalitarian, painless, anesthetizing, euthanizing" (DP1 223/305). When

Dr. Guillotin proposed his six articles to the Constituent Assembly on October 10, 1789, he was seen as a reformer and the guillotine as a humane form of execution (one might even say he was 187 years ahead of his time, arguing for a form of capital punishment that was neither "cruel" nor "unusual"). Here are Guillotin's two most widely cited articles:

> Article 1. Crimes of the same kind shall be punished by the same kinds of punishment, whatever the rank or estate of the criminal.

> Article 6. The method of punishment shall be the same for all persons on whom the law shall pronounce a sentence of death. . . . The criminal shall be decapitated. Decapitation is to be effected by a simple mechanism.[11]

Progressive, egalitarian, painless, the "simple mechanism" of the guillotine brings aid, humanitarian aid, to the criminal, so as to soften (*adoucir*) the blow of capital punishment and put an end to cruelty. The guillotine was thus also interpreted as *progress*—"progress toward the end of cruelty, a bloody, sanguinary cruelty" (DP1 199/276).

And this is where the irony of a double-edged sign cuts both ways— death by decapitation becomes almost pleasurable. Derrida muses:

> The guillotine, inasmuch as it is supposed to act instantaneously [by means of a simple mechanism] . . . would be what relieves pain, what puts an end to pain . . . one could say that it is a little like what is called in American English . . . a "painkiller." The guillotine is not just a killer, it's a painkiller [in an even more colloquial American English, we might say that it is a *killer painkiller*]. . . . And it kills pain because in a certain way, reducing time to the nothing of an instant, to the nothing but an instant, it kills time. (DP1 226/308).

In this satirical vein, Derrida brings together the theme of the *Augenblick*, the instant as blink of an eye, and the theme of absolute noncruelty, of euthanasia, of anesthesia: "These two themes—instantaneity and anesthesia, the almost intemporal instantaneity and insensibility, non-pain, non-cruelty, even gentleness—are indissociable" (DP1 225/308). But this philosophical irony on Derrida's part is already the parodic echo of a satirical piece that appeared in 1789 two weeks after Guillotin's proposed articles and that suggests that the abolition of time is not only painless but also pleasurable or almost pleasurable: "Gentlemen [says Guillotin's caricature], with my machine, I chop off your head in the blink of an eye and without your feeling the least pain. . . . The punishment I have invented is so gentle that one . . . feel[s] nothing but a slight coolness on the neck" (DP1 226/309).

Cruelty and Its Vicissitudes

Following in this vein, we might say that the language of parody takes a further and *exceptionally ironic* turn when, in Badinter's book *L'Exécution*, we read that Claude Buffet, the man who killed two hostages in 1971, wrote to Georges Pompidou, the president of the French Republic, asking Pompidou *not* to pardon him for his crime. In *L'Exécution*, Badinter in fact describes Buffet's murderous and suicidal drive as a death drive:

> The death drive took possession of Buffet; it escorted him, carried him to the guillotine. It exerted a power of fascination over him. . . . It had been waiting for him for all eternity, so it seemed. . . . In the wake of the razor, the dagger with which he had killed, the huge knife would now slit his throat in one clean stroke. This was the secret and long-awaited apotheosis.[12]

In his letter to Pompidou, Buffet asks *not only* that he *not* be pardoned ("If I am pardoned, I will kill again. I will commit other murders in whatever prison I happen to be in") but also—and this is the detail I wanted to underscore—that he be executed lying on his back so that he could look death in the face, that is, so he could watch the blade *falling* on him (FWT 224n1/223n1). This second request was denied. Perhaps because Pompidou sensed that *that* ironic turn, or trope, would be one turn too many . . . too much pleasure, *un trop de plaisir*. As if pleasure in punishment were an indictment of punishment. Or pleasure in cruelty an homage to cruelty such that cruelty would know no end.

Thus, Victor Hugo's signs of progress, signs that involve the imminent and ineluctable end of the death penalty, point to an end of cruelty that may in fact have no simple end: "Sign of decrepitude. Sign of imminent death," writes Hugo. And Derrida comments: "The death penalty is going to die, agony; end" (DP1 201/279). The "sign" by which Hugo recognizes the imminent demise of the death penalty,[13] the "sign" of signs, is the moving of the guillotine out of Paris. The hideous machine is being moved, away from la place de Grève, because it failed to work, because it "malfunctioned in a terrifying and barbaric way" (DP1 204/282). And there is nothing gentle (*doux*) about the impossibility of killing that Hugo describes in two gruesome executions. In both cases, Dr. Guillotin's blade does its job poorly, and the condemned one is tortured before being killed: "Seen from a certain angle," writes Hugo, "the[se] frightful executions . . . are *excellent signs*. The guillotine is hesitating. It has begun to misfire. All the old scaffolding of the death penalty is breaking down" (DP1 207/285, modified). Though it would take almost another 150 years for the guillotine to break down permanently in France, the signs of the senescence of this exceptional—and exceptionally bloody—cruelty are there for Victor Hugo as early as 1832. For Hugo, thus, all signs lead to the end of bloody cruelty, that is, to the day when the "merciful law of Christ will at last suffuse the legal code, which will glow with its radiance" (FWT 143/231, modified).

But the death penalty survives the death of the guillotine. The end of bloody cruelty is not the end of cruelty. The death penalty survives, and its very survival testifies, as we will see, to a more originary history at the heart of cruelty, namely, the possibility of psychical cruelty.

Cruelty and Its Vicissitudes (Psychoanalysis)

The history of the death penalty is a bloody history. But in this history of blood there is another history, an alternative history, a history *without* blood (*sans sang*), one that involves the disappearance of blood and a nonbloody process of interiorization. In this way, the history of blood in Derrida's *Death Penalty* seminars takes us from the *bloody experience* of the guillotine in France to the *end of blood* by lethal injection in the United States. We move from "blood that flows, red blood . . . blood that exhibits, by pouring out, and lets one see the inside on the outside" to "experiences of the bloodless, experiences of the becoming bloodless [*du devenir exsangue*], of reabsorption, drying up, or the disappearance by interiorization of blood, of the visibility of blood" (DP1 191–92/267).

The etymology of "cruelty" is bloody: *Cruor* is blood (specifically the blood that flows from a wound), "a stream of blood," according to Lewis and Short.[14] But not all cruelty is bloody. Indeed, cruelty "can be and is no doubt *essentially* psychical (pleasure taken in suffering or in making suffer in order to make suffer, to see suffering; *grausam*, in German, does not name blood)" (FWT 142/229, my emphasis). By passing from the Latin *cruor* to the Germanic *Grausamkeit*, one passes from bloody cruelty to a cruelty without blood (and the move from decapitation or the electric chair, which can still be bloody, to lethal injection or the gas chamber is part of this same movement). This is why, as Derrida says in "Psychoanalysis Searches the States of Its Soul," the end of bloody cruelty does not signal the end of cruelty but rather a shift in both the form and the visibility of cruelty: "One can staunch bloody cruelty . . . one can put an end to murder by the blade, by the guillotine, in the classical or modern theater of bloody war, but according to Freud or Nietzsche, a psychical cruelty will always take its place [*y suppléera toujours*] by inventing new resources" ("PSS" 239/10). It is this essentially psychical, bloodless (*exsangue*) or nonbloody (*non sanglante*) cruelty that makes cruelty not only so "difficult to *determine* and *delimit*" but also, as Derrida insists, "one of the horizons *most proper* to psychoanalysis" ("PSS" 239/10, my emphasis).

Indeed, in "Psychoanalysis Searches the States of Its Soul," Derrida's address to the International Psychoanalytic Association at the Estates General of Psychoanalysis in July 2000, delivered in the space/time separating *The Death Penalty, Volume I* from *The Death Penalty, Volume II*, "psychoanalysis" has become the name of the royal road to psychical cruelty:

> If there is something irreducible in the life of the living being, in the soul, in the psyche . . . and if this irreducible thing . . . is indeed the possibility of cruelty . . . then no other discourse—be it theological, metaphysical, genetic, physicalist, cognitivist, and so forth—could open itself up to this hypothesis. They would all be designed to reduce it, exclude it, deprive it of sense. The only discourse that can today claim the thing of psychical suffering as its own affair [*comme son affaire propre*] would indeed be what has been called, for about a century, psychoanalysis. . . . "Psychoanalysis" would be the name of that which, without theological or other alibi, would be turned toward what is most *proper* to psychical cruelty. Psychoanalysis would be another name for the "without alibi." ("PSS" 239–40/12–13)

Nonbloody cruelty, psychical cruelty, would be the *proper* affair of psychoanalysis, one of its most *proper* horizons, as we saw in Chapter 6. What is *properly* psychoanalytic would be turned toward what is *properly* cruel (*proper* to psychical cruelty). It is as if psychical cruelty were "the ultimate ground" on which the figure of psychoanalysis took its proper shape ("PSS" 239/11), as if psychoanalysis had become not only the name but also the proper name for (thinking about) psychical cruelty. A psychical cruelty, a cruelty of the *psyche*, would belong to the life and soul of psychoanalysis. This is because, unlike other discourses, psychoanalysis does not turn elsewhere (*alibi*) or close itself off to the hypothesis of a cruelty essential to life and therefore indestructible (a cruelty, which, following the publication of *Beyond the Pleasure Principle* in 1920, Freud will reinscribe in the logic of aggressive and destructive drives that are inseparable from the death drive). Rather psychoanalysis would open up the interrogation of the meaning of the word "cruelty," opening itself up to "this obscure and enigmatic concept" ("PSS" 245). Psychoanalysis would be, *in its very project*, turned toward the language of cruelty, its "grammatical syntax, conjugations, reflexivities, and persons" ("PSS" 240/13).

Hence what Derrida calls the "psychoanalytic revolution" (DP2 134/185) will have been a sign: a sign not of the *possibility of progress* but of "this irreducible thing in the life of the animate being" ("PSS" 239/12) that is the *possibility of cruelty*. Which is why, as we saw in Chapter 6, psychoanalysis can appear "terrifying, terribly cruel, pitiless" (FWT 173/281). In short, Derrida reads the psychoanalytic revolution as the sign of the impossibility of reading signs as the pure, simple, and definitive possibility of progress.

But in "Psychoanalysis Searches the States of Its Soul," two terms, two nouns, "cruelty" and "sovereignty," enter the scene together. We have already seen how psychical cruelty is the proper affair of psychoanalysis. But if Derrida credits psychoanalysis with having in principle heard and understood the necessity of a discourse "without alibi," it is also because psychoanalysis does not yield to the phantasm of sovereignty or to the alibi of an "invincibly transcendental or ontological structure" (WA xxvii). On the contrary, as we have seen, the psychoanalytic revolution becomes "an invincible force" (FWT 172/280) when it goes against a certain history of reason, a force that can provoke thought "beyond even 'power' and the 'drive for power' . . . and therefore the drive for sovereignty" (FWT 173/280).[15]

Just as a deconstruction of what is most hegemonic in philosophy must pass through a deconstruction of the death penalty, so too a deconstruction of the death penalty must pass through psychoanalysis, through its revolutionary critique of the sovereignty of autonomy. This is why Derrida turns to the psychical (and phantasmatic) dimension of the death penalty in the penultimate session of *The Death Penalty, Volume I*. For it is indeed a *phantasm* that "underwrites or *alibis* the death penalty."[16] This phantasm, which will be the topic of Chapter 9, involves putting an end to the "principle of indetermination . . . [to] the incalculable chance whereby a living being has a relation to what comes, to the to-come [*à l'à-venir*] and thus to some other as event [*à de l'autre comme événement*]" (DP1 256/347). The scandal of the death penalty, its madness and its cruelty, lies in the desire to put an end to (this) chance by imposing an end in a calculable place at a calculable time. The power to master time/the future/the "irruption of other," this would be the ultimate phantasm, the phantasm that lies at the "origin of phantasm" (DP1 258/349), the phantasm that, as I argue in Chapter 9, would be a *primal phantasm*.

In fact, one might say that Derrida's Freudian heritage is unmistakable in his description of the "phantasm" or "dream" that guarantees the survival of the death penalty:

> Since this experience is constitutive of finitude, of mortality, since this phantasm is at work in us all the time . . . well, the fascination exerted

by the real phenomena of death penalty and execution . . . has to do with its effect of truth . . . we see . . . actually take place what we are dreaming of all the time—what we are dreaming of, that is, what in a certain way we desire, namely, to give ourselves death and to infinitize ourselves by giving ourselves death in a calculable, calculated, decidable fashion; and when I say "we," this means that in this dream we occupy, simultaneously or successively, all the positions, those of a judge, of judges, of the jury, of the executioner or the assistants, of the one condemned to death, of course, and the position of one's nearest and dearest, loved or hated, and that of the voyeuristic spectators who we are more than ever. And it is the force of this effect of phantasmatic truth that will probably remain forever invincible, thus guaranteeing forever, alas, a double survival, both the survival of the death penalty and the survival of the abolitionist protest. (DP1 258/349–50)

Derrida cannot help but echo Freud when he speaks of the multiple positions occupied by the dreamer in the dream, that is, when he uses the first-person singular to speak of the singular plural of the dreaming ego ("when I say 'we'"). In *The Interpretation of Dreams*, Freud tells us that dreams are the expression of an unbridled and ruthless egoism. The ego, "my ego," says Freud, "may be represented . . . many times over, now directly and now through identification with extraneous persons" (SE 4:322–23 / GW 2/3:327–28).

But more than the multiple positions occupied by the dreamer in the dream, Derrida's phantasm echoes a concept of phantasy that Freud (briefly) evokes in *The Interpretation of Dreams*. This is the concept of a "ready-made phantasy [*einer fertig vorgefundenen Phantasie*]" (SE 5:495 / GW 2/3:499), a "long-prepared phantasy [*seit langem fertige Phantasie*]" (SE 5:497 / GW 2/3:501), a phantasy that is stored up in memory and so is available—arousable—at a moment's notice. The ready-made phantasy, Freud tells us, explains how a dreamer can compress a superabundant quantity of material into the short period elapsing between the perception of an external stimulus and the moment of waking. What should arouse *our* interest, however, is not only the concept but also the example that Freud gives of a "ready-made phantasy."[17] The example is the "guillotine phantasy [*Guillotinenphantasie*]" (SE 5:497 / GW 2/3:502), and it harks back to a dream discussed by Freud 470 pages earlier—a dream reported by the French physician Alfred Maury. In this dream, which Freud recounts at some length, Maury is brought before the revolutionary tribunal during the Reign of Terror; he is questioned, condemned, and "led to the place of execution surrounded by an immense mob" (SE 4:27 / GW 2/3:28). When the blade of the guillotine falls, Maury wakes up and discovers that the top of his bed has collapsed and struck his neck just in the way in which the blade of the guillotine would actually have struck it. "Stored up ready-made [*fertig aufbewahrt*]" (SE 5:496/GW 2/3:500), "composed already [*bereits komponiert*]" (SE 5:496/GW 2/3:500), the guillotine phantasy is thus ready to hand within the nexus of Maury's dream thoughts. But one is equally struck by the force of Freud's descriptive powers when it comes to this particular phantasy:

> If the piece of wood had struck the back of Maury's neck while he was awake, there would have been an opportunity for some such thought as: "That's just like being guillotined." But since it was in his sleep that he was struck by the board, the dream-work made use of the impinging stimulus in order rapidly to produce a wish-fulfilment.... It can hardly be disputed, I think, that the dream-story was precisely of a sort likely to be constructed by a young man under the influence of powerfully exciting impressions. Who ... could fail to be gripped by narratives of the Reign of Terror, when men and women of the aristocracy, the flower of the nation, showed that they could die with a cheerful mind and could retain the liveliness of their wit and the elegance of their manners till the very moment of the fatal summons? How tempting for a young man to plunge into all this in his imagination—to picture himself bidding a lady farewell—kissing her hand and mounting the scaffold unafraid! ... how tempting for him to take the place of one of those formidable figures who, by the power alone of their thoughts and flaming eloquence, ruled the city in which they were led by their convictions to send thousands of men to their death and who prepared the way for the transformation of Europe, while all the time their own heads were insecure and destined to fall one day beneath the knife of the guillotine—how tempting to picture himself as one of the Girondists, perhaps, or as the heroic Danton! (SE 5:496–97/GW 2/3:500–1)

How tempting, how exciting, how wish fulfilling the fantasy of the guillotine is! No wonder it comes, with flaming eloquence, to exemplify the ready-made fantasy. In fact, one might say that Freud's exquisite lyricism registers, on yet another level, the force of the effect of Derrida's "phantasmatic truth." And in so doing, it points the way to a *ready-made alliance* between psychoanalysis and deconstruction.

Thus, if Derrida echoes Freud at this moment, it is because this "phantasm," this "we," signals an alliance with psychoanalysis in the deconstruction of the death penalty, an alliance with a revolutionary force that offers

Cruelty and Its Vicissitudes

the best and perhaps the only chance of transforming this phantasmatic structure. Indeed, as Derrida tells us in *The Death Penalty, Volume II*, there is no way forward, no way to think abolition, without psychoanalysis: "If there is to be a transformation . . . of international law and of the very axiomatics of law, ethics, and politics . . . this transformation passes and must pass through a consideration . . . of something like the psychoanalytic revolution" (DP2 134/185).

And perhaps there is no better *sign* of this psychoanalytico-philosophical alliance—however surprising or shocking this may seem—than what we call the Jewish joke, what in French is called "une histoire juive." For in both "Psychoanalysis Searches the States of Its Soul" and *The Death Penalty, Volume II* Derrida suddenly and unexpectedly interrupts his analysis (of psychical cruelty, of the history of blood) to tell a Jewish joke, one that he relates, explicitly in one case, implicitly in the other, to psychoanalysis. Of course, Derrida is not the only one to crack a joke with the death penalty looming in the background. Freud opens his 1927 essay on "Humor" with a joke—not a Jewish joke but a joke, told by a Jew, about a criminal who is about to be hanged. The joke is about a dead man walking, or, in this case, a dead man joking. Freud's joke is a one-liner. A criminal is being led out to the gallows on a Monday morning and has only this to say: "'Well, the week's beginning nicely [*Na, die Woche fängt gut an*]'" (SE 21:161 / GW 14:383).

Derrida's jokes, I think you will agree, are a little funnier, or at least the second one is. In the first one, which sets the scene for the second, the joke is on psychoanalysis's *turn* to psychical cruelty: "I will not exploit this reflection on psychical cruelty, that is, bloodless or not necessarily bloody cruelty, on the acute pleasure derived from the soul in pain, to recall a Jewish joke: the psychoanalyst who declared he chose this therapeutic discipline because he could not stand the sight of blood" ("PSS" 239/11). You will notice that Derrida tells this first joke in the form of a negation ("I will not exploit this reflection . . ."). In Freud's "Negation" essay (1925), the famous example of negation is of course the mother ("'You ask who this person in the dream can be. It's *not* my mother.' We emend this to: 'So it *is* his mother'" [SE 19:235 / GW 14:11]). Well, in Derrida's second joke he says just this, that it is all about the mother. And not just any mother but the mother of mothers, Jesus's mother.

In what is explicitly set off as a parenthetical remark, as a break from the Christian, European political theology of the death penalty, Derrida reminds us that the history of blood is not only a history of violent death and death sentences: "It is also that of birth, of filiation, and lineage. One inherits from one's parents, and in the Jewish tradition one inherits from one's mother by blood" (DP2 216/290). It is in this context that Derrida tells his joke:

> I will not resist ... the temptation, however vulgar and explosive it may seem, to tell a story, which is more or less a Jewish joke, the story of a Jew who intends to demonstrate by means of a four-part proof that Jesus was not only born Jewish, as everyone knows, born of a Jewish mother and of Jewish blood, but that he remained Jewish, up until the end, 100 percent Jewish by blood. ... The *bon mot* of this Jewish joke about a Jew condemned to death, the *mot d'esprit*, the *Witz* that I didn't make up is at once ridiculous and profound, vulgar, laughable, and nonetheless abyssal.
>
> First of the four proofs of the Jewishness of Jesus, then: he lived with his mother until he was 28.
>
> Second proof: he believed his mother was a virgin.
>
> Third proof: his mother thought he was the son of God.
>
> Fourth proof: he inherited a tiny little artisanal carpentry shop and, [starting from nothing!] from a few pieces of wood and nails he founded a multinational corporation. (DP2 217/290–91, modified)

However "vulgar and explosive" such a joke may seem (*si vulgaire et détonant que cela paraisse*), one thing is clear: Derrida's "Jewish joke," his "histoire juive," invokes, in its preamble, a 100 percent Freudian heritage: "*le mot d'esprit, der Witz*" (*Le mot d'esprit et sa relation à l'inconscient* is the title of *Der Witz und seine Beziehung zum Unbewußten* [*Jokes and Their Relation to the Unconscious*] in French). The verb *détoner* (written with one *n*, as Derrida does in his original typescript) means to detonate, to explode. But when one is telling a Jewish joke in an academic setting one more readily hears its homonym, the verb *détonner* (two *n*'s): *il détonne, ses manières vulgaires détonnent dans ce milieu*, he is out of place, his vulgar manners are out of place in this setting. *Détonner* (two *n*'s) is also to be out of tune or out of harmony ("incongruous" is how the translator chose to correct Derrida's "typo"). And Derrida's Jewish jokes are all of these things at once: explosive, out of tune, and literally out of place (whether parenthetically as in *The Death Penalty, Volume II* or in the caesura separating *The Death Penalty, Volume I* from *The Death Penalty, Volume II*).

And yet if we read the Jewish joke as the sign of a psychoanalytico-philosophical alliance that begins by deconstructing the political onto-theology of sovereignty, the sign of an alliance that is *explosively* out of tune

Cruelty and Its Vicissitudes 137

with the political theology of the death penalty, then perhaps we can say that a mutation of philosophy is *already* underway.

Swan's Wake

To conclude this chapter, I would like to return to the epigraph with which I began in order to add a final, discordant, and literary note to this psychoanalytico-philosophical alliance *qui détonne*. On September 15, 1848, Victor Hugo spoke his famous words to the Constituent Assembly that I alluded to earlier: "I vote for the pure, simple, and definitive abolition of the death penalty" (DP1 97/147). But Victor Hugo is not only famous for his political speeches or for wanting to read signs of the end of the guillotine as signs of progress. He is also one of the dominant, literary figures of French Romanticism. So I wanted to turn to a scene in his literary work that is also about signs of beneficence and humane gestures. The context is the following: A man and his son are standing by the edge of a pond. There are swans on the pond, and the boy is holding a half-eaten brioche. The man, urging his son to have pity on the animals, tells him—"Sois humain. Il faut avoir pitié des animaux"[18]—before taking the brioche from the boy and throwing it into the water. The swans, however, are preoccupied with other things, and they do not see the bourgeois or the brioche. Frustrated by the swans, the man begins to gesticulate "telegraphically," at which point the swans take notice of the man and begin to swim in his direction. The man, now very pleased with himself, turns to the boy and says: "Les cygnes comprennent les signes." This means of course "swans understand signs." But because *cygne* (c-y-g-n-e: swan) is a homonym for *signe* (s-i-g-n-e: sign) in French, we may hear this line as "swans understand signs," or as "signs understand swans," or "as signs understand signs," or perhaps even as the self-understanding of swans, "*swans* understand swans." But if we read this story as the sign of signs, then what it tells us is that there may be no simple end to this story of signs.

Indeed, this same line—"Les cygnes comprennent les signes"—is used as an epigraph, as a heading, as an *en-tête*, in the very first chapter of Villiers de l'Isle Adam's book *Tribulat Bonhomet* (1887). The title of this first chapter, which immediately precedes the Hugo quote, as if the Hugo quote were a kind of subtitle to it, is "Le tueur de cygnes [The Killer of Swans]," and in the course of this chapter Dr. Bonhomet stalks and kills swans by crushing their necks with the steel teeth of his medieval gloves. In other words, "The Killer of Swans," a chapter that ends with an orgasmic putting to death of swans, ironizes the understanding of signs and injects cruelty into a scene of beneficence, thereby inscribing the survival of cruelty on a humane gesture. It is as if the chapter titled "The Killer of Swans" were wringing the neck of its own heading, wringing the neck of its *en-tête*, turning its own epigraph into an epitaph, twisting a telegraphic communication into a deathly stranglehold.

But Villiers's dark humor reminds us that it is not only the fate of swans but also the fate of signs that is at stake here. For *le tueur de cygnes* (the killer of swans) is both the sadistic Dr. Bonhomet *and* the chapter title that ends by turning Hugo's "si(cy)gnes" into swan songs. What this literary turn may suggest, in other words, is the cruelty of signs. And yet . . . Villiers's literary coup de grâce, the final and ironic twist of "The Killer of Swans," leaves us not so much with *dead swans* as with a *killer title*. And if Derrida's *Death Penalty* seminars turn out to be the *swan song* of the death penalty in a few more American states, then perhaps *his* killer title will have been a good sign.

CHAPTER 8

The "Question" of the Death Penalty

In this chapter, I will address the *question* of the death penalty in Derrida's *Death Penalty* seminars: the *question* of the death penalty, if there is *one*, that is, if there is "*la* question de la peine de mort." For nothing is less certain. Not only, as we will see, must we speak of the two sets of triple questions in both seminars, and not only must we speak of the transformation or mutation of the question of the death penalty from one seminar to the other (in *The Death Penalty, Volume I*, the question of the death penalty is primarily the question of the political onto-theology of sovereignty; in *The Death Penalty, Volume II*, it becomes the question of reason as the principle of reason). But we must also, as we saw in Chapter 6, speak of Derrida's question about the question, about the authority of the question or the questioning form. Indeed, at the very end of *The Death Penalty, Volume II*, Derrida will point to the future of the question. How do the possibility and the reality of the death penalty, how does the *question* of the death penalty, force us to ask a question not only about what comes before the question but also about the future of the question, that is, about the future of reason, the principle of reason, and what is *proper* to man?

If someone came to you and said, "You know, Derrida's *Death Penalty* seminars are just a series of questions," what would you say? One might first be tempted to say—too quickly: Yes, you're right. Unless with these questions he is trying to rethink the question of the death penalty as the question of questions (as *the* question for philosophy), not to mention the death penalty's *questionable* future. Look at what Derrida says at the end of *The Death Penalty, Volume I*:

> Even when the death penalty will have been abolished, when it will have been purely and simply, absolutely and unconditionally, abolished on earth, it will survive; there will still be some death penalty [*il y en aura encore*]. . . . Let us harbor no illusion on this subject: even when it will have been abolished, the death penalty will survive; it will have other lives in front of it, and other lives to sink its teeth into [*d'autres vies à se mettre sous la dent*]. (DP1 282–3/380)

One would then be tempted, upon reflection, not to respond so quickly and to leave the question suspended.

Derrida's *Death Penalty* seminars are driven by questions, proliferating questions, questions suspended, strung together, sometimes on the wings of a kite: "I will begin with these . . . questions . . . and leave them suspended," Derrida writes at the beginning of *The Death Penalty, Volume II*, "three questions . . . on the wings, or on the tail, or at the head of a kite [*trois questions . . . sur les ailes, ou à la queue ou à la tête d'un cerf-volant*]" (DP2 4/22–23).[1] Whether these questions find themselves at the head or on the tail or on the wings of a kite, one thing is clear: Guiding these seminars and at their *heart*—indeed, one might even say that the heart is at the wheel in these seminars, *le cœur au volant*—are two sets of questions, two triple questions, two ternary figures of questions, two nodal unities, two knots: "What is an exception?" "What is sovereignty?" "What is cruelty?" in the case of *The Death Penalty, Volume I*, and "What is an act?" "What is an age?" "What is a desire?" in the case of *The Death Penalty, Volume II* (DP2 2–4/21–23).

The question of the death penalty is 2 × 3 questions, or a flow of questions that becomes impossible to seal off (*étancher*): "What is the death penalty?" (DP1 22/49), "What is the essence and the meaning of the death penalty?" (DP1 22–23/49), "What is the theologico-political?" (DP1 23/51), "What is a political death penalty?" (DP1 172/243), "What is a punishment?" (DP2 31/55), "What is a president?" (DP2 14/35, 24/47), "What is the figure of the president in this history of the death penalty?" (DP2 14/35), "What is the *res publica*?" (DP2 60/92), "What is a war?"

The "Question" of the Death Penalty   141

(DP1 82/127), "What is a civil war?" (DP1 81/125), "What is a public enemy?" (DP1 82/127), "What is self-defense?" (DP2 36/61), "What is blood?" (DP1 192/267), "What is an interest?" (DP1 140/201), "What is the secret interest that drives . . . discourses of absolute disinterest?" (DP1 141/203), "What is progress?" (DP2 21/44), "What is it to believe?" (DP2 68/103), "What is man?" (DP1 236/322, DP2 210–11/282), "What is it that is proper to man?" (DP1 236/322), "What is death?" (DP1 237/323), "And what is life?" (DP2 111/154), "What is a sur-vival?" (DP1 270/365), "What is a game?" (DP2 136/187), "What is a calculation?" (DP2 144/197).

And I have only cited those questions (and not even all of them) that are in the form "What is . . . ?" These questions, and such is Derrida's expressed intention, make our head spin:

> We have asked ourselves, or we have pretended to ask directly in a classical philosophical form, the form of What is . . . ? a certain number of questions, such as: What is an exception? What is cruelty? What is blood? What is man? What is it that is proper to man or to the humanitarian? and so forth.
>
> This was not just playing with what are called "rhetorical questions" in English, that is, simulacra of questions whose answer is known in advance, and inscribed in the very form of the question. But neither were they questions to which we expected an immediately satisfying or reassuring response. They were above all questions meant to show, with their own inadequation, the *vertigo* or the abyss of their own impossibility, the *vertigo* above or around their own impossibility, what makes them turn on themselves until they make the head turn, namely, that to articulate themselves, to take shape, they would have to pretend to know at least what they are talking about at the very moment they seem to be asking about it. And this *vertigo* is not only, I believe, the one that can be induced by the *dizziness* of a simple hermeneutic circle, even though there is indeed a sort of hermeneutic circle that lets us suppose a pre-comprehension of that about which we are asking. (DP1 236–37/322, my emphasis)

The vertigo brought on by these questions (a vertigo [*vertige*] that exceeds or compounds the mere dizziness [*tournis*] of a hermeneutic circle) entails precisely the collapse of the guardrail or safeguard, the barrier, the rigorous oppositional partition that is supposed to separate the conceptual couples upon which all thinking about the death penalty has always relied: inside/outside, self/other, *poena naturalis/poena forensis*, auto-/hetero-punishment, suicide/execution, condemned to die/condemned to death, cruel/noncruel, act/nonact, active/passive, doing/letting be done—and ultimately, life/death.

Indeed, by challenging the "knowledge, judged to be indubitable, of what separates a state of death from a state of life" (DP1 238/324), the question of the death penalty ends up destabilizing the supposed knowledge of all great philosophies of death. Without the "supposed or supposedly possible knowledge of this clear-cut, sharp limit [*cette limite tranchée, tranchante*]" (DP1 238/324) separating death from life, no philosophy of death can know or claim to know what it is talking about. The simple idea of a limit between life and death, the simple idea of the "supposed existence of an objectifiable instant that separates the living from the dying, be it of an ungraspable instant that is reduced to the blade of a knife or to the *stigmē* of a point" (DP1 238/324), this simple idea orders, organizes, orients all of the great meditations on death (from Luther to Heidegger to Levinas). Hence, the question of the death penalty triggers something like a *disorientation* in thinking. And it does so by displacing the question not only from death to death penalty but also from the alternative life/death or living/dying to the manner, apparatus, theater, scene, or phantasm "of giving-death, indeed of giving-oneself-death" (DP2 6/25).[2]

Could one not say, then, that Derrida is *putting* philosophy *to the question* here? Is he not putting philosophy to the question of the death penalty just as he put psychoanalysis to the question of cruelty in "Psychoanalysis Searches the States of Its Soul" (as we saw in Chapter 6)? In the case of philosophy, this putting to the question would also be a putting into question of the question, of the essential question, the question of essence, the question of being, if we understand philosophy to be from its very beginning, from its inaugural moment *a question*, the question "*ti esti* . . ." "what is . . .?" This putting into question does not always come in the form of questions, of course. And it is not limited to philosophical thinking, as we will see. However, its trajectory is marked over and over again, in *The Death Penalty* seminars and Derrida's other published writing on the death penalty,[3] by a term that draws sparks, sparks in the form of scare quotes (you might think of a key on the string of a kite in a lightning storm): This key-term is "fact." I am going to mention three of these "facts" that illustrate the onto-theologico-political reach (*portée*) of the deconstruction of the death penalty in Derrida's writing.

The first fact is a "troubling" and "highly significant" "fact" ("'fait' . . . troublant, et hautement significant") (FWT 140/224):

> Almost everywhere, as statistics show [so it's an empirico-statistical fact], those who are the most violently opposed to abortion, those who sometimes try to kill doctors in the name of the "right" to life, those very people are often the most ardent supporters of the death penalty. (FWT 140/224–25, modified)

In this way, the so-called unconditional defenders of life are at the same time militants for death. And what is more, it is often Christian fundamentalists who embrace both struggles: the struggle against abortion and the struggle against abolition (FWT 140/225).

This troubling and highly significant "fact" leads, via Christianity, to another fact, this time an "undeniable *fact* [fait *indéniable*]" (FWT 143/230), namely, that there has never been any *political* opposition to the death penalty by the Catholic Church:

> Up to the twenty-first century, almost without exception, the Catholic Church has been in favor of the death penalty. Sometimes in an active, fervent, militant way. It has always supported state legislation on the death penalty. (FWT 141/226)

Although Vatican City did finally abolish the death penalty in 1969 (the death penalty had been legal from 1929 to 1969), the engagement of the church and the Vatican in the abolitionist struggle has been virtually nonexistent (until now).[4] I say virtually because one can find a short YouTube video, dated November 30, 2011, of former Pope Benedict reading seven lines of greeting to a delegation taking part in a meeting on the theme "No Justice without Life."[5] But what follows is a far more telling example of the former pope's thinking on the death penalty. In his July 9, 2004, letter to the US bishops (so he is writing to bishops as their superior, and to bishops in the United States, where at the time thirty-eight states still had not abolished the death penalty), then Cardinal Ratzinger writes:

> Not all moral issues have the same moral weight as abortion and euthanasia. *For example*, if a Catholic were to be at odds with the Holy Father on the application of capital punishment or on the decision to wage war, he would not for that reason be considered unworthy to present himself to receive Holy Communion. While the Church exhorts civil authorities to seek peace, not war, and to exercise discretion and mercy in imposing punishment on criminals, it may still be permissible to take up arms to repel an aggressor or to have recourse to capital punishment. There may be a legitimate diversity of opinion

even among Catholics about waging war and applying the death penalty, *but not however with regard to abortion and euthanasia.*⁶

And this undeniable fact, namely, that no pope (until just recently) has formally engaged the church and the Vatican in the abolitionist struggle, seems to contradict "*another* Christianity, another spirit of Christianity" (FWT 143/230), which is best represented by the example of Victor Hugo. In the name of an unconditional abolition—the "pure, simple, and definitive abolition of the death penalty"—Hugo appeals to the "merciful law of Christ" and to the day when this law "will at last suffuse the Code, which will glow in its radiance" (FWT 143/231). Indeed, this contradiction will lead Derrida to speak of the internal tension, division, self-contestation, self-deconstruction at the heart of Christianity.

Now these two facts (the troubling fact, the undeniable fact) lead to a third "fact." This is the "massive and highly significant 'fact' [*'fait' massif et hautement significant*]" (FWT 147/239) that we encountered in Chapter 7 but whose full deployment—as *fait*, *donnée*, and *constat*—I will now bring into focus. In the very first session of *The Death Penalty, Volume II*, Derrida refers to

> the strange and stupefying and shocking fact [*fait étrange et stupéfiant et interloquant*] that never, but never, it turns out, has any philosophical discourse as such, in the system of its properly philosophical argument, opposed the principle, I repeat, the principle, of the death penalty, which indicates, as shocked as we are by this fact, the magnitude of the difficulty or the task: is it possible to oppose the *principle* of the death penalty or to oppose it with something that is called an unconditional principle. (DP2 2/20)

Or again in *For What Tomorrow . . .*, he tells us that he will proceed

> from what has long been for me the most significant and the most stupefying—also the most stupefied—fact [*la donnée la plus signifiante et la plus stupéfiante*] in the history of Western philosophy: never, *to my knowledge*, has any philosopher *as such*, *in his properly philosophical discourse*, never has any philosophy *as such* contested the legitimacy of the death penalty. From Plato to Hegel, from Rousseau to Kant . . . they all expressly, each in his own way . . . took a stand *for* the death penalty. (FWT 145–46/235–36, modified)

Finally, in "Peine de mort et souveraineté," he speaks of this "fact" as guiding a new "abolitionist" discourse:

The "Question" of the Death Penalty

> I am guided by the need to elaborate a new "abolitionist" discourse—
> and by the massive, stupefying, stupefied fact [*et par le constat massif,
> stupéfiant, stupéfait*] that no philosophy, no philosopher as such, has,
> to my knowledge, ever objected to the very principle of the death
> penalty in a philosophical and systematic discourse. ("PMS" 14, my
> translation).

We must face the facts. And the fact is that no philosopher as such in the history of Western philosophy has objected to the principle of the death penalty in a systematic way. Now, one of the interesting things has been the way these passages get under people's, and in particular philosophers', skin. And the response is always the same: anger or irritation followed by the need to find exceptions, *factual* exceptions to the rule. It is a little as if the response were trying to eliminate or to abolish this "strange and stupefying and shocking fact" by countering it with other "facts," that is, precisely by mistaking the principial nature of the "fact" and thereby turning the question of the death penalty into just another question for philosophy.

Perhaps we could even say that the "whack, whack, whack, whack" (Plato, Hegel, Rousseau, Kant)[7] that Derrida delivers to the history of philosophy elicits an Oedipal response. Oedipus, you will remember, was whacked on the head by Laius at the crossroads: "The old man . . . waited till I was passing his chariot, and whacked me [*mou kathiketo*] on the head with his double-pointed goad."[8] It's true that Oedipus is responding to a blow he has received and that he returns whack for whack (a whack for a whack, an eye for an eye . . . would this not be a modern version of talionic law?). Indeed, I have suggested that Derrida is *putting* philosophy *to the question* and that he means to provoke. But Oedipus, says Sophocles, pays the "penalty with interest [*ou mēn isēn g' eteisen*; not only equal he paid]" (l. 810). Perhaps we could just say that the responses to Derrida's provocative statements seem to bring out—*precisely in the name of abolition*—a curiously *corrective* impulse. An impulse that may not be entirely unrelated to a history of the erasure of facts (a history that includes a torture known euphemistically as *la question*).[9]

But the question of the death penalty is not only the question of the political onto-theology of sovereignty—and here I will say a few words about the "future" of the question of the death penalty in Derrida's seminars. The question of the death penalty is also, as Derrida suggests in *The Death Penalty, Volume II*, the question of the principle of reason, of the interpretation of reason as the "principle of reason," and of the interpretation of the "principle of reason" as the principle of calculability (in particular through a reading of Heidegger's *Der Satz vom Grund*). Reason understood as calculating reason, says Derrida, insures and reassures. It is an insurance system, a machine that generates insurances and in particular life insurances (Derrida, like Heidegger, muses on the fact that Leibniz, the inventor of the "formalizing formulation" [DP2 149/203] of the principle of reason, namely, *nihil sine ratione*, was also the inventor of life insurance). According to this reading, *law*, including the death penalty, can simply be interpreted as one of the modalities of life insurance, whether one is *for* or *against* the death penalty, whether one condemns the death penalty in the name of the inalienable right to life or whether one sees in the death penalty a force of deterrence that would be in the service of the security and survival of the social body. In this way, the history of the death penalty, or at least its modern history, says Derrida, can be interpreted as a history of life *insurance* or social *security* (DP 150/204–5).

Is there a way out of this life-insuring, death-dealing game? In *The Death Penalty, Volume II*, Derrida imagines a party game, which he likens to "un jeu de l'oie" (game of the goose), in which every possible response (historical, religious, philosophical, anthropological) to the question "what is man?" "what is proper to man?" becomes a square in the finite series of squares (*cases*) that make up the track of the board game. One would move from square to square according to the roll of a die (these would be the rules of the game). In Derrida's version of the game, the squares would be called things like "language," "reason," "law," "politics," "freedom," "responsibility," "sovereignty," "laughter," "tears," "the experience of death," "time as such," "rights," "modesty," "clothing, hearth and home," "technology," "foolishness [*bêtise*]" (DP2 211/282–83, 219/292–93). And one square would be called "death penalty." But since this square (a bit like the prison square in the game of the goose) would be just another square on this finite track, that is, just another figure for what is proper to man, the game would continue in its circular, finite way. Indeed, even if one hid or removed one of squares, for example the "death penalty" square—even if one abolished it—the game would go on, since all of the other squares would remain the same: "The game master or the philosopher croupier would say to you: nothing has changed, carry on, place your bets, the square 'death penalty' is closed, it has disappeared, it's abolished, but this changes nothing" (DP2 213/285). Nothing changes because what is proper to man is still represented by all the other squares, and each one involves a metonymic or synecdochic relation to the rest. In other words, the possibility of the death penalty—qua possibility—remains.

As does the question: "Is there a way out of this game?" (DP2 213/285). Is there a future for the *animal rationale*, "a future for the future of what is proper to man [*un avenir pour l'avenir du propre de l'homme*]" (DP2 219/292)? If the "death penalty" is not just one square among others and the question of the death penalty is not just one question among others—and not even simply a question about death (that is, the alternative life/death)—then there is perhaps, if not a way out, at least a way *for-ward*, or at least a turn toward the "for," *le pour*.

In order to *goose up* the reader's interest in these seminars, I will not say much more. I will simply point to three disseminal moments. The first moment is philosophical: Derrida literally refers to "the disseminal opening of all the meanings of 'for' [*l'ouverture disséminale de tous les sens du 'pour'*]" at the very end of the penultimate session of *The Death Penalty, Volume II*. Such an opening would disrupt the logic of the calculable equivalence, the calculating and prosthetic formalization of the "for" of talionic law: an eye *for* an eye, a tooth *for* a tooth. To die *for* the other, on the other hand (and to understand the full force of Derrida's argument here one would have to go back to his readings of Kant, Heidegger, and Freud),[10] would mean not only *for* the other in the sense of a replaceability, a prosthetic substitution or a sacrifice. No, an "I" dies for the other, says Derrida, "in the disseminal opening of all the senses of 'for'": 'Je meurs et je ne meurs que *pour* l'autre . . . [ce qui] ne signifie pas que cela, ma mort, ne m'arrive pas [I die and I die only *for* the other . . . this does not mean that this, my death, does not happen to me]" (DP2 242/323).

The second moment is psychoanalytic. In *The Death Penalty, Volume II*, in the months following his address to the Estates General of Psychoanalysis in Paris, Derrida returns to the question of "revolution as psychoanalytic reason" (DP2 159/216). Only this time he does so from the side of philosophy and the history of reason.[11] In fact, in *The Death Penalty, Volume II*, Derrida speaks not once but twice of the psychoanalytic revolution. The very same remarks on the need to believe in, and hope for, the *mondialisation*, the becoming-worldwide or the worldwide-ization of psychoanalysis occur, as it were, twice (the first time, one might add, as irony):

> I wouldn't want my irony last time on the subject of the worldwide-ization [*mondialisation*] of psychoanalysis to give rise . . . to any confusion. We must believe in and hope for the worldwide-ization of psychoanalysis, however uncertain, obscure, and indirect its paths. Beyond all possible or real caricature, it is certain, as I was saying, that

if a transformation (already underway, in fact, and in any case so necessary) of international law and the very axiomatics of law, ethics, and politics is to come to pass, right down to their most fundamental concepts and principles . . . well then, this transformation passes and must pass through a consideration [*prise en compte*], direct or indirect, explicit or implicit, by conscious or unconscious contagion, of something like revolution, or even psychoanalytic reason, revolution as psychoanalytic reason. At issue here is a history of reason and the mutation that something like psychoanalysis might inscribe in it—which is not an irrationality but perhaps another reason, another putting into play [*mise en jeu*] of reason. (DP2 159–60/215–16).

However long and circuitous its path, we must believe in the worldwideization of psychoanalysis, which promises to transform the fundamental concepts and principles of law, ethics, and politics. And yet, in a way, we can already begin to read this disseminal opening in the passage that takes us from a *prise en compte* to a *mise en jeu*, from a "consideration"—or more literally a "taking into account"—to a "putting into play." To *take* the psychoanalytic revolution *into account* here, the history of reason (as the reason that calculates or takes *into account*) has to put itself at risk (*en jeu*). What is at stake (*en jeu*) when reason takes account of psychoanalytic reason is the conceptual hold or grasp (*prise*) of reason (as the principle of reason). Hence this high-stakes game (a game that gives full play to reason, *un jeu qui donne du jeu à la raison*) involves not only the history of reason but also the future of philosophy. Indeed, a few months after *The Death Penalty, Volume II*, in his interview with Élisabeth Roudinesco in *For What Tomorrow . . .*, Derrida will describe deconstruction's relation to its philosophical heritage in such a way that it becomes possible to hear "something like" a *mise en jeu* of philosophical reason by another reason:

> Deconstruction is seen as hyperconceptual, and indeed it is . . . but only to the point where a certain writing, a writing that thinks, exceeds this conceptual grasp or mastery [*la prise ou la maîtrise conceptuelle*]. It therefore attempts to think the limit of the concept; it even endures the experience of this excess; it lovingly [*amoureusement*] lets itself be exceeded. It is like an ecstasy of the concept: a *jouissance* of the concept to the point of overflowing. (FWT 5/17, modified)

A *jouissance* of the concept, an experience of excess to the point of overflowing, an experience that must be endured, undergone, suffered . . . in other words, *la mise en jeu* of philosophical reason by something like "psychoanalytic reason" would lead not to death—that is, to a big, spectacular death, whether symbolic or real (castration or decapitation)—but rather to a little death, *une petite mort*, a little death that cannot be separated from desire or interest, that is—and I have always loved this phrase—"la vie la plus intense possible [the most intense life possible]" (LLF 52/55). Translating from French to French, one might say that deconstruction *se meurt d'amour pour le concept, elle se meurt d'amour pour l'autre, pour le concept de l'autre*.

The third moment, finally, is literary.[12] In Charles Dickens's *David Copperfield*, Mr. Dick is an eccentric whose tragic past includes abuse at the hands of a cruel brother and confinement in an insane asylum. Though Aunt Betsey rescues Mr. Dick from the asylum and takes him into her guardianship, he is not quite right in the head (some say that he is mad, others that he is simpleminded, *qu'il a le cerveau lent*). Mr. Dick keeps trying to write his Memorial but is constantly interrupted by the head of King Charles the First, which was cut off in 1649 and is repeatedly inscribed in Mr. Dick's text. Aunt Betsey tells David that King Charles I is Mr. Dick's name for his troubles: "[King Charles the First] is his allegorical way of expressing it. He connects his illness with great disturbance and agitation, naturally, and that's the figure, or the simile, or whatever it's called, which he chooses to use. And why shouldn't he, if he thinks proper?"[13]

So Mr. Dick is a madman or a simpleton for whom the question of the execution of King Charles the First, the question of the death penalty, is not just any question but *the only* question: It is *the* question over which he has lost his head. But if I mention Mr. Dick and his troubles here, it is because of the crazy, simpleminded way he engages this question: He suspends it *on the wings of a kite (cerf-volant)*. Here is David Copperfield's description of it:

> I was going away, when [Mr. Dick] directed my attention to the kite.
> "What do you think of that for a kite?" he said.
> I answered that it was a beautiful one. I should think it must have been as much as seven feet high.
> "I made it. We'll go and fly it, you and I," said Mr. Dick. "Do you see this?"
> He showed me that it was covered with manuscript, very closely and laboriously written; but so plainly, that as I looked along the lines, I thought I saw some allusion to King Charles the First's head again, in one or two places.
> "There's plenty of string," said Mr. Dick, "and when it flies high, it takes the facts a long way. That's my manner of diffusing 'em. I don't know where they may come down. It's according to circumstances, and

the wind, and so forth; but I take my chance of that." (DC 177, my emphasis)

Unlike the Oedipal response to the "strange and stupefying and shocking fact" of philosophy's alliance with the principle of the death penalty, Mr. Dick does not deny the facts or erase the facts (or counter the facts with other facts). He diffuses or disseminates them: "When it flies high, it takes the facts a long way. That's my manner of diffusing'em." Like psychoanalytic reason, literary unreason would be not an irrationality but another reason, another putting into play (or flight) of reason. Indeed, we might think of Mr. Dick—and with him the modern institution of literature—as the *voice of unreason* of philosophy.

In order, then, to think this "*exceptionally cruel* thing that is the death penalty" (DP1 69/109), philosophy would have to let itself be altered by the mutation that something like psychoanalysis or literature inscribes in the history of reason. It would have to pass through some taking into account of the cruelty of the question and the questioning form:

> If there is something cruel, it is perhaps, to begin with, the question itself, the putting into question as putting to the question that initiates torture and that threatens, in the course of an interrogation, in the course of a quest, an inquest, a requisition, an inquisition, a perquisition, to cause the subject in question to lose his or her head. (DP1 167/236–37)

But to speak of the future of the question is never simply to speak of a dizzying proliferation of questions. It is also to speak of questions that remain perilously suspended:

> Let us leave these questions hanging over our heads; we'll see later where they fall. And if they fall, if they fall, as a sign of coherence or consistency, on their feet, or on their head or on whose head, and which head they cause once again to fall. (DP1 167/236)

This suspension is anything but reassuring. And yet one cannot help but wonder whether this very *insecurity* is not itself a sign: the sign of what remains to be thought beyond the (life-insuring) principle of reason as the principle of calculation, that is to say, beyond the terrible reckoning of the death penalty.

CHAPTER 9

A New Primal Scene
Derrida and the Scene of Execution

> It's a hell of a thing, killin' a man. Take away
> all he's got and all he's ever gonna have.
>
> —CLINT EASTWOOD, *Unforgiven*

Prologue: An "American" Vision

As we know, the United States is an exception. Of the 195 independent states that are members of the United Nations or have observer status, 140 have abolished the death penalty in one form or another: 104 of them (53 percent) have abolished the death penalty for all crimes (in these states, no crime is punishable by death), seven of them (4 percent) have abolished the death penalty for ordinary crimes (that is, only crimes committed in exceptional circumstances are punishable by death, such as crimes committed in time of war), and twenty-nine of them (15 percent) have abolished the death penalty in practice (though still legal in these states, the death penalty has not been used for at least ten years).[1] In other words, a supermajority of the world's independent states, 72 percent of them to be exact, qualify as "abolitionist" according to the Death Penalty Information Center: These countries are either "abolitionist for all crimes," "abolitionist for ordinary crimes," or "abolitionist in practice," and they stand in marked contrast to those countries, highlighted in red on the website, that the DPIC classifies as—and here there would be more to say about this term and its anal-sadistic

151

resonances²—"retentionist."³ Of the fifty-five "retentionist countries," countries that maintain or *retain* the death penalty for ordinary crimes, I will list just a few: Afghanistan, China, Iran, Iraq, North Korea, Pakistan, Saudi Arabia, Sudan, the United Arab Emirates, Yemen—*and the United States.* How is it, one might ask, that the United States, "the most Christian democracy in the world" (DP1 192/267), as Jacques Derrida has called it, stands not with the Christian, European West ("old Europe") when it comes to the death penalty but with countries whose human rights abuses have so often been decried by its own State Department? How is it that the United States is today "the only great, Western so-called democracy with a European-Judeo-Christian culture" (DP2 2/20–21) that *retains* the death penalty?

In *Democracy in America*, Alexis de Tocqueville famously speaks of American exceptionalism: "The American position is, therefore, *entirely exceptional* and it is quite possible that no democratic nation will ever be similarly placed."⁴ When abolition, as a European and international trend, has become "irresistible" (FWT 145/235), how do we explain America's surprising retentiveness?⁵ How do we account for its peculiar retentionist tendencies? One may of course conclude that America is a uniquely violent and unforgiving place, a perpetual Wild West. Or one may dismiss it, as Freud did, as a kind of cultural aberration. Following his visit to Clark University in 1909, Freud is reported to have said to Ernest Jones: "America is a mistake, a gigantic mistake, it is true, but nonetheless a mistake."⁶

But what if we read the American exception otherwise? What if we read it not only as an *example* of aberration, which it most certainly is, but also, at the same time, as an *exemplary* aberration? What if, in other words, the American exception allowed us to see the death penalty differently: not as a freak and unfortunate accident of history but as the figure—indeed the privileged figure—of a more originary aberration or desire, one that could never simply be abolished by law (American or otherwise)? What does the example of American retentionism tell us about the difficulties that lie in the path of an "effective end" (DP1 282/380) to the death penalty? And how would such an understanding help us in the abolitionist struggle?

With these questions in mind, let me turn for a moment to a rather spectacular vision of the death penalty, one that brings together, with great irony, the death penalty, the (im)possibility of its abolition, and the "American spirit." Here, then, is that vision:

> I would like to see a law passed which would abolish capital punishment, except for those states which insisted on keeping it. Such states would then be allowed to kill criminals provided that the killing is not

impersonal but personal and a public spectacle: to wit that the executioner be more or less the same size and weight as the criminal (the law could here specify the limits) and that they fight to death using no weapons, or weapons not capable of killing at a distance. Thus, knives or broken bottles would be acceptable. Guns would not.

The benefit of this law is that it might return us to moral responsibility. The killer would carry the other man's death in his psyche. The audience, in turn, would experience a sense of tragedy, since the executioners, highly trained for this, would almost always win. In the flabby American spirit there is a buried sadist who finds the bullfight contemptible—what he really desires are gladiators. Since nothing is worse for a country than repressed sadism, this method of execution would offer ventilation for the more cancerous emotions of the American public.[7]

The author of this fight-club phantasy—this unadulterated American Gladiators–meets-Thunderdome scenario—is Norman Mailer. The same Norman Mailer who would, some twenty years later, go on to write the Pulitzer Prize–winning "true life story" *The Executioner's Song* (1979), which depicts in 1,109 pages the events surrounding the execution of Gary Gilmore by the state of Utah in 1977 (Gary Gilmore was the first person to be executed in the United States after the reinstatement of the death penalty in 1976). *The Executioner's Song* is, of course, also the title of a 1982 NBC film starring Tommy Lee Jones and Rosanna Arquette.[8]

But before the book, and before the movie, Mailer wrote a short article, titled "A Program for the Nation," from which I have just quoted an excerpt. This article was written in response to a survey from *Esquire* in 1959 in which 150 famous people were queried about the 1960 US presidential election: "What, to your mind, should be the most important issues in the election" (PP 10)? Mailer's article, written "at two or three in the morning in February, 1959" (PP 305), as he reports, lists what he takes to be the five most important issues for the next president.[9] Besides his proposed legislation for "A New Capital Punishment" (PP 9), these issues include: a bill abolishing all forms of censorship; a bill legalizing the sale of drugs ("it must be recognized that the right to destroy oneself is also one of the inalienable rights" [PP 12]); the sharing of American diseases with the Russians ("since the Russians seem to have more vigor than we do at the moment, I would make every effort to pass them our diseases" [PP 12]); and, finally, the sentencing to mortal combat of cancer researchers who fail to make progress in their work after two years. In all five cases, whether he is advocating the imposition of stricter deadlines on cancer research, germ warfare as the best solution to the Cold War, the right to self-destructive self-determination, or a form of therapeutic execution ("this method . . . would offer ventilation for the more cancerous emotions of the American public"), Mailer's humor consists in highlighting issues that could never be addressed by a US presidential candidate in 1960 (or in 2016, for that matter)—the first among them being capital punishment.

Now if I turn to Mailer's program for the nation here, it is not only because he addresses capital punishment as an important, presidential issue. It is also because he insists on the *scene* of execution in America. There is a scene, says Mailer, that is not being seen: a hidden and invisible and perhaps even disavowed scene. This scene, says Mailer, must be made visible; it must be *literally* seen (this is his irony): "Those states which insisted on keeping [capital punishment] . . . would . . . be allowed to kill criminals provided that the killing is . . . a public spectacle." America must see what it refuses to see: the *scene* of execution. What Mailer goes on to describe, however, is a rather un-American scene: no lethal injection here (or to put it less anachronistically: no hanging, no electric chair, no gas chamber here). Instead Mailer stages his American scene of execution as an epic historical drama; he *re-presents* an *archaic* scene, a Roman scene (which is also a scene of desire), as an American tragedy ("the audience . . . would experience a sense of tragedy"). In Mailer's vision of it, then, the scene in question is not something that can simply be located in (historical) time or (geopolitical) space; rather it exceeds the bounds of its particular, twentieth-century American context. Such that one might ask the following question: What would it mean to read an American scene of execution as a virtual Roman scene? Or, to ask the same question in a more (psycho)analytic vein: What would it mean to read the American scene of execution as an archaic or (anal-)sadistic scene?

Indeed, what Mailer's phantasy makes visible—by staging and glorifying, by *gladiatorifying*, the violence of capital punishment in America—is not only a Roman scene. It is also a second (or even third) scene, which is really a kind of primal scene: "In the flabby American spirit there is a buried sadist who finds the bullfight contemptible—what he really desires are gladiators." In the deep, dark, fleshy recesses of the American soul lies a desire that is older, younger, more primitive, more archaic than a desire for (European) bullfights. It is a desire for cutting or thrusting weapons (for what are called in French *les armes blanches*: swords, knives, or broken bottles) and a desire for human, rather than animal, sacrifice. Thus, Mailer's insistence on the scene of capital punishment leads him, as it were, behind the scene(s) to the scene's latent structure: "Since nothing is worse for a

A New Primal Scene   155

country than repressed sadism, this method of execution would offer ventilation for the more cancerous emotions of the American public."

The scene, then, in Mailer's vision of it, would be something that exceeds its particular (empirical, social, political, historical) context. Or to put it more provocatively, there is no such thing as an *American* scene of execution, which does not mean that people are not executed in the United States. What it does mean, however, is that there remains something excessive, something fundamentally out of joint, temporally and spatially dislocated, about what is called the "American" scene.

It should come as no surprise, therefore, if I move to another scene, another theater, this time the Amphi*theater* at L'École des hautes études, where, every Wednesday from 5:00 to 7:00 p.m., from December 1999 to March 2000 and then again from December 2000 to March 2001, Jacques Derrida delivered his seminar on the death penalty. One might say that, like Mailer, Derrida calls our attention to the *scene* of execution—to the essentially theatrical and spectacular nature of the death penalty. Unlike Mailer, however, the scene in question involves not a literal seeing but a virtual or phantasmatic seeing—that is, a specific kind of visibility that has important consequences for thinking the death penalty (and its future). In this chapter, I will highlight two moments of this other visibility: The first is Derrida's insistence on the *virtualization* of the spectacle ("the spectacle will have continued; it still continues by becoming virtual" [DP1 205/284]), in particular in his critique of Foucault's thesis of "despectacularization" (DP2 220/294) in *Discipline and Punish*; the second is Derrida's appeal, in the penultimate session of *The Death Penalty, Volume I*, to the explicitly *phantasmatic* dimension of the death penalty. As we will see when we get to the phantasm, there is no escaping the *scene* of execution because there is no escaping the *dream* of execution; one does not simply put an end to a "phantasmatic truth" (DP1 258/350). But if this "ready-made phantasy" (SE 5:495 / GW 2/3:499) is the case, if there is something invincible about the dream of execution, then what would it mean to think—perchance to dream—*beyond* the death penalty?

Scene 1: The Strategy

But let me begin again. New starting point. Change of scene:

> It is dawn, then. Early light, earliest light. Before the end, before even beginning, before the three blows are struck, the actors and the places are ready, they are waiting for us in order to begin. (DP1 3/26)

These lines appear in the opening session of *The Death Penalty, Volume I*. Derrida is setting the scene for a seminar in which he gestures again and again to the "theater of the death penalty" and the "theater of cruelty." For there is no escaping the theater when it comes to the administration of capital punishment: "Always the theater," "condemned to the theater" (DP2 56n1, 56/87n1, 87), he says in *The Death Penalty, Volume II*. Or as Mailer says at the very end of *The Executioner's Song*: "Executions must be a spectator sport."[10]

The idea of spectacle is analytically contained or included in the idea of legal execution. There can be no legal *mise à mort* without a *mise en scène*. Here is what Derrida says in the opening pages of *The Death Penalty, Volume I*:

> By definition, in essence, by vocation, there will never have been any invisibility for a legal putting to death [*une mise à mort légale*], for an application of the death penalty; there has never been, on principle, a secret or invisible execution for this verdict. The spectacle and the spectator are required. The state, the polis, the whole of politics, the co-citizenry—itself or mediated through representation—must attend and attest, it must testify publicly that death was dealt or inflicted, it must *see die* the condemned one. (DP1 2/25)

There can be no invisibility for a legal putting to death. Capital punishment—*by definition, in essence, in principle*—requires a public: "The death penalty must be accessible to the public in its procedures of judgment, verdict, and execution. . . . Where this is not the case . . . it is not certain that we can, in all rigor, speak of the 'death penalty'" (FWT 154/249). Nothing is more "publicly theatrical or theatrically public" (DP2 60/92) than a punishment that is administered by the state. Nothing is less private than the criminal law in the name of which a person is condemned to death. "The state," says Derrida, "must see die [*doit voir mourir*] the condemned one." This *seeing-die*, this *voir-mourir*, is, for Derrida, a *must-see*; it is essential to capital punishment. But let there be no literal or literalizing misunderstanding here. When Derrida says "the state, the polis, the whole of politics, the co-citizenry—*itself or mediated through representation*" (my emphasis), it is clear that to be public does not mean, as it did for Mailer (or as it will for Foucault), that the public must *literally* see the execution or that the death penalty must be visible to everyone. Nor does it mean that it is *literally* possible to see die (that is, to locate or pinpoint, *épingler*, as Foucault might say) the "objectifiable instant that separates the living from

A New Primal Scene

the dying" (DP1 238/324). Rather, as we will see, a certain virtuality is already inscribed in the very act of witnessing an execution.

But the quotation continues. After pointing to the *spectacular* dimension of legal execution, Derrida shifts his attention to its *specular* dimension. In short, staging becomes *self*-staging:

> It is at that moment, in the instant at which the people having become the state or the nation-state *sees die* the condemned one that it best sees itself. It best sees itself, that is, it acknowledges and becomes aware of its absolute sovereignty and that it *sees itself* in the sense in French where "il se voit" can mean "it lets itself be seen" or "it gives itself to be seen" [or, as Derrida adds during the session, "it sees itself"]. Never . . . is the sovereignty of the state more *visible* in the gathering that founds it than when it makes itself into the *seer* and the *voyeur* [voyante *et* voyeuse] of . . . an *execution*. For this act of witnessing—the state as witness of the execution and witness of itself, of its own sovereignty, of its own almightiness—this act of witnessing must be visual: an eye witness. It thus never happens without a stage. (DP1 2–3/25)

In the scene of execution, sovereignty makes a spectacle of itself; it makes an absolute spectacle of itself. For it is "at that moment, in that instant" in which the state sees die the condemned one, and perhaps not without jubilation, that it "acknowledges and becomes aware of its absolute sovereignty." In this sense, in the sense that the scene of execution is the site of the coming-to-visibility of sovereignty to itself, the scene of execution might also be called the *mirror stage* of sovereignty. In a way too, and though I hate to say it, I don't think it can be avoided here, in this context of optics and self-reflection, the spectacle of capital punishment becomes a kind of *super-selfie*: It is the *sovereign selfie*.

But it is also through this sovereign selfie that the light of a more archaic or foundational scene begins to come into focus. Indeed, Derrida points not only to the coming-to-visibility of sovereignty (to itself) but also to the coming-to-visibility of sovereignty "in the gathering that founds it": "Never," says Derrida, "is the sovereignty of the state more *visible* in the gathering that founds it [*en son rassemblement fondateur*] than when it makes itself into the *seer* and the *voyeur* . . . of an *execution*" (DP1 3/25). Never is sovereignty more visible *in its foundational gathering*, never is sovereignty more visible in the assembling/gathering (*Versammeln*) that is its dawn and first light, than in the state's act of witnessing an execution. To be most visible in its foundational gathering: What does this mean? What would it mean to see a *primal* gathering? Does one *see* a primal scene?

Now I should also point out that the above-quoted passage (up through the words "seer" and "voyeur") was posted on the American Psychoanalytic Association's (APsaA) openline listserv on May 17, 2015, two days after Dzhokhar Tsarnaev was sentenced to death in Boston for his role in the 2013 Boston Marathon attack. If I mention this, it is not because I think APsaA should have the last word on this passage but rather because I take it as a sign of an identification or an alliance with Derrida's reading; it is as if psychoanalysis in America (APsaA is, after all, the oldest and the largest psychoanalytic organization in the United States) were seeing *itself* in Derrida's deconstruction of the genealogy of sovereignty (a genealogy that passes, in *The Death Penalty* seminars just as it does in *Totem and Taboo*, "by way of cruel murder" ["PSS" 244/20]).

But let me return to Derrida's starting point:

> It is dawn, now, we are at dawn. In the first light of dawn. In the whiteness of dawn (*alba*). Before beginning, let us begin. We would begin. (DP1 1/23)

Why begin in this way? Why set the scene in such a "deliberately pathos-laden fashion" (DP1 2/24)? Why begin a seminar on the death penalty by "pretending to begin before the beginning" (DP1 1/23)? Derrida has in mind, of course, to "analyze the 'scene,' the history of its visibility and of its 'public' character generally" (DP1 xv/16). But if he marks the stage in this way, if he "play[s] without playing at the theater . . . as theatrically but also as nontheatrically as possible" (DP1 3/26), it is also because he desires to change the scene. It is because he wants to *bring down the curtain* on the death penalty: "It is obvious that in my argumentation and in the pathos you will hear, my discourse is going to be abolitionist" (DP1 5n7/28n1). That is, it is a strategy. It is a strategy for thinking a dramatic turn of events—a *coup de théâtre*. For when all is said and done, it may be impossible to deconstruct "the essential voyeurism that attaches to a putting to death" (DP1 4/26) "*in absentia* or *in effigie*" (SE 12:108/GW 8:374). In fact, and despite his early programmatic statement to the contrary ("deconstruction . . . is not the psychoanalysis of philosophy" ["FSW" 196/293]), Derrida's strategy here resembles nothing so much as that of an analyst who, in bringing the theater of a patient's phantasies to the fore in an analytic setting, gives place to the nontheatrical at the heart of the theatrical, the place from which these phantasies can be analyzed and thus potentially transformed.

Just like the analyst who plays without playing at the theater as theatrically but also as nontheatrically as possible, Derrida is laying the groundwork for thinking the possibility of change. Thus, in the final lines of the first session, he shows us the map:

> We are here—permit me to recall this because it is essential and decisive at this point—neither in a courtroom or on a witness stand, nor in a place of worship, nor in a parliament, nor in print, radio, or televised news. And neither are we in a real theater [*Nous ne sommes pas non plus dans un vrai théâtre*]. To exclude all of these places, to exit from all of these places, without exception, is the first condition for *thinking* the death penalty. And thus for hoping to change it in some way. (DP1 27/55)

To exclude or exit the theater (in all of its juridico-theologico-political manifestations), this would be the first condition for thinking and for changing the death penalty in some way. But just as there can be no transference interpretation without transference, so too there can be no *coup de théâtre* without the theater. In other words, we must begin, as Derrida does in *The Death Penalty* seminars, by making the scene of execution as visible and as manifest as possible.

Scene 2: The Virtualization of Visibility

But we have already seen it—and right from the start. By insisting at every turn on visibility, on the essential *mise en scène* of the death penalty ("by definition, in essence, by vocation, there will never have been any invisibility for a legal putting to death"), Derrida disputes Michel Foucault's claims regarding the progressive disappearance of the spectacular visibility of torture and execution in *Discipline and Punish*. Foucault's thesis, you will recall, is that at the end of the eighteenth and the beginning of the nineteenth century "punishment had gradually ceased to be a spectacle [*La punition a cessé peu à peu d'être une scène*]."[11] "Punishment-as-spectacle [*le châtiment-spectacle*]" (DP 9/15) had disappeared and with it the theater of public execution. In the recently published 1972–1973 lectures at the Collège de France, entitled *The Punitive Society*, Foucault even describes the 1757 execution of Robert-François Damiens (with which *Discipline and Punish* famously begins) as the "final staging [*la dernière mise en scène*]"[12] of the great sovereign spectacle of torture and punishment. Instead of the "tortured, dismembered, amputated body" (DP 8/14) and the meticulous ceremonials that belonged to the display of sovereign power in premodern times, the beginning of the nineteenth century ushers in a "new age for penal justice" (DP 7/13). Punishment, which for Foucault simply includes capital punishment, loses its "visible intensity" (DP 9/15); it is less immediately physical, and the sufferings that accompany it, subtler and more muted, are "deprived of their visible display" (DP 8/13). The theater closes its doors. It is replaced by the prison and the geo- and biopolitics of incarceration, where what "gets erased" (*s'efface*) is no longer the criminal but the sovereign spectacle. Hence, *Discipline and Punish* marks a division, a rupture, a passage from one *episteme* to another. I quote Foucault here:

> At the beginning of the nineteenth century . . . the great spectacle of physical punishment gets erased [*S'efface donc . . . le grand spectacle de la punition physique*]; the tortured body was avoided; the theatrical representation [*la mise en scène*] of pain was excluded from punishment. The age of sobriety in punishment had begun. (DP 14/19, modified)

We move, in other words, from "one art of punishing" (DP 257/261) to another, from one "penal style" and "economy of punishment" (DP 7/13) to another, from one "technique of power" (DP 24/28) to another—from a society of spectacle and public execution to a society of surveillance where punishment "tend[s] to become the most hidden part of the penal process" (DP 9/15).

Now it is precisely this shift in the administration of penalties, a shift from the spectacular to the hidden, from the visible to the invisible, that Derrida calls into question.[13] This is why, and it is somewhat compulsive, whenever Derrida mentions the name "Foucault" in his writing on the death penalty—and I will give three examples of this—he does so in order to highlight another logic, another modality of visibility, one that extends the field of the visible beyond "the 'how,' the 'where,' and especially the 'when'" (DP1 219/300) of the premodern "spectacle."[14]

This other logic, which is that of the "virtual," follows closely upon any mention of "Foucault" (and though this is not exactly Derrida's point in these passages, we might also wonder about the effects of *virtual surveillance* on Foucault's thesis of despectacularization—in fact, as I was writing this, the Chicago police began to wear body cameras on their uniforms: "'Everybody acts better on film,' said police Supt. Gary McCarthy, who said the [police body-camera pilot] program was 'off to a great start'").[15] The first example is from *The Death Penalty, Volume I*, and it is the only explicit reference to Foucault in the whole first year of the seminar. Though Derrida praises *Discipline and Punish* ("it is a rich and important book, a very precious one for us, which I recommend you read or reread" [DP1

A New Primal Scene

42/74]), though he quotes its opening pages and uses the last words of poor Damiens, "Pardon, Lord," to connect his own past seminars on "perjury and pardon" to his present seminar on the death penalty,[16] he cannot help but point to a visibility beyond visibility that complicates the orderly, historical sequence of *Discipline and Punish*:

> Foucault's book [*Discipline and Punish*] is not a book on the death penalty, but it is a book that deals among other things with the historical transformation of the spectacle, with the organized visibility of punishment, with what I will call, even though this is not Foucault's expression, the *seeing-punish* [voir-punir], a *seeing-punish* essential to punishment, to the right to punish as right to see-punish(ed), or even as duty-to-see-punish(ed) [*devoir de voir-punir*], one of Foucault's historical theses being that at the beginning of the nineteenth century, what "gets erased" is, I quote, "the great spectacle of physical punishment; the tortured body is avoided; the staging of suffering is excluded from the punishment. The age of punitive sobriety begins." . . . I am not so sure of this, but perhaps there is here a technical, tele-technical, or even televisual complication of seeing, or even a virtualization of visual perception. (DP1 42–43/75).

Or again in an interview with Élisabeth Roudinesco in *For What Tomorrow* . . . (where Derrida is speaking of his seminar on the death penalty):

> Contrary to what Foucault says, I don't believe that there is a shift from the visible to the invisible in the administration of penalties beginning in the eighteenth century. While I recognize the relative legitimacy of this analysis, according to certain limited criteria, I would be tempted to say that in the evolution of punishments, we shift not from the visible to the invisible but rather from one visibility to another, more virtual, one. In [my] seminar on capital punishment, I am trying to demonstrate that the same process is oriented toward another modality, another distribution of the visible (and therefore of the invisible) that can even, on the contrary, extend the virtual field of the spectacular and the theatrical, with decisive consequences. (FWT 12/28)

Or again in *The Death Penalty, Volume II* (where he is speaking of *The Death Penalty, Volume I*):

> Last year we took issue with Foucault's thesis of despectacularization, his claims about the modern detheatricalization of punishment; I suggested instead that punishment, which is in the end always public, did

not become invisible but only changed its form and its place of visibility by virtualizing itself [*en se virtualisant*]. (DP2 220/294)

By becoming virtual, the spectacle will have continued: "Today we can no longer speak of . . . the death penalty without film and television; we have proof of this every day and it is an essential change in the given state of affairs" (DP1 247/336). Film and television but also the media and the internet will have transformed and extended the field of the visible. Never, says Derrida, "have things been as 'visible' in the worldwide space as they are today; this is itself an essential element of the problem—and of the struggle. Spectral logic invades everything" (FWT 159/256, modified). Spectral logic, here the logic of the "virtual," makes it such that the scene of punishment and execution is never simply visible (or invisible) in Foucault's sense but always marked by the trace of another visibility, of a non-present visibility (that is, the trace of something that is not visible determines our experience of the visible, so there is no pure visibility; visibility is always marked by the trace of another visibility). Thus, although it is true, *in a certain sense*, that punishment and execution have become less and less visible, less and less theatrical, more and more hidden and invisible, it is also true that we have more and more visibility through technical, teletechnical, and televisual means.

What this means, however, is that there is something *visibly unmasterable*, abyssal, and unattributable about the scene of punishment and execution. Hence Foucault's own masterful attempt to locate power in the organized visibility/invisibility of punishment finds itself unmastered by this logic. Indeed, one might hear in Derrida's language of "virtualization" another way of pushing Foucault to think "beyond the power principle," as it were. Now before I jump to the phantasmatic scene of execution in the penultimate chapter of *The Death Penalty, Volume I*, I would like to turn briefly to a strange moment in *Discipline and Punish* where Foucault describes the "real subjugation [*assujettissement réel*]" that results from a "fictitious relation [*relation fictive*]" (DP 202/204). In this passage, which is remarkable in many ways, one might say that Foucault sees without seeing, and knows without being able to take into account, what Derrida has been saying all along, namely that "capital punishment remains fundamentally [*en son fond*] . . . a spectacle"—and just to make my point in advance, I will tell you that this last quotation comes not from Derrida's *Death Penalty* seminars but from *Discipline and Punish*.[17] What Foucault describes in this passage is a fictional, a phantasmatic or virtual scene, an internalized spectacle in which the prisoner in the Panopticon sees himself being seen.

A New Primal Scene

Although Foucault sees only a "calculated, organized, technically thought out" (DP 26/31) subjection in this scene of self-surveillance, I will suggest instead that it presents us with a scene from which we can begin to think an excess of play in the panoptic machine.

In "The Means of Correct Training," the chapter that immediately precedes "Panopticism" in the "Discipline" section of *Discipline and Punish*, Foucault points to the importance of the examination in the rise of disciplinary power. The examination, says Foucault, "combines the techniques of an observing hierarchy and those of a normalizing judgment" (DP 184/186). It is a technique of surveillance designed to single out and judge individuals. Foucault devotes several pages to the examination in both its medical and educational applications before advancing a statement, which seems to follow directly and rather unproblematically from the central thesis of *Discipline and Punish*: "*The examination transformed the economy of visibility into the exercise of power*" (DP 187/189). Such a sentence, one has to admit, beautifully summarizes the movement away from visibility that I have pointed to in Derrida's critique of Foucault. Yet this is not what Foucault says, at least not in French. In French the line reads: "*L'examen intervertit l'économie de la visibilité dans l'exercise du pouvoir*"—that is to say, *the examination reverses* (intervertit) *the economy of visibility in the exercise of power*. It is not, in other words, that we move from an economy of visibility, on the one hand, to an exercise of power, on the other, which is how the translator understands it (here, by being too Foucauldian, he forgets to read Foucault). Rather we move from one economy of visibility to another economy of visibility when we move from a society of spectacle to one of surveillance. The examination reverses or inverts what is visible; it changes who or what is seen. Thus, the very process of despectacularization is not only a move from visibility to invisibility; it is also, at the same time, a repositioning or repositing of visibility. What Foucault goes on to say makes this perfectly clear:

> Traditionally, power was what was seen, what was shown and what was manifested [these are all reflexive verbs in French: *le pouvoir, c'est ce qui se voit, ce qui se montre, ce qui se manifeste*]. . . . Those on whom it was exercised could remain in the shadows [*dans l'ombre*]; they received light only from that portion of power that was conceded to them, or from the reflection of it that for a moment they carried. Disciplinary power, on the other hand, is exercised through its invisibility; at the same time it imposes on those whom it subjects a principle of compulsory visibility [*un principe de visibilité obligatoire*]. In discipline, it is the

subjects who have to be seen. Their visibility assures the hold of the power that is exercised over them. It is the fact of being constantly seen, of being able always to be seen, that maintains the disciplined individual [*l'individu disciplinaire*] in his subjection. (DP 187/189)

Thus, Foucault describes the passage from relations of sovereignty to relations of discipline as a chiasmic reversal. The power that was visible ("Traditionally, power was what was seen") becomes invisible ("Disciplinary power, on the other hand, is exercised through its invisibility"), while the reverse is true for those who are on the receiving end of punishment. Traditionally, those on whom power is exercised remain invisible, "in the shadows," whereas now they are driven into the limelight ("Disciplinary power . . . imposes on those whom it subjects a principle of compulsory visibility"). But what remains constant and completely unchanged in this reversal is the principle of visibility/invisibility as a principle of power or mastery. Power (whether sovereign or disciplinary) is the power to make visible and/or invisible.

And nowhere is this power more explicit or more literal than in the "political anatomy" (DP 208/210) of "Panopticism." "The Panopticon," says Foucault, "is a machine for dissociating the see/being seen dyad: in the peripheric ring, one is totally seen, without ever seeing; in the central tower, one sees everything without ever being seen" (DP 201–2/203). The Panopticon makes completely visible those in the peripheric ring while making completely invisible those in the central tower. The reason for this distribution of visibility/invisibility is that when it comes to the power of disciplinary power, less is more: The less visible, the less external, the less physical a mechanism, the more effective, the more efficient, and the more insidious its power. But nothing quite compares to the marvel that is the Panopticon—"The Panopticon," says Foucault, "is a marvelous machine [*une machine merveilleuse*]" (DP 202/204):

> [With the Panopticon] it is not necessary to use force to constrain the convict to good behavior, the madman to calm, the worker to work, the schoolboy to application, the patient to the observation of regulations. . . . He who is subjected to a field of visibility, and who knows it, assumes responsibility for the constraints of power; he plays them out spontaneously on himself [*il les fait jouer spontanément sur lui-même*]; he inscribes in himself the power relation in which he simultaneously plays both roles [*il joue simultanément les deux rôles*]; he becomes the principle [*principe*] of his own subjection. By this very fact, the external power may throw off its physical weight; it tends to the non-corporal;

and, the more it approaches this limit, the more constant, profound and permanent are its effects: it is a perpetual victory that avoids any physical confrontation and which is always played out in advance [*toujours jouée d'avance*]. (DP 202–3/204, modified).

What Foucault is describing here—and what he calls "panopticism"—is the process whereby intersubjective relations are transformed into intrasubjective ones ("he inscribes in himself the power relation [*il inscrit en soi le rapport de pouvoir*]"). The power relation is transposed in phantasy from the "outside" to the "inside"; it is taken within the psyche such that the relation of subjection is lived out on the intrapsychic level. Freud called this process "internalization [*Verinnerlichung*]," and he too found it to be "something very remarkable [*etwas sehr Merkwürdiges*]" (SE 21:123/GW 14:482). Whether or not Foucault intends to limit this internalization process to societies of surveillance (which would mean, I suppose, no superego before the eighteenth century), one thing is clear: There is a fictional and even theatrical dimension to this process. To be seen is at the same time—"spontaneously," "simultaneously" says Foucault—to see oneself being seen. Thus, the disciplined individual (the convict, the madman, the worker, the schoolboy, the patient) sets up an agency within himself to watch over him, "like a garrison [*Besetzung*] in a conquered city" (SE 21:124/GW 14:48); he plays and replays for himself a scene of surveillance. In this scene, he *plays both roles*, "il joue . . . les deux rôles"; he *plays them out* on himself ("il les fait jouer . . . sur lui-même"): He occupies both roles, *à tour de rôle*, as one might in a dream—he is inmate *and* guard, schoolboy *and* examiner, patient *and* doctor, victim *and* executioner. The echo is thus not only Freudian but also Baudelairean: "Je suis la plaie et le couteau!/ . . . Et la victime et le bourreau! [I am the wound and the blade!/ . . . The victim and the executioner]."[18] In becoming the "principle of his own subjection," the convict, the madman, the schoolboy, the patient is also the *principal* actor or *star* player in a *scene* of subjection. Or to put it another way: In this phantasmatic scene of (self-)surveillance, the disciplined individual becomes the *master of ceremonies*.

To play both roles, to become the master of one's own subjection, where does this lead us? For Foucault it leads only to "a real subjection" (DP 202/204). By taking the Panopticon into himself and establishing his own private Panopticon ("he inscribes in himself the power relation in which he simultaneously plays both roles"), the prisoner *plays* into the hands of the other, of the external power, precisely because this external power is now inside him ("non-corporal" and invisible). In other words,

Foucault sees the *play* between inside/outside, auto-surveillance/hetero-surveillance, auto-punishment/hetero-punishment as merely the effect of a disciplinary machination. Thus, although Foucault may rage against the machine and its "calculated management of life,"[19] the victory of external power is "always played out in advance" (DP 203/204, modified). It is always played out in advance because we are part of its mechanism (*rouage*).

But what if we saw the "fictitious relation" (that is, the phantasmatic scene of surveillance) in a more Freuderridean vein? What if we saw the scene as precisely exceeding, or better yet e-luding (and the French here would be *dé-jouer*), the grip of our common sense (or conscious) belief in the oppositional distinction between inside/outside, internal/external, auto- and hetero-? What if, in other words, we read the scene of self-surveillance not only as a scene of "real subjection" but also, as I have suggested with and against Foucault, as a scene of *virtual mastery*? Indeed, what if what this scene of virtual mastery *made visible* was something essential to punishment?

Perhaps, then, we might read Foucault's disavowal of the theatrical nature of modern punishment—the fact that he sees without seeing that punishment remains fundamentally a spectacle—as a different sort of recognition.[20] One that would lead us to ask a different sort of question: What if there were something about the scene of virtual mastery that made it not only unthinkable for a thinker wedded to the modern detheatricalization of punishment but also intolerable? Might there not be something intolerable about a virtual collusion with (and to collude is to play with, *colludere*) "real subjection"?

Scene 3: The Dream of Deconstruction

But here I would like to recall a difference—namely that, unlike Foucault, for whom the death penalty becomes but another example of power-knowledge in a specific regime of punishment, Derrida considers the death penalty to be the example par excellence of sovereign power. Along with war, the death penalty remains the "best emblem of the sovereign power of the state over the life and death of the citizen" ("PSS" 245/21). This is why the deconstruction of the death penalty is not simply "one necessity among others, a particular point of application" (FWT 148/240). Rather "deconstruction is perhaps always, ultimately . . . the deconstruction of the death penalty, of the logocentric, logonomocentric scaffolding in which the death penalty is inscribed or prescribed" (DP1 23/50).

As a result, the theater of the death penalty is not simply one theater of punishment among others. Indeed, if Derrida returns again and again to the scene of execution, it is because, as we have seen, it is the primal or foundational scene of sovereignty; it is the moment in which sovereignty becomes most visible "in the gathering that founds it" (DP1 3/25). But if he insists on the logic of virtualization—against Foucault's logic of "devisibilization" (DP1 205/283)—it is because this primal scene of sovereignty is bound up with future scenes of punishment, that is, with the very question and possibility of abolition (with the question of the abolition of the death penalty but also, by extension, with the question of prison abolition). To disavow the spectacle—to see without seeing the virtualization of visibility, as Foucault does—is thus also to disavow the way in which the scene of the foundational gathering of sovereignty is *projected* into the future. It is to miss not only the foundational element of the spectacle but also its temporalization: the relation between primal and future scenes of punishment. In the end, I hope to show how the linking of these questions (the question of what comes before with the question of what comes after) throws new light on the "actual" theater of the death penalty and on its future projections.

Derrida begins Session 9 of *The Death Penalty, Volume I* with a question: "When to die finally [*Quand mourir enfin*]?" (DP1 218/299). When to die, in the end, since we are all fated or "condemned to die"? "What is the right age to die, if there is one?" (DP2 5/24). These questions lead him to imagine a scenario, a kind of thought experiment: "If . . . I was given the choice between being condemned to death at age seventy-five (guillotined) or being condemned to die at age seventy-four (in my bed)" (DP1 218/299), what would I choose? Indeed, this same choose-your-own-death adventure reappears in the opening pages of *The Death Penalty, Volume II*:

> If, condemned to dying sooner or later, like everyone else, I had the choice between, *on the one hand*, dying at such and such an age, tomorrow or later today, of natural causes, as the result of an automobile accident or an illness (like almost everyone, in fact), and, *on the other hand*, of dying at another age, later, the day after tomorrow, in a year, ten years, twenty years, in a prison, because I will have been sentenced to death by capital punishment (the guillotine, the electric chair, lethal injection, hanging, the gas chamber), what would I choose, what age would I choose for my death? (DP2 5–6/24–25)

The point obviously is not to choose but rather to show that what is at issue in this "choice," and thus what is at issue when it is a question of the death penalty, is a "certain modality, a certain qualification of living and dying . . . a theater, a scene of giving-life and of giving-death, indeed of giving-oneself-death" (DP2 6/25). The choice is thus not between life and death, between living or dying, or even between two objective ages of death; the choice is between two modes of an "unavoidable and always imminent death" (DP2 6/25), between two theaters of death, or—and Derrida will use the word "intolerable" here to characterize both sides of the alternative—two relations to calculation, mastery, decidability, and the question of "when":

> The alternative is terrible and infinite: I may deem it intolerable, and this is the case of the death penalty, to know that the hour of my death is fixed, by others, by a third party, at a certain day, a certain hour, a certain second, whereas if I am not condemned to death but only to die, this calculable knowledge is impossible. But conversely, I may deem it intolerable not to know the date, the place, and the hour of my death and thus I may dream of appropriating this knowledge, of having this knowledge at my disposal, at least phantasmatically, by getting myself condemned to death and thus by arriving in this fashion at some calculable certitude, some quasi-suicidal mastery of my death. . . . By knowing at what hour, on what day I will die, I can tell myself the story of how death will not take me by surprise and will thus remain at my disposal, like a quasi-suicidal auto-affection. (DP1 218–19/300)

To know, or not to know "when"—that is the question that divides, "as with a knife blade, two deaths or two condemnations, the condemnation to die and the condemnation to death" (DP1 219/301). Whether it is more intolerable to know the moment, the date, the precise hour of one's death (the "'given moment' or the 'designated place' of the given moment of 'my death'" [DP2 5/24]) or not to know at which instant death will come, and by opposing this nonknowledge with the calculable certainty of the death penalty, arrive at some quasi-suicidal mastery of my death.

However paradoxical it may seem, both positions are not only possible but also inseparable. For both are predicated on a relation to a force that comes "into" me from a beyond that is greater than I am. Indeed, the point is that, *in both cases*, my time-of-life-and-death, the (im)possibility of my future, is determined by what comes to me from the outside, from the other. On the side of the death penalty, it is too obvious, but it is an "obscure obviousness that one must begin by recalling" (DP1 250/339). Let me quote, therefore, four short passages in order to recall this obvious fact, the fact that the death penalty is first and foremost *la mort venue de l'autre*, "death that comes from the other":

> The death penalty, as the sovereign decision of a power [*comme décision souveraine d'un pouvoir*], reminds us perhaps, before anything else, that a sovereign decision is always the other's [of some other: *une décision souveraine est toujours de l'autre*]. Come from the other [*Venue de l'autre*]. (DP1 1/24)

> Even in cases ... where the death sentence might be obscurely, compulsively, irresistibly sought, desired—as desire itself—by the condemned one ... the death penalty is always, by definition, death that comes from the other [*la mort venue de l'autre*], given or decided by the other, be it the other within oneself. The possibility of the death penalty ... begins where I am delivered into the power of the other [*livré au pouvoir de l'autre*], be it the power of the other in me [*fût-ce au pouvoir de l'autre en moi*]. (DP1 249–50/339)

> The death penalty ... [is] a death that comes from the other [*venue de l'autre*], decided and calculated by the other, in the hands of the other. (DP1 251/341)

> Where death comes to me from the other [*où la mort me vient de l'autre*], the death penalty is the only experience that, in principle, allows the very moment of death, the *given* moment of death to be a moment that is both *desired* [*voulu*] and publicly dated. (DP2 4/23)

The death penalty is death that comes from the other. It is death that is given, decided, calculated by the power of the other (be it the power of the other in me, the power of the outside inside me). It implies, in principle, "that the other knows and sometimes that I know, to the second, to the minute, in a way that is therefore calculable, the moment of 'my death'" (DP2 4/23). To be condemned to death, in other words (and here we must distinguish the condemnation to death from the condemnation to die), implies the power of the other as the one who decides, sovereignly: "You will die and you will die in such a way and you will die on this day, at this hour" (DP2 137/188). And what is decided by the power of the other, what is "delivered up to the calculating decision of the other," is my time of life and death: "the time given or the time taken, time that becomes the calculation of the other" (DP1 220/302). In the case of the death penalty, what comes to me from the other is, one might say, my death date, the given moment of my death.

But this death that comes to me from the other is also, says Derrida, the only example of a death whose instant is calculable by a machine or by machines (in the plural)—"not by someone, finally, as in a murder, but by all sorts of machines: the law, the penal code, the anonymous third party, the calendar, the clock, the guillotine or another apparatus" (DP1 257/348–49). This is why one must also speak, as Derrida does, of the "machine of the death penalty" (DP1 257/349) or, as Harry Blackmun did in *Callins v. Collins* (1994), of the "machinery of death."[21] The worst, that is to say, the most intolerable but also, as we will see, the most fascinating and the most seductive of these machines, is the clock. Indeed, one cannot think the torture and cruelty of the calculating decision without thinking its relation to clockwork: "You will die . . . in that calculable place, and from blows delivered by several machines, the worst of which is perhaps neither the guillotine nor the syringe, but *the clock and the anonymity of clockwork*" (DP1 256/347, my emphasis).

In the end, what is intolerable (in the first sense) and what we oppose when we oppose the death penalty is not death, or even the fact of killing, the fact of taking a life. What we oppose when we oppose the death penalty is the calculating decision, the calculation imposed on what is, and should remain, an incalculable future. And this is where the foundational element that distinguishes Derrida's thinking of the death penalty from Foucault's is also strangely—how shall I put it?—"heartening," for what comes to us originally from the other is both death- *and* life-giving. For there is no way for me to speak of "my life," that is, of my relation to an "incalculable and undecidable future," without first naming what "comes from the other," or from what Derrida lyrically calls the "heart of the other" (DP1 256/347)[22]:

> The insult, the injury, the fundamental injustice done to the life in me, to the principle of the life in me, is not death . . . it is rather the interruption of the principle of indetermination, the ending imposed on the opening of the incalculable chance whereby a living being has a relation to what comes. . . . It is because my life is finite, "ended" in a certain sense, that I keep this relation to incalculability and undecidability as to the instant of my death. It is because my life is finite, "finished" in a certain sense, that I do not know, and that I neither can nor want to know, when I am going to die. Only a living being as finite being can have a future, can be exposed to a future, to an incalculable and undecidable future that s/he does not have at his/her disposal like a master and that comes to him or to her from some [or the] other [*qui lui vient de l'autre*], from the heart of the other [*du cœur de l'autre*]. So much so that when I say "my life" . . . I have already named the other in me . . . the other who . . . lets me be me, the other whose heart is more interior to my heart than my heart itself. (DP1 256–57/347–48)

In other words, what comes to me from the other is not only death, calculation and decision, the calculable decidability of the instant of my death, but also life, the relation to incalculability and undecidability, the relation to the "coming of the to-come [*venue de l'à-venir*]" (DP 1 256/347). What comes to me from the other, *from the heart of the other*, is thus a certain *undecidability* as to the instant of my death. And here we would have to think the heart *with* the machine, for a heart is also a machine: It's a time machine, a ticker. We would have to think the "heart" as an excess in relation to the machine itself, at once a machine and something that eludes (*déjoue*) machinelike calculation. We might have to think the heart as something like the "ghost in the machine."

The "I" is thus "invested" by the other. What comes to me from the other, from "the heart of the other," is the *force* that affirms life in me (the force that "lets me be me") rather than the *power* or the decision to give me death. "Only thanks to the other," says Derrida, "by the grace of the other heart that affirms life in me" (DP1 257/348), can the finite being that I am have a future, be exposed to a future, to an incalculable and undecidable future that I do not have at my disposal like a master.

One might put this another way, and here we return to the other possible position, that of the second "intolerable." What is intolerable, and that of which I am relieved by the calculating decision, is precisely my exposure to an unmasterable future. By eliminating the principle of indetermination, by determining the instant of my death, by providing protection against what comes from the outside, the calculating machine has a strangely reassuring and pleasurable effect.[23] Whence its seductive power, as we saw in Chapter 7: We are "fascinated by the power and by the calculation . . . fascinated by the end of this anxiety before the future that the calculating machine procures" (DP1 258/349). I may thus dream of appropriating or securing the power-knowledge of the calculating machine by getting myself condemned to death. For it is precisely in putting an end to *life* that the calculating machine gives the impression of putting an end to *finitude*: "It *affirms* its power over time; it *masters* the future; it *protects* against the irruption of the other" (DP1 258/349, my emphasis). But of course it only *seems* to do this; it only seems to do this because "this calculation, this mastery, this decidability, remain *phantasms*" (DP1 258/258, my emphasis).

To put an end to finitude, to put an end to the principle of indetermination that comes to us from the other (from some other)—this would be our ultimate but also our most fundamental desire: "It would no doubt be possible to show," says Derrida, "that this [desire for calculation, mastery, decidability] is even the origin of phantasm in general" (DP1 258/349).²⁴ *Never is the origin of phantasm more visible, one might say, never is its foundational gathering more manifest, than in the scene in which we give ourselves death* (that is, in a scene in which the end of finitude is *represented* as the end of life). Thus, what the phantasm of the end of finitude makes *visible* is a primal or final scene of self-protection: self-destruction as self-protection against what threatens to irrupt or break into us from the outside. Why be anxious if there is no future, that is, if the future can be mastered?

But "an end will never put an end to finitude," says Derrida, "for only a finite being can be condemned to death" (DP1 258/349). An end will never put an end to finitude, one might say, because it is already too late. The fear of irruption is the fear of an irruption that has already taken place—in a time before the beginning of time. We are always too late when it comes to the other: "So much so that when I say 'my life,' or even my 'living present' . . . I have already named the other in me" (DP1 257/348). I am invested by the other, says Derrida, "as one is by a force greater than oneself and that occupies you entirely by pre-occupying you"; the other is "before me in me" (DP1 257/348).²⁵ What comes before, from the heart of the other, is the incalculability of the instant of my death. And it is to this *primal* incalculability that the calculating decision tries to put an end—by making a scene, as it were. Indeed, we would have to say that the virtuality of *any scene* of execution (the fact that the visibility of the death penalty is never simply literal but always also virtual) is already a sign or symptom of this primal relation to incalculability. To calculate the incalculable: This would be what "sets [us] to dreaming" (DP1 240/326).

And now for the scene, a scene that is not only a primal scene but also a primal projector (it is a self-projecting scene). It is a much more unsettling scene than the scene of self-surveillance in *Discipline and Punish*. Here is how Derrida stages it (as we saw, in a much abbreviated form, in Chapter 7):

> Since this phantasm is at work in us all the time, even outside any real scene of verdict and death penalty . . . since we cannot keep ourselves from permanently playing out for ourselves the scene of the condemned one whom we potentially are . . . the fascination exerted by the real phenomena of death penalty and execution, this fascination of which we could give so many examples, has to do with its effect of truth or of acting out: we then see it <as> actually staged [*comme mise en scène effective*]; we project it as one projects a film or as one projects a project; we see in projection actually enacted [*nous voyons en projection s'effectuer en acte*] what we are dreaming of all the time—what we are dreaming of, that is, what in a certain way we desire, namely, to

A New Primal Scene

> give ourselves death and to infinitize ourselves by giving ourselves death in a calculable, calculated, decidable fashion; and when I say "we," this means that in this dream we occupy, simultaneously or successively, all the positions, those of a judge, of judges, of the jury, of the executioner or the assistants, of the one condemned to death, of course, and the position of one's nearest and dearest, loved or hated, and that of the voyeuristic spectators who we are more than ever. And it is the force of this effect of phantasmatic truth that will probably remain forever invincible, thus guaranteeing forever, alas, a double survival, both the survival of the death penalty and the survival of the abolitionist protest. (DP1 258/349–50)

What keeps the death penalty alive, as it were, is a dream, a desire, a fabulous and virtual scene of mastery in which we occupy all the roles, all the positions, all at once or successively. But if the death penalty fascinates and seduces us, if it promises us the fulfillment of our oldest wish for omnipotence, it is also because it allows us to *externalize* what is otherwise always (*en permanence*) *internally* occurring. In the real phenomena of death penalty and execution, we see *actually* staged, *actually* enacted, *in* projection what we are dreaming of all the time. What we are dreaming of all the time: What can this mean except that *the death penalty is a dream come true*? But to express it in this way is also, I hope, to convey something of its obscenity, for what the death penalty tries to play out as "actual" theater is a kind of "internal" primal relation to an "outside" that can never simply be located—and mastered or eliminated—in this way.[26]

So where does this leave us? In a way, one might read Derrida's two-year seminar on the death penalty as a kind of *Thanatology of Spirit* in which the phantasm of the end of finitude (which "is at work in us all the time") is both the final scene and the opening scene in the spectacle of the death penalty. Or then again one might read the seminar as a kind of Dream Book. For Derrida not only speaks of the dream of "giving ourselves death in a calculable, calculated, decidable fashion." He also speaks of the "dream of deconstruction" in a somewhat *play*ful manner (indeed, as the dialogue between two angels). And what does deconstruction dream of, you may ask? Why, of deconstructing death, of course, of putting death to death: "Hey [*eh*]," says one of the angels, "at bottom that is the dream of deconstruction, a convulsive movement to have done with death, to deconstruct death itself . . . to come to blows with death and put it out of action. No less than that. Death to death [*Mort à la mort*]" (DP1 240–41/327).

In his first moment of temptation ("My angel, who is . . . my temptation" [DP1 241/327]), Derrida describes the dream of deconstruction in terms that belong to a scene of mastery, that attest to a phantasm of omnipotence over death ("Death to death"). But immediately another angel (who is perhaps the same—"the same other angel of deconstruction" [DP1 241/327]) calls Derrida back to order and tells him that he will not get off so easily, that the dream of deconstruction is not what we would call a "wish-fulfilling" dream: "It is not enough to deconstruct death," says this same other angel, "in order to assure one's salvation . . . in order to survive. . . . For neither does life come out unscathed by this deconstruction. Nothing comes out unscathed by this deconstruction" (DP1 241/327–28). What we are left with—let me put it this way—is a dream, the same and another, a dream that dares us to think this unprecedented thing: a theater that resists its own spectacle, that is to say, "its specular and spectacular temptation" ("PSS" 256/44).

Epilogue

In conclusion, I would like to return briefly to the American scene and to a rather remarkable episode in *The Executioner's Song*. Although Mailer's description of the scene of execution certainly accentuates its theatrical elements—"Gary's end of the room was lit . . . and the rest of the room was dark. He was up on a little platform. It was like a stage" (ES 1011–12)—I would like instead to bring up an earlier and eerier scene in which Gary is preparing for his execution. In this scene, which takes place the day before the execution, Gary is insisting that his uncle deliver a posthumous gift to his girlfriend: "Gary said, 'Look, take this watch. I don't want anybody to have it but Nicole.' He had broken it and taped it with the hands set at 7:49" (ES 1014). Gary's parting gift to his girlfriend is a watch. But not just any watch. It's a watch he has broken and taped so that its hands are forever set at the given time of his death: *dawn*, January 17, 1977.[27] It is a little as if he were trying to stage, from beyond the grave, his mastery over the "clock and the anonymity of clockwork."

But I do not want to end on a morbid note. So instead I will describe a new product on the market called "Tikker." Fredrik Colting, its inventor, calls it "The Happiness Watch" and claims it was designed to help people make the most of their lives. Here is how you will find the watch advertised online (at mytikker.com):

> *Anger or forgiveness? Tic-toc. Wearing a frown or a smile? Tic-toc. Happy or upset? Tic-toc.*

A New Primal Scene

> THAT'S WHY WE'VE CREATED Tikker, the death watch that counts down your life, just so you can make every second count.
>
> Tikker is a wrist watch that counts down your life from years to seconds, and motivates you to make the right choices. Tikker will be there to remind you to make the most of your life, and most importantly, to be happy.[28]

Colting, who came up with the idea for the "death watch" following the death of his grandfather, explains it this way:

> For all of us, life comes with a best-before date. . . . While death is non-negotiable, life isn't. All we have to do is learn how to cherish the time and the life that we have been given; seize the day and follow our hearts. . . . From years to seconds [Tikker] presents time ever moving, never standing still, and our lives dwindling towards the final rest. . . . I think that if we were more aware of our own expiration . . . we'd make better choices while we are alive.[29]

The idea of the Tikker is for its wearers to know "when" they will die, that is, to be constantly aware of their "death date." And although the website does not go into much detail about the process, it is clear that Colting has developed an algorithm to calculate this date. Consequently all wearers are asked to fill out a questionnaire in order to set their Tikkers. They are asked not only about their medical history (including allergies and illnesses, how often they drink or smoke) but also about their families' history of cancer, diabetes, and other diseases. They are asked about their physical activity and their weight, and they receive a "score." Their age is then deducted from this "score," and they are given a "death date" . . . at which point the countdown begins.

However perverse we may find the Tikker and its maker—to say nothing of the algorithm that calculates the wearer's "death date"—there is clearly a market for such products. Records indicate that 2,162 backers pledged $98,665 on Kickstarter to help bring the Tikker to life. For there is something unique, even if uniquely intolerable, about an everyday accessory that brings together "this strange coincidence, this bizarre synchrony" (DP1 250/340) of subjective and objective time, ticker and Tikker, heart and clockwork, the condemnation to die and the condemnation to death, the virtual event (Kickstarter) and the calculating machine, happiness and death. Indeed, for all its perversity, the "death watch" puts a certain death penalty back on stage as if to submit it to the "hypothesis of a mutation" ("PSS" 256/44). It is a little as if the Tikker campaign were saying: If there will always be some death penalty, if, as Derrida says at the end of *The*

Death Penalty, Volume I, the future of the death penalty lies in the figures that will be invented for it, why not invent a figure for the death penalty, a symbolic deathwatch, we can live with? Why not a virtual death penalty?

And yet even this figure of the death penalty may give us pause. For it repeats, albeit symbolically, the illusion that the future is a countdown and the heart merely a ticking machine.

Since this epilogue is already very long, I will simply end by quoting my good friend and colleague Michael Naas, who, bless his heart, had only this to say when I told him about the Tikker watch: "Let's just hope," he said, "your Tikker gives out before your ticker does." By which I took him to mean—but who can say for sure, we were talking on the phone—that there would always remain something undecidable about what comes to us from the other.

APPENDIXES
Crib Notes

APPENDIX A

What Is at Play in Play?
Derrida's *Fort/Da* with Freud's *Fort/Da*

In order to add a final twist to the question of contingency, I would like to use this (double) appendix to illustrate the chances/risks of translation. To do so I will need to take the reader behind the scenes of the Derrida Seminars Translation Project (aka "D(u)ST(u)P").[1] My hope is that these scenes will illustrate both the serious play and the play of chance that are involved in any translation of Freud or Derrida.

In thinking about the last ten years of DSTP, I gave in to a temptation: the temptation to compare our task—that of translating forty-two years of Derrida's seminars—to the task undertaken by James Strachey, between 1953 and 1966, of rendering two million words of Sigmund Freud's into English. Now I don't need to tell you what a monumental achievement *The Standard Edition of the Complete Psychological Works of Sigmund Freud* is, but what you may not realize is that Strachey translated twenty-three volumes in thirteen years. Twenty-three volumes in thirteen years: That's 1.7692 volumes per year, though it sometimes worked out—in 1955, for example—to five volumes in a single year. Just to compare: In the last ten years, DSTP has published five seminars in translation, that is, one volume every two years.

This temptation to compare DSTP's task to Strachey's also led me to reread the General Preface to the *Standard Edition*, in which Strachey discusses, among other things, the difficulties, both stylistic and technical, of translating Freud. And what I found, much to my surprise, is that, for Strachey, it all comes down to a certain conception of "English." So, I wanted to begin by going behind the scenes of DSTP and offering two examples of DSTP's dust-ups over English, of the back and forth, *fort* and *da*, between English and English. These scenes of serious play, I will suggest, not only bring out the stylistic and technical difficulties of translating Derrida. They also echo a number of earlier scenes, one might even call them primal scenes, of *intra*linguistic translation within Derrida's own texts. That is, this movement back and forth, *fort* and *da*, between English and English, also translates the back-and-forth movement between French and French, which, in my third and fourth examples, is further marked, literally marked, becomes remarkably literal, in the *passage* between the French of Derrida's seminars and the French of his published texts. In the end, all of this back and forth returns us—how could it not?—to the *fort/da* game, or, as we will see in Derrida's 1975–1976 seminar *Life Death*, to a French idiom that goes a little *overboard* when it comes to this game. And if I say "a little overboard," it is not because I want to rock the boat. It is because it is hard not to get carried away and lost in translation when one is exploring, as will be the case in these examples, "the dominance of the pleasure principle" (SE 18:17/GW 13:7).

The Battle of the Englishes (Examples 1 and 2)

It is perhaps no surprise that Strachey begins his discussion of translation with the description of a *fantasy* (two years in analysis with Freud will do this to you!). This fantasy is presented as a kind of solution: a translator's solution to what Strachey calls the "problem of style" (SE 1:xviii). How to turn a stylist like Freud, a man whose literary merits cannot possibly be dismissed, into a writer of good English prose? Strachey's solution is to imagine Freud as a native and eloquent speaker of the Queen's English. Here is what Strachey says in his General Preface:

> The imaginary model which I have always kept before me is of the writings of some English man of science of wide education born in the middle of the nineteenth century. And I should like, in an explanatory and not patriotic spirit, to emphasize the word "English." (SE 1:xix)

What Is at Play in Play?   181

Though I will not interpret Strachey's "imaginary model" here (or what it might mean to turn Freud into a jewel in the crown of the British Empire), suffice it to say that this scene is immediately complicated, in Strachey's own account, by the conflicting need for more literal translations and technical language.

Stylistic elegance, the fantasy of uninhibited flow or fluidity, must pay the price when it comes to "the primary question of the correct rendering of Freud's *meaning*" (SE 1:xix). For in such cases, Strachey laments, "it is necessary to swallow whole into the translation quite a number of technical terms, stereotyped phrases and neologisms which cannot with the best will in the world be regarded as 'English'" (SE 1:xix). Here, of course, we might think of Strachey's Latinizations (his translation of *Es, Ich, Überich* as "id," "ego," "superego") or his recourse to Greek (his notorious translation of *Besetzung* as "cathexis," for example).

But to swallow whole in this manner raises not only historical questions; it also raises structural questions. Indeed, how not to hear, in Strachey's comments on his translation of technical terms (on his translation of *Trieb*), an attempt to think precisely the limits of monolingualism?

> My choice of this rendering ["instinct" for *Trieb*] has been attacked in some quarters with considerable, but, I think, mistaken severity. The term almost invariably proposed by critics as an alternative is "drive." There are several objections to this. First, I should like to remark that "drive," used in this sense is not an English word and, as I have explained in my preface, this translation aims at being a translation into English. This use of the word "drive" is not to be found in the large Oxford dictionary, or in its first supplement of 1933 (though this was sufficiently up to date to include "cathexis"). (SE 1:xxiv–xxv)[2]

Thus, the word, "cathexis," a neologism (one coined by the very same James Strachey in 1922, as we read in the "large Oxford dictionary"), the very thing that, with the best will in the world, could not be regarded as "English," has been swallowed whole into the English language, as attested by the *OED*. What Strachey seems to be saying when he points to the 1933 supplement of cathexis, in other words, is that English, what we call "English," is never simply itself. "Drive," on the other hand, is simply *un-English*—and here I think we might emphasize the word "English" in its *patriotic* spirit, for how else to account for this very *British* repression, the repression of what, at least as far back as 1925 in the American psychoanalytic journals, was being called the "sex drive"? In spite of this repression, however, I would argue that Strachey's comments on translation are driven by a kind of reflection on the double postulation of *Monolingualism of the Other*: "'We only ever speak one language,' and 'we never speak only one language'" (MO 27/50). What would it mean, then, to translate into English if English is never only one language?

Which brings me to DSTP. In the case of DSTP, of course, there could be no fantasy of "English" (that is, no single, shared fantasy) because there was always more than one "English" from the very beginning (there was British, American, Canadian, New Zealand English). We began with English*es*, that is, with competing Englishes. It wasn't the battle of the sexes; it was the battle of the Englishes. I will give just two short DSTP examples in which the lines between Englishes, between British English and American English, could not be clearer.

First example. It's 2009, and we are going over Geoffrey Bennington's translation of *The Beast and the Sovereign, Volume II*. In the fifth session of this seminar, Derrida stages a back and forth between himself and his audience. What if, says Derrida, Robinson Crusoe were buried alive, swallowed up alive (like a neologism in a translation)? We, his audience, Derrida says, would not believe him:

> "But that's not true," you would object firmly . . . that's not what happened . . . Robinson Crusoe was not buried alive, he was not swallowed up alive. . . . In fact, as we know, he came back from his island alive and well [*bien vivant*, says Derrida, *en pleine forme*]." (BS2 128/190)

Now our disagreement as translators had nothing to do with Robinson Crusoe being swallowed up alive. Had he been swallowed up alive, there would have been no problem. What we argued about was how best to describe his state of health when he came back from his island. For many of us, the translation seemed clear and straightforward, totally unproblematic: *Il est rentré de son île bien vivant, en pleine forme*, he came back from his island alive and well, in good health (or in good shape: *en pleine forme*). But for Geoff, and his British ear prevailed in the end—Robinson Crusoe was, after all, returning to England—another idiom came to mind: "He came back from his island alive and well, *in fine fettle*" (BS2 128/190, my emphasis). It's sad and funny. It's the collapse of an Empire when "in fine fettle" sounds to an American ear about as hale and hearty as "namby-pamby." In the end, however, the Empire struck back; "in fine fettle" has now completely replaced "fit as a fiddle" in our everyday vocabularies—and not only in jest. At bottom, one might say—and I use this expression because it would make Geoff wince—*at bottom*, "in fine fettle" was our "cathexis."

Second example. In this case, we were all in agreement. We were celebrating a rather remarkable coincidence: the successful rendering of one untranslatable idiom by another (this time, an American idiom). It's the first session of *The Death Penalty, Volume II* (so it's my translation—and this is by far the best thing in the whole volume; the reader will be disappointed by the rest). Derrida is talking about how best to approach the problem of the death penalty, and he tells us he is going to multiply his points of departure by dissociating and diversifying his angles of attack through a series of multilateral advances, on different fronts, along different wings ("wings" in French is *ailes*). One of these wings will be the figure of the "President," of the sovereign known as "President." At which point, the figure of the president and the figure of wings converge:

> Voici maintenant une autre avance, sur une autre aile [Here, now, another advance, along another wing (*aile*)]. Surnommons-la la présidentielle, la présidentiaile. (DP2 21/43)

You can hear the adjective *présidentielle*, which is the same in English, *presidential*, but you can also hear that the adjective ending *-elle* and the word "wing," *aile*, are homophones, hence Derrida's playful repetition and neologism *presidenti-aile*. So how does one do this in English? How does one translate a homophonic play? And in particular one that brings together "president" and "wing"? Here's the translation:

> Here, now, another advance, along another wing. Let us call it the "presidential," the "West-wing." (DP2 21/43)

We might speak here of an American Empire, at least insofar as English is concerned. Where the expression "in fine fettle" finds little response (or laughter) among American speakers of English, the phrase "West Wing" (made famous by the NBC show), a phrase that designates an architectural detail of the White House complex, is immediately and universally recognizable.

Excusing His French

PLAYING AND PLEASURE (THIRD EXAMPLE)

Now, in my next two examples, it is the intralinguistic *play*, this time between French and French, that must be taken seriously.[3] And not only because, as we know from D. W. Winnicott, "it is in playing and only in playing that the individual . . . is able to be creative."[4] No, if this play must be taken seriously in the examples that follow, both of which are taken from Derrida's discussion of Freud in his 1975–1976 seminar *Life Death*, it is because it is only in *playing up* the "game-like character" (LVLM 343) of Freud's speculation on the death drive that we are able to think the forward movement, the *fort*, of Derrida's—but also Freud's—"unconditional affirmation of life" (LLF 51/54). A lot is at work, you might say, in this play.

Third example. In the penultimate chapter of *Beyond the Pleasure Principle*, you may recall, Freud wonders just how seriously he takes his own speculative hypotheses of the repetition compulsion and the death drive. How convinced is he? How seriously does he believe what he is saying?

> It may be asked whether and how far I am myself convinced of the truth of the hypotheses that have been set out in these pages. My answer would be that I am not convinced myself and that I do not seek to persuade other people to believe in them. Or, more precisely, that I do not know how far I believe in them. (SE 18:59/GW 13:63–64)

In other words, Freud stages his own uncertainty. He goes back and forth with himself, *fort* and *da*, somewhat "narcissistically" (cf. LVLM 341). In this way, Freud stages his uncertainty but also, ultimately, as Derrida claims, his pleasure.

If I say "pleasure," then, it is not only because of this narcissistic turn, this lifting of a long-suppressed desire to speculate. If I say "pleasure," it is also because Derrida draws attention to what he, Derrida, understands to be Freud's pleasure in this line of thought. Freud takes pleasure in thinking beyond the pleasure principle. In both *Life Death* and "To Speculate—on 'Freud,'" Derrida seems pleased by this new pleasure; he goes so far as to imagine Freud defending himself (that is, this new pleasure) against his would-be critics. Here is what Derrida says in "Speculate" where he plays at imitating Freud's riposte to his critics:

> "Allez donc vous faire voir. . . . L'hypothèse de la pulsion de mort, moi j'aime ça."

> "You can all go to hell [and not 'go look for yourself,' as the translator mistakenly translates it]. . . . This hypothesis of a death drive, that's what I like." ("SoF" 385/411, modified)

But "To Speculate—on 'Freud'" is already the polite version of Derrida's imaginary scene. As we now know from his 1975–1976 seminar, there existed an earlier, unexpurgated, version of Derrida's formulation of Freud's expression of pleasure:

> "Allez-vous faire foutre, moi ça me plaît, l'au-delà du plaisir tel est mon bon plaisir, l'hypothèse de la pulsion de mort, moi j'aime ça."
>
> "Screw you all [or as Geoff and David might say: bugger off!], I myself am rather pleased with this, the beyond of pleasure, that's my pleasure; the hypothesis of a death drive—that's what I like." (LVLM 344)

No need to excuse Derrida here—or rather to excuse his French. For whether we screw ourselves or go to hell, one thing is clear: Speculative play, the hypothesis of the death drive, gives Freud—*and Derrida*—pleasure. Though perhaps I could put it this way: Derrida's language, its exuberance, and its color remind us that there is always *an element of play* in the death drive that keeps the very possibility of pleasure alive. Still, to imagine a Freud who would take pleasure in the hypothesis of the death drive, "one has to have ideas," "il faut avoir des idées" ("SoF" 317/337, modified).

Derrida's Ideas (Fourth Example)

Which brings me to Derrida's ideas about Freud or rather, in this case, about the *fort/da* game. Fourth example. The *fort/da* game is about difference and translation: The difference in German between *fort* and *da*, or rather between "a loud, long-drawn-out 'o-o-o-o'" (SE 18:14 / GW 13:12), which Freud takes to be the German word "*fort*" ("gone"), and a "joyful '*da*'" ("there") (SE 18:15 / GW 13:12). But it is also a Game of Zones; it is a symbolic representation that repeats an unpleasurable experience as a pleasurable one by throwing a reel *fort*, that is, by banishing it to the "gone" zone, and then bringing it back again, into the *da* zone. I will briefly quote Freud's description of the game in order to bring out what is *en jeu* (at stake and in play) in Derrida's modified translation of this passage in *Life Death*. Here is what Freud says in Chapter 2 of *Beyond the Pleasure Principle* (and I have Americanized Strachey's English translation):

> The child [this of course is Freud's grandson Ernst] had a wooden reel with a piece of string tied round it. It never occurred to him to pull it *along the floor* [*am Boden*] behind him, for instance, and play at its being a carriage. What he did was to hold the reel by the string and very skillfully throw it over the edge of his curtained crib [Strachey famously says "cot," but a cot in American English is a collapsible bed; it is not a crib], so that it disappeared into it [*so daß sie darin verschwand*], at the same time uttering his expressive "o-o-o-o." He then pulled the reel *out of the crib again* by the string [*zog dann die Spule am Faden wieder aus dem Bett heraus*] and hailed its reappearance with a joyful "*da*" ["there"]. This,

then, was the complete game—disappearance and return. As a rule, one only witnessed its first act, which was repeated untiringly as a game in itself, though there is no doubt that the greater pleasure was attached to the second act. (SE 18:15 / GW 13:12–13, modified, my emphasis)

Just to be clear, because I think it is very clear, both in English and in German: Ernst is not pulling the reel along the floor behind him (this is Freud's fantasy). Rather, he is standing and throwing the reel over the edge of the curtained crib in such a way that the reel disappears behind the curtain; he is making "gone [*fort*]" with it. That is the first part of the game and sometimes even the whole of the game, even if it is not the complete game, according to Freud. The complete game includes hailing the return of the thing: reeling the reel back in, out of the crib. In other words, what is thrown *into the crib* is *fort* and what is pulled *out of the crib* is *da*.

Here, now, are Derrida's comments on this passage in *Life Death*:

Freud seems surprised by the fact that the child never had the idea to pull the reel along behind him and play at its being a carriage. Freud's problem is this: why does he not play at its being a carriage, which would be normal, pulling the thing behind him. That is Freud's problem, who would have apparently preferred to play at its being a carriage and who is surprised that the idea never occurred to Ernst. . . . Freud finds Ernst's choice to be strange, but you have to admit that Freud's desire is no less strange when you consider that all this is taking place *in a crib* and that it has only ever taken place *in a crib with curtains*. One has to wonder how Ernst would have gone about playing at the reel being a carriage by pulling it behind [him] *in a curtained crib*. In order to have the reel—or the vehicle—behind oneself *in a crib*, one has to have ideas. What is surprising, then, is not that Ernst never had these ideas but that the Pépé considers them the most natural. (LVLM 309–10, my emphasis, modified)

What is surprising and strange, says Derrida, is how natural the idea of playing at the reel being a carriage seems to Freud. What could be more natural for an analyst who is always sitting behind his patient than to imagine a scene in which the Re(a)l remains out of sight, uninscribed in the Symbolic? But how are we to read Derrida's strange idea here, his insistence that the play take place *in a crib* (*dans un lit*), *in a crib with curtains* (*dans un lit avec des rideaux*), *in a curtained crib* (*dans un lit à rideaux*), that is, to put it simply, *in bed*? In fact, when I first read this passage, I thought it was a joke: All this is taking place *dans un lit*, in a bed, and perhaps between the sheets. How do we end up *in bed* with Derrida when Freud's idea was

What Is at Play in Play?   187

precisely to drag the reel "along the floor [*am Boden*]"? Has Derrida just missed the boat here?

I will not analyze Derrida's (conscious? unconscious?) desire, his desire to challenge Freud's strange idea with his own strange idea. Nor will I interpret the fact that where Freud "might have wished that Ernst had played more seriously on the floor ... without attending to the bed" ("SoF" 315/336, modified), Derrida makes all the world a bed, and Ernst a *player* in it. Instead I will point to a strange French idiom, one that seems to have crept into Derrida's translation of Freud's text. One can only speculate that it is the proximity of the verb *jeter* (to throw) and the word *bord* (edge) that has pushed the translation over the edge here. I will quote Derrida's translation of Freud (in my own translation):

> The child had a wooden reel ... with a string tied around it. Not once did the idea ever occur to him ... for example, to drag the reel behind him, that is, to play carriage with it. (LVLM 309)

I will continue now in French so that you can hear the idiom (and as far as I know, this is Derrida's own translation—he is not quoting Samuel Janké-lévitch's translation here, as he does elsewhere):

> Mais il jetait la bobine ... avec une grande adresse par-dessus bord, le bord de son petit lit entouré d'un rideau [but with great dexterity he threw the reel overboard (*par-dessus bord*), over the edge (*le bord*) of his curtained crib] (LVLM 309)

The French idiom *jeter par-dessus bord*, like the English idiom "to throw overboard," does not take an article; one does not throw over *the* board but simply *overboard*. Indeed, one might say that everything hinges on the disappearance of the definite article here. For when the article disappears—"overboard"—the reel goes in one direction and one direction only: out of the boat (or crib). Hence Derrida's strange idea of having Ernst play carriage with the reel in the crib. Only if Ernst is *in the crib* can he throw the reel *overboard*. So how are we to read Derrida's move here? What does it mean to make (a) game of the game, to play *fort/da* with Freud's/Ernst's *fort/da*?

Now, I want to quote the published version of this passage in "To Speculate—on 'Freud.'" In the published text, as you will see, Derrida replays the scene; he playfully corrects his own (mis)reading of the *fort/da* game in *Life Death* by distancing himself from it. He takes himself out of his text. Just like Ernst who, in *Beyond the Pleasure Principle*, not only plays *fort/da* with the reel but also plays at making himself "gone," *fort*, by crouching down in front of a mirror. Derrida too, I will suggest, "plays at being *fort*ified . . . by his own disappearance" (LVLM 312, my emphasis):

> [Freud] seems surprised, adding to this surprise a confident regret that the good little boy never seemed to have the idea of pulling the reel behind him and playing at its being a carriage. . . . Why doesn't he play train or carriage? Wouldn't that be more normal? And why doesn't he play carriage by pulling the thing behind him? For the thing is a vehicle in motion. . . . Too bad that the idea never occurred to him (for example!) to pull the reel behind him on the floor, and thus to play carriage with it. . . . Instead of playing on the floor (*am Boden*), he insisted on putting the crib into the game, into play, on playing with the thing over the crib, but also in the crib. *Not in the crib as the place where the child himself would be, for contrary to what the text and the translation have often led many to believe (and one would have to ask why), he is not in the crib at the moment when he throws the reel, it would seem.* He throws it from outside the crib over its edge, over the veils or curtains that surround its edge. ("SoF" 314–15/335–36, modified, my emphasis)

Derrida may have pulled Ernst from the crib and returned him to solid ground, but he, Derrida, is still occupied with, not to say "cathected on," the crib. Much like Ernst, who *insists* on giving it a pivotal role in his game. You might even say that Derrida and Ernst are *in the same boat* when it comes to putting the bed into play.

But let us also note Derrida's somewhat cryptic (though humorous) remark about his own earlier interpretation. Derrida takes himself *out of* the picture when he takes the child *out of* the bed. He mentions only the "many" who *may have gone overboard* in interpreting what it means "to play with a reel in a crib." I hate to say it, but Derrida is right, even when he's wrong. People have often assumed that the child was *in* the crib. The question is why: Why might we think or *want* to think that Ernst is *inside*, rather than *outside*, the crib? I don't have the answer to this question, but I will suggest that there is something about the playful movement of this game, about the "long-drawn-out 'o-o-o-o'" and the "joyful '*da*,'" something about this *awakening* to language, that places the child—and his words—at the center of the scene: inside, rather than outside, the crib. Yet these words also drive us from the comforts of the crib. They throw us outside the language we thought we were in. They remind us that we never speak just one language. Where *da* was, there *fort* shall be, they say.

So where does this leave us? Are we to remain hopelessly *at sea* over this *fort/da* with Ernst? Perhaps, though, we could pause for a moment and take a step back. What if we read the relevant sections of *Life Death* and "To Speculate—on 'Freud'" as a kind of double session with Freud, one in which Derrida was acting out—playing out—his relationship with Freud? After all, we must remember that, just as Derrida plays *fort/da* with Ernst, putting Ernst both inside and outside the crib, so too he plays *fort/da* with himself, placing himself both inside and outside Freud's text.

There is something else, at any rate, that we cannot remain blind to. And that is that what brings out this play, what brings play into play, is the movement—the chance opportunity (*Gelegenheit*)—of translation: from "o-o-o-o" . . . to *o*-verboard. Which is not to say that translation is all fun and games. On the contrary. When translating a stylist like Freud or Derrida, one is not always in *fine fettle*. There are days—and here I speak from experience—there are days when one feels one has gotten up *on the wrong side of the bed*.

APPENDIX B

Devouring Figures
Little Red Riding Hood and the Final Seminars of Jacques Derrida

I thought I would end, just as I began, with an anecdote, in this case one that takes me back to the very beginning of the Derrida Seminars Translation Project (DSTP)[1] but also forward to what, in Derrida's final seminars, gives "life" the last word.

The date is July 8, 2008. Nine of us (four of our team members—Pascale-Anne Brault, Peggy Kamuf, Michael Naas, and I—and five students from doctoral programs in comparative literature, French, and philosophy) are sitting around a seminar table in a room known as "la boulangerie" at the Institut Mémoires de l'Édition Contemporaine (IMEC)[2] in Caen, France. It's late afternoon on day 2 of DSTP's inaugural workshop, and we are preparing to read through Geoffrey Bennington's 350-page translation of the first volume of *The Beast and the Sovereign, mot-à-mot,* line by line (we've got a lot to do in this boulangerie, *on a du pain sur la planche*). We have been discussing some of the translation difficulties in the opening sessions of the seminar, in particular the untranslatability of the terms *bête* and *bêtise*. *Une bête* is of course a beast or an animal, but *bête* is also a common and idiomatic term for "stupid": *Être bête comme ses pieds* is to be "too stupid for words," to be "thick as a brick." The translation of *bête* by "stupid" or of *bêtise* by

Devouring Figures 191

"stupidity" thus loses everything that marks the idiomatic element in French, namely, the proximity of stupidity to animality. In seminars that set out to explore, among other things, the analogy between *bête* (beast) and sovereign, and the limits between what is called "the animal" and what is called "man" (who alone can be *bête*, *la bête n'est pas bête*), the semantic loss is just too great. *Bête* and *bêtise* must be left in the original in order to convey the force of the particular association network of the French idiom.

At this point, if I remember correctly, I became concerned with what seemed to me to be the nonidiomatic quality of the word "maw" that Geoff had used to translate the very colloquial *gueule* several times in the first session (for example, *en pleine gueule*, "right in the maw"). Was it better, I asked, to err on the side of the beast ("maw" being, according to the *OED*, "the jaws or throat of a *voracious* animal"), or was it better to err on the side of the idiom ("jaw" or "jaws" translating more accurately the idiomatic quality of *gueule* in French)? Was it better to stress the *voracity* of the voracious, devouring mouth ("maw") or the linguistic performance of the talking, speaking mouth ("jaw")? I argued for the latter and appealed to the fabular language of children in my defense: "Would there ever be a 'maw' in Little Red Riding Hood?" I asked. I thought I had clinched the matter with my question when the team weighed in, first Michael and then Peggy. In response to my provocation, "Would there ever be a 'maw' in Little Red Riding Hood?" Michael answered without even missing a beat: "Grandmaw"! To which Peggy made the following, untranslatable rejoinder: "My, what *bêtises* you have!"

But if I begin with this story about my colleagues' jaw-dropping display of rhetorical brilliance, it is not only because it is a funny story. It is also because the buccal cavity and the figure of orality (which is to say, not simply the mouth but also the face, and not simply the face but also the word, the spoken word or word of mouth, the voice and its *vociferations*) play a crucial role in Derrida's final seminars, and in particular in the movement between *The Beast and the Sovereign, Volume I* and *The Beast and the Sovereign, Volume II*. In other words, it is no accident that *gueule* should have been the site of a vociferous argument among translators. It is no accident because *The Beast and the Sovereign, Volume I* identifies the figure of orality, the figure of the face, with the "figure of the figure" (BS1 23/46). Hence, there is something excessive about *la figure de la figure*, something that demands more than one iteration, more than one translation, more than one *figure*. One is reminded here of the serial figures (or quasi-figures) for deconstruction that appear in Derrida's work. These are figures of the impossible or the "impossible unconditional," figures such as hospitality, the gift, forgiveness, autoimmunity, the event, figures whose very *seriality* testifies to the necessity of proliferating gestures.

The Big Bad Wolf

Now Derrida does, in fact, refer to Little Red Riding Hood in *The Beast and the Sovereign, Volume I*. He draws our attention to "Grandmother-Wolf [*Grand-mère-Loup*]" (BS1 12/32), who belongs to a long and illustrious line of wolves in this seminar. In the seminar that Derrida calls "my genealogy of the wolf, my book of wolves, my genelycology" (BS1 64/99, modified), Derrida tracks the wolf: from the tyrant-wolf or wolf-tyrant of Plato's *Republic* to the wolf of "The Wolf and the Lamb" in La Fontaine's fable to Freud's Wolf Man. One path, the one that eventually leads to Grandmother-Wolf, tracks the philosophical, rhetorical, political history that takes us from Plautus's *homo homini lupus*—through Rabelais, Montaigne, and Bacon—to Hobbes's famous *homo homini lupus*, against which Rousseau thinks and writes the *Social Contract*. The wolf is thus a privileged (political) figure in *The Beast and the Sovereign, Volume I*, whether sovereign or outlaw, sovereign and outlaw:

> One cannot be interested in the relations of beast and sovereign, and all the questions of the animal and the political, of the politics of the animal, of man and beast in the context of the state, the *polis*, the city, the republic, the social body, the law in general, war and peace, terror and terrorism, national and international terrorism, etc., without recognizing some privilege to the figure of the "wolf." (BS1 9/28)

What is more, the figure of the wolf that is privileged (whether in Plato, Hobbes, or Rousseau) is that of the big bad wolf, the "devouring wolf" (BS1 12/32). Which means that the *face* of this privileged figure—*la gueule du loup*, the mouth of the wolf—is not just any face. Indeed, in a long parenthetical remark that literally interrupts the *Social Contract* at the word "devour," Derrida stops and warns us: "The devouring wolf is not far away, the big bad wolf, the wolf's mouth, the big teeth of Little Red Riding Hood's Grandmother-Wolf ('Grandmother, what big teeth you have')" (BS1 12/32).

As it turns out, Derrida quotes Little Red Riding Hood twice in the opening session of *The Beast and the Sovereign, Volume I*, and each time her words point to a different *portée* (reach, range, aspect, carry) of orality. One might say that the big bad wolf is the face of orality par excellence: whether in its oral (OR) form—"Grandmother, what big teeth you have" (BS1

12/32)—or in its aural (AUR) form—"Grandmother, what big ears you have" (BS1 23/46).

As we have seen, the big bad wolf first appears as a "power of devourment":

> Devourment and voracity. *Devoro, vorax, vorator.* It's about mouth, teeth, tongue, and the violent rush to bite, engulf, swallow the other, to take the other into oneself. (BS1 23/46)

The big bad wolf devours, swallows, takes the other into himself. In fact, by the time Little Red Riding Hood arrives at her grandmother's house, the wolf has already engulfed her grandmother. When Little Red Riding Hood sees his teeth, that is, he is already a Grandmother-Wolf. He is a Grand Maw, a maw in GrandMA's clothing. On the one hand, thus, the figure of the *face*, namely the *face* of this privileged figure, Grandma's large-toothed face, marks the *place of devourment*.

On the other hand, however, and this will be the second place, the other place that we encounter the words of Little Red Riding Hood, the figure of the devouring wolf marks the *place of vociferation*. The story of Little Red Riding Hood does of course provide us with a devouring-speaking wolf, a wolf who speaks in a big voice (*la grosse voix du Loup*, writes Perrault) and even softens his voice in order better to deceive Little Red Riding Hood, but Derrida will use the example to gesture instead to what is the reach or carry (*portée*) of the voice:

> But what goes via interiorizing devourment, i.e., via orality, via the mouth, the maw, teeth, throat, glottis, and tongue—which are also the sites of cry and speech, of language—that very thing can also inhabit that other site of the visage or the face, i.e., the ears, the auricular attributes, the visible and therefore audiovisual forms of what allows one not only to speak but also to hear and listen. "Grandmother, what big ears you have, she says to the wolf." (BS1 23/46)

Thus orality has a double tongue, a double carry (*double portée*), and a double place. On the one hand, there is the devouring tongue, the voracious reach or carry of the teeth that lacerate and cut to pieces ("Grandmother, what big teeth you have"); this is the place of devourment. On the other hand, there is "the carry of the tongue that speaks" (BS1 65/100), "the place of what carries the voice, the *topos* of the *porte-voix* ... the place of *vociferation*" (BS1 23/46).[3] When Derrida quotes Little Red Riding Hood for the second time, in other words, the figure of orality has shifted from the place of *devourment* to that of *vociferation*—it has shifted to the voice-carrying place, to the place that carries the voice to "that other site of the visage or face, i.e., the ears, the auricular attributes": "Grandmother, what big ears you have."

In this way, the figure of orality becomes, as Derrida says, the place of "vociferating devourment or devouring vociferation," and the "figure of the face" (*la figure de la figure*) becomes the "figure of figure" (*la figure de la figure*):

> Devourment, vociferation, there in the figure of the face [the translation has "figure of figure" here], in the face, smack in the mouth, but also in the figure as trope, there's the figure of figure [*voilà dans la figure de la figure, dans le visage en pleine gueule, mais aussi dans la figure comme trope, voilà la figure de la figure*], vociferating devourment or devouring vociferation. (BS1 23/ 46, modified)

Here, between the first *figure de la figure* and the second *figure de la figure*, the figure of the face, but also the *face* of the figure, the *face* of the wolf, seems to have been effaced, erased, devoured, swallowed up by "the figure as trope" (the *face* only appears in a footnote in the translation). As indeed it must be if the figure of the *face* is to be the figure of figure. The figure of figure must devour the *face* of the figure as the condition of its vociferation.

Yet the maw always comes back to bite us. We have seen how the *face* of this figure is anything but benign. If the figure of *face* is indeed the face *of* figure (the face of figuration, the figure of figure) *and* this face is a maw, then the figure (as *face*) is also, as Derrida says, a figure that swallows up figures *as* it vociferates (it's the Grand *Maw* of figuration, the Grand *Maw* that is structured into trope, a *devouring* vociferation). And it's not a pretty face: It's the *face* of a figure that vociferates by chewing up or swallowing. We are not far, in other words, from the figure of a sovereign "capable of devouring those he commands, namely *cattle*" (BS1 11/31).

The Phantasm of Devourment

I am going to jump now, briefly, to *The Beast and the Sovereign, Volume II* and to the place where Derrida turns to the figure of devourment, indeed to the phantasm of being devoured alive, swallowed alive, buried alive. This is the great or fundamental phantasm of *Robinson Crusoe*, according to Derrida:

> The great gesture, the great phantasmatic *gesta* of the book, which rules its whole vocabulary, its speech, its mouth, its tongue and its

teeth, is that of eating and devouring, eating the other, that's all we ever hear about, the fear of being devoured by wild beasts or by savage cannibals, and the need to eat beasts. (BS2 55/92)

The fundamental, foundational fear, the basic fear [*peur de fond*] from which all other fears are derived and around which everything is organized, is the fear of going to the bottom [*au fond*], precisely of being "swallow'd up alive." . . . [Robinson Crusoe] is afraid of being swallowed up or "buried alive" . . . thus of sinking alive to the bottom . . . as much because of an earthquake as because of wild or savage beasts, or even because of human cannibals. He is afraid of dying a living death [*mourir vivant*] by being swallowed or devoured into the deep belly of the earth or the sea or some living creature, some living animal. (BS2 77/122)

The phantasm that rules Robinson Crusoe's speech, mouth, tongue, and teeth does not lead, as it did in the case of Little Red Riding Hood, to "the *visible* and therefore *audiovisual* forms of what allows one . . . to hear and listen" (BS1 23/46, my emphasis). It does not lead, that is, to the ears or the "auricular attributes" (BS1 23/46). Rather it is a phantasm that leads to the bottom, to the bowels, to "the deep belly of the earth or the sea or some living creature." It's about mouth, throat, gullet, and *belly* (and in this context we should recall that "maw" comes from *maga* [Old English], *maag* [Dutch], *Magen* [German], the stomach).

This all-consuming phantasm, this "obsessional terror" (BS2 93/146), this great, fundamental, foundational fear of devourment has, for Derrida, a specifically autoimmune logic. To be swallowed up by the earth or the sea is not the same thing as to be eaten by beasts or cannibals. Earth and sea, says Derrida, are "non-living . . . anonymous and inanimate" whereas beast and cannibal are fellow living beings (BS2 142/208):

The devouring beast is similar [*semblable*] to its victim insofar as it is alive. . . . Devourer and devoured are both living beings; but the anthropophagic cannibal is *more* similar to his victim than the beast, precisely because he is an anthropoid (only an anthropoid can be anthropophagic). The cannibal is thus more similar to his victim and thus also, paradoxically, more *other*, more of an other than the beast. (BS2 142/208)

Devourment by the cannibal, by the anthropophagic anthropoid, is the most terrifying because the cannibal devours itself when it devours "its own kind" (these are Defoe's words). Only the cannibal—because he is more similar to his victim, more human, and thus, ironically, less human, that is to say, more *inhuman*—reveals the "hyperbolic point, the absolute excess of this being eaten by the other" (BS2 139/204), that is, the autoimmune process of self-destruction that is at work in the phantasm of devourment. From a figure-eating-figure, from a Grand Maw that devours *others*, for example, grandm*others*, we move to an autoimmune figure, a self-eating figure of devourment.

What the phantasm of devourment is thus able to "figure or configure [*figurer ou configurer*]" (BS1 148/217) is the inconceivable, the unthinkable, the impossible: "that state in which the dead man is alive enough . . . to live his own death . . . to be present at his death and beyond, without however failing to die, to survive his death while really dying, to survive his death" (BS2 148/217). Of course, dying a living death can only be a phantasmatic virtuality, a fiction: "One cannot presently be dead, die, and see oneself die" (BS2 130/192).

Yet, as Derrida playfully insists, Robinson Crusoe *was* buried alive, he *was* swallowed up alive. What can this mean? As the name not of the character but of the book, *Robinson Crusoe* is eaten alive. This is because any book, any trace, is "both alive and dead or, if you prefer, neither dead nor alive. . . . A book is living dead [*un mort vivant*], buried alive and swallowed up alive" (BS2 130/193). In fact, it is this alliance of the dead and the living that Derrida calls *survivance*: "The book lives its beautiful death. That's also finitude, the chance and the threat of finitude, this alliance of the dead and the living. I shall say that this finitude is *survivance*" (BS2 130/193). A book (or a seminar) is a dead thing that precisely resuscitates and lives again with every "reanimating reading" (BS2 132/195).

We can understand this living death, I will suggest, through the notion of vociferating devourment or devouring vociferation. Like the *face* of the figure, Robinson Crusoe is swallowed up by the book *Robinson Crusoe* that "lives its beautiful death [*vit de sa belle mort*]" (BS2 130/193). In this way, the *survivance* of the book *Robinson Crusoe*—a book that "has been read and will be read, interpreted, taught, saved, translated, reprinted, illustrated, filmed, kept alive by millions of inheritors" (BS2 130/193)—would be the *survivance* of an autoimmune or self-eating figure, the *survivance* of a figure that eats itself to death and has its life too, a self-devouring vociferation or vociferating self-devourment. In these seminars whose "ultimate criterion" is "the immense question of the living" (BS2 176/239), seminars that try to think "the living in life [*le vivant de la vie*]" (BS2 219/292), *survivance* would point to "a beyond of the opposition between being or not being, life and death, reality and fiction or [ph]antasmatic virtuality" (BS2 130/193).

Devouring Figures

We can also follow life death in *The Beast and the Sovereign* seminars by tracking another word that appears in both seminars and whose movement between seminars is for me particularly resonant. Derrida begins the last session of his last seminar with this word: "Que veut dire *porter*? Nous nous sommes déjà souvent demandé, en plus d'une langue, ce que signifie *porter*, *to carry, to bear, tragen* [We have already often wondered, in more than one language, what *porter, to carry, to bear, tragen* mean]. . . . *Die Welt ist fort, ich muß dich tragen*" (BS2 258/357). We have already seen *la double portée*, the double aspect, range, reach, carry between maw and jaw in *The Beast and the Sovereign, Volume I*, the *double portée* between devourment and vociferation, between the ravenous tongue and the talking tongue. But *porter* has another *portée*, if I can say this, and not only another *portée* but another *double portée*. Whenever Derrida refers to the verb *porter* in *The Beast and the Sovereign, Volume II*, he insists on the *double portée* between birth and mourning, life and death:

> At bottom, the true sense of the word "porter" (*tragen, ertragen*) is just as much the sense determined by the carrying or bearing [*portée*] of life (the mother who carries her child) as it is by the carrying or bearing [*portée*] of death by life, of the dead by the living. (BS2 153/222, modified)

In the end, I would suggest that *porter* returns us to the many movements of oscillation that characterize and give life to these seminars. And it reminds us that they belong to a lifework that bears (*porte*) the name Jacques Derrida.

The verb *porter* also reminds us, though, in one of its carries, of the *belly*, a mother's belly. Which leads me to my conclusion . . .

Coda

In conclusion, I would like to look very briefly at the end of Little Red Riding Hood in Charles Perrault's 1697 version of it. In this version, the fairy tale ends with a moral: Young ladies should never talk to strangers, for even gentle wolves are dangerous. The moral fits the tale. After all, Perrault's story ends with an unmitigated devourment: "Grandmother, what big teeth you have. All the better to eat you with. And, saying these words, this wicked wolf fell upon Little Red Riding Hood and ate her all up [*Et, en disant ces mots, ce méchant Loup se jeta sur le petit chaperon rouge, et la mangea*]."[4]

Now the 1857 Grimm version of this tale (which is, in fact, far less grim) changes Perrault's ending. Where, in Perrault, the wolf eats Little Red

Riding Hood, and the story ends, in Grimm the story goes on after the wolf eats her. It goes on to recount two further incidents. At the very end, following what will be her rescue from the belly of the wolf by a hunter, we get a Hollywood ending. Little Red Riding Hood has learned her lesson: When she meets another wolf on her way to her grandmother's house, she doesn't stop to speak to him. He follows her home and hides on the roof, but she tricks him by putting out fresh sausage (it's a *German* version): "The smell of sausage rose up into the wolf's nose [*Da stieg der Geruch . . . dem Wolf in die Nase*]. He sniffed and looked down . . . and he began to slide. He slid off the roof, fell into the great trough, and drowned."[5]

But it is the rescue from the belly of the wolf, the immediate sequel to Perrault's story, that is most fabulous here. Not only because it brings the figure of the devouring wolf and the phantasm of devourment together, and not only because it rewrites death as life, but because translation, in this case, brings technology with it: namely, another set of jaws. In the Grimm sequel, as soon as the original wolf has finished off his tasty bite, he climbs back into bed and falls asleep. A hunter who hears him snoring enters the house. The hunter understands what has happened, takes out a pair of scissors (*eine Schere*), and cuts open the wolf's belly (*Bauch*). Out jumps Little Red Riding Hood with her grandmother right behind her. They fill the wolf's body with large heavy stones, and the wolf dies. So, in the end, we have a Grandmother-Wolf, a Grand Maw who becomes a Ma by giving birth to Grandma and Little Red Riding Hood and whose belly is then filled with stones.

In this German rewriting of a French fairy tale, death by devourment is rewritten as birth by cesarean. I would even argue that the question of translation itself is being reconfigured here as a question of carrying or bearing (and in English *every* translation is a carrying: a *translatio*, a transference): from a death-bearing *gueule* to a life-bearing *Bauch*. And a few stones. But I wanted to end not with the survival of Grandma and Little Red Riding Hood but with the technē of the hunter's scissors in order to insist that it is translation—that other figure for deconstruction—that carries us from *the jaws that bite* to the *Jaws of Life*.

ACKNOWLEDGMENTS

For whatever merits this book may possess, I am indebted to many people. Were I to thank them all, however, this acknowledgment would risk adding another chapter to what is already a lengthy work. So I will limit myself to the four who have fashioned my world in its essential being, the four who are my fourfold: Peg Birmingham, Pascale-Anne Brault, Cathy Caruth, and Michael Naas.

Earlier versions of several chapters of this book were originally published elsewhere. A shorter version of Chapter 1 appeared in the *Journal of Speculative Philosophy* 28, no. 3 (2014): 134–45. A section of Chapter 2 was published in *Parrhesia* 21 (2014): 13–22. An early version of Chapter 3 appeared in the *Revue internationale de philosophie* 71, no. 282 (2017): 445–56. A version of Chapter 4 was first published in *Paragraph* 40, no. 3 (2017): 310–28. A revised version of Chapter 6 appeared in *A Companion to Derrida*, ed. Zeynep Direk and Leonard Lawlor (London: Blackwell, 2014), 304–20. An abbreviated version of Chapter 7 appeared in *The Southern Journal of Philosophy* 50 (Spindel Supplement, 2012): 143–59. Shorter versions of Chapter 8 and 9 were originally published in the *Oxford Literary Review*, the first in volume 35, no. 2 (2013): 189–204; and the second in volume 38, no. 2 (2016): 188–220. A first version of Appendix A originally appeared in *Mosaic, an interdisciplinary critical journal* 51, no. 4 (2018): 93–103. An early version of Appendix B appeared in *Philosophy Today* 55 (SPEP Supplement, 2011): 183–88.

Finally, I would like to express my gratitude to Rebecca Comay and Elissa Marder for their generous comments on this book.

NOTES

INTRODUCTION: *FREUDERRIDA*

1. Monique David-Ménard, *Éloge des hasards dans la vie sexuelle* (Paris: Hermann, 2011), 19–20, hereafter abbreviated EHVS.

2. Although, technically speaking, the MMPI test puts forward statements, such as "I feel blue," to which the test-taker is asked to respond "true" or "false," these "statements" not only read as questions but are also tabulated as such by the test administrators ("questions not answered," "answering similar/opposite question pairs inconsistently," "answering questions all true/all false," etc.). See http://en.wikipedia.org/wiki/Minnesota_Multiphasic_Personality_Inventory.

3. Charcot's great admiration for his own teacher Duchenne de Boulogne is expressed in similar terms: "How is it that, one fine day, Duchenne discovered a disease [namely, muscular dystrophy] which had probably existed since the days of Hippocrates?" G. T. Guillain, *Jean-Martin Charcot: His Life, His Work*, trans. P. Bailey (New York: Hoeber, 1959), 105, modified.

4. Hélène Cixous, *Philippines*, trans. Laurent Milesi (Cambridge, MA: Polity, 2011), 43, 75; *Philippines: Prédelles* (Paris: Galilée, 2009), 67, 40, hereafter abbreviated P.

1. PSYCHOANALYSIS AND NEUROSCIENCE (FOREIGN BODIES I)

1. Karen Kaplan-Solms and Mark Solms, *Clinical Studies in Neuro-Psychoanalysis: Introduction to a Depth Neuropsychology* (London: Karnac, 2000), 251, hereafter abbreviated CS.

2. Mark Solms and Oliver Turnbull, *The Brain and the Inner World: An Introduction to the Neuroscience of Subjective Experience* (New York: Other Press, 2002), 294–95, hereafter abbreviated BIW.

3. See *Clinical Studies*, where the language of correlation appears on almost every page. Indeed, one might go so far as to say that the "correlate" becomes the linguistic figure for the hyphen in "neuro-psychoanalysis": "[Neuropsychology] is devoted precisely to the problem of correlating the phenomena of mental life with the structures and functions of the brain" (CS 5); "This, we hope, will suffice to convince the reader . . . that it is now

possible to discover the neurological correlates of our psychoanalytic understanding of the structure of the human mind" (CS 68); "An analysis of the psychological mechanisms . . . enables us to gradually identify the neural correlates of the basic metapsychological functions that comprise the human mental apparatus as a whole" (CS 115); "We hope . . . to gain an understanding of the neural correlates of our psychoanalytic model of the mind" (CS 149); "We can therefore correlate what we have been able to discover in psychoanalysis from the viewpoint of psychic reality with what we have been able to discover in neuroscience from the viewpoint of material reality" (CS 251). Correlation is the name of the game ("in our quest to correlate psychoanalysis with neuroscience" [CS 235]), and "neuro-psychoanalysis" is the method or science best equipped to succeed in this quest.

4. Michael S. Gazzaniga, "The Split Brain Revisited," *Scientific American* 279, no. 1 (1998): 54.

5. For a reading of Freud's 1891 monograph *On Aphasia* as a "radical departure from orthodox German neurology," see Mark Solms and Michael Saling, "On Psychoanalysis and Neuroscience: Freud's Attitude to the Localizationist Tradition," *International Journal of Psychoanalysis* 67 (1986): 397–416. See also John Forrester's description of Freud's departure from neurology in his *Language and the Origins of Psychoanalysis* (New York: Columbia University Press, 1980), 30.

6. Here we must be careful not to confuse Freud's attitude toward the localizationalist tradition of neurology with his notion of "psychical localities." Even though Freud describes unconscious and conscious systems as "localities [*Lokalitäten*] in the mental apparatus" (SE 5:610/GW 2/3:615)—even though "a certain spatiality" remains "inseparable from the very idea of the system" and "irreducible" to it ("FSW" 215/318)—such localities have nothing to do with anatomical reality: "I shall carefully avoid the temptation to determine psychical locality in any anatomical fashion" (SE 5:536/GW 2/3:541).

7. It is interesting to note that Foucault scrupulously avoids any mention of Freud when he speaks of the fundamental "*spatialization*" of pathology at the birth of modern medicine. See Michel Foucault, *The Birth of the Clinic*, trans. A. M. Sheridan Smith (New York: Random House, 1973), xi; *Naissance de la clinique* (Paris: PUF, 1963), viii, hereafter abbreviated BC. Foucault reads the spatializing shift of modern medicine as a mutation at every level of medical experience, one that affects not only medical knowledge but also "the very possibility of a discourse about disease" (BC xix/xv). Yet nowhere does Foucault mention neurology and its specific, even literal, history of "localization." And though he will argue against Bergson's privileging of time over space in the constitution of the differentiated form of the individual—"Bergson is strictly in

error when he seeks in time and against space . . . the conditions with which it is possible to conceive of the living individuality" (BC 170/175)—he overlooks the very thinker whose work might be said to exemplify a recognition of, and departure from, "the value of a rule of localization" (BC 140/142), namely, Freud. In fact, it is not until the very end of *The Birth of the Clinic* that Foucault even broaches the problem of disorders in which there is no apparent lesion, that is, no localized lesion (e.g., nervous disorders and fevers). But, again, just as he avoids the history of neurology as "localization," so too he avoids the psychoanalytic study of nervous disorders and instead turns to the question of fevers (BC 174ff./177ff.). In other words, Foucault skirts both the history of neurology as localization and the history of psychoanalysis as the confrontation with neurology's fundamental "spatialization" of pathology.

8. Catherine Malabou, *Ontology of the Accident: An Essay on Destructive Plasticity*, trans. Carolyn Shread (New York: Polity, 2012), 30; *Ontologie de l'accident: Essai sur la plasticité destructrice* (Paris: Léo Scheer, 2006), 34, hereafter abbreviated OA.

9. For another reading of hysteria as a form of resistance to the psychiatric "reality" of illness, see the final session of Foucault's *Psychiatric Power*. Michel Foucault, *Psychiatric Power: Lectures at the Collège de France, 1973–1974*, ed. Jacques Lagrange, trans. Graham Burchell (New York: Picador, 2006), 297–333; *Le pouvoir psychiatrique: Cours au Collège de France, 1973–1974* (Paris: Seuil/Gallimard, 2003), 299–337, hereafter abbreviated PP. Since the hysteric is someone whose symptoms defy the power-knowledge (*pouvoir-savoir*) of nineteenth-century psychiatry, one might expect psychoanalysis's attentiveness to the symptoms of hysteria (or its insistence on the traumatic sexual etiology of hysteria) to put it on the side of antipsychiatry. But the opposite is true. Though Foucault identifies Freud and the psychoanalytic movement with a form of depsychiatrization, depsychiatrization is not antipsychiatry: "These . . . forms of depsychiatrization . . . which retain and preserve power . . . are opposed by antipsychiatry" (PP 344/349). Instead, Foucault will associate psychoanalysis with a "reconstitution of a truth-producing medical power" (PP 343/349), and, in a move that is as interesting as it is symptomatic, he will associate psychoanalysis with eugenics: "Eugenics and psychoanalysis are the two great technologies that arose at the end of the nineteenth century to give psychiatry a hold on the world of instincts." See Michel Foucault, *Abnormal: Lectures at the Collège de France, 1974–1975*, ed. Valerio Marchetti and Antonella Salomoni, trans. Graham Burchell (New York: Picador, 1999), 133; *Les anormaux: Cours au Collège de France, 1974–1975* (Paris: Seuil/Gallimard, 1999), 124.

10. "On the Psychical Mechanism of Hysterical Phenomena: Preliminary Communication" was first published by Freud and Breuer in a Berlin

periodical, the *Neurologisches Zentralblatt*, in two installments (January 1 and 15, 1893), before being republished as the introduction to *Studies on Hysteria* in 1895.

11. See also "Some Points for a Comparative Study of Organic and Hysterical Motor Paralyses," where Freud redefines the "lesion" in hysterical paralysis as an abolition of associative networks in the wake of trauma: "The lesion in hysterical paralysis will therefore be an alteration of the *conception*, the *idea*, of the arm, for instance. . . . The lesion would therefore be *the abolition of the associative accessibility of the conception of the arm*. The arm behaves as though it did not exist for the play of associations" (SE 1:170/GW 1:52). For a fascinating account of the changing meaning of the word "lesion" in Freud, see Katja Guenther, "The Disappearing Lesion: Sigmund Freud, Sensory-Motor Physiology, and the Beginnings of Psychoanalysis," *Modern Intellectual History* 10, no. 3 (2013): 569–601, esp. 589–93.

12. See also Lacan, who reminds us in his seminar on the psychoses that "we always have to come back to the disturbances of memory [*troubles de remémoration*] to know what the departure for psychoanalysis was." Jacques Lacan, *The Seminar of Jacques Lacan, Book III: The Psychoses, 1955–1956*, trans. Russell Grigg (New York: Norton, 1993), 104; *Le séminaire, livre III: Les psychoses, 1955–1956*, ed. Jacques-Alain Miller (Paris: Éditions du Seuil, 1981), 119.

13. See, for example, "On the Psychical Mechanism of Hysterical Phenomena: A Lecture" (SE 3:27–39/N 183–95); "The Neuro-Psychoses of Defense" (SE 3:45–61/GW 1:59–74); "Heredity and the Aetiology of the Neuroses" (SE 3:143–56/GW 1:407–22), "The Aetiology of Hysteria" (SE 3:191–221/GW 1:425–59).

14. Although hysterical reminiscences may be both "unremembered" and "unforgettable," one must distinguish them from memories that are "unrememberable and unforgettable." In his famous 1969 article, Alvin Frank explores memories that are subject to a "passive primal repression." These memories are not directly recoverable because of the "immaturity of the mental apparatus at the time when the significant impressions occurred"; they are repressed as a result of a "developmental rather than a defensive vicissitude." We could certainly speculate that some hysterical memories are not only "unremembered" but also "unrememberable," but this is hardly Freud and Breuer's point in *Studies on Hysteria*. See Alvin Frank, "The Unrememberable and the Unforgettable: Passive Primal Repression," *The Psychoanalytic Study of the Child* 24 (1969): 48–77.

15. When it comes to the etiology of hysteria, Freud challenges not only Charcot's notion of an *agent provocateur* but also his theory of the *famille névropathique*: "The theory of the *'famille névropathique'* is certainly in urgent need of revision. . . . The conception of the *'famille névropathique'*—which,

incidentally, embraces almost everything we know in the form of nervous diseases, organic and functional, systematic and accidental—could scarcely stand up to serious criticism" (SE 1:142–43 / N 164). In fact, one might read Freud with Foucault here and say that Charcot's rhetoric of *la famille névropathique* is a way of giving body to hysteria at the very moment that hysteria can no longer be located in the anatomical body of an individual—"so one invents, one marks out [*découpe*] a sort of huge fantastical body of the family affected by a mass of illnesses" (PP 271/273, modified).

16. In his obituary notice for Charcot in 1893, Freud has already begun "qualifying" his admiration for Charcot. On the one hand, of course, there are those discoveries that have a "permanent place in the storehouse of science" (SE 20:13 / GW 14:38). By his efforts, Charcot was able to lift hysteria out of the "chaos of the neuroses" (SE 1:12 / N 41); he was able to differentiate hysteria from other conditions with similar appearance; he was able to provide hysterical illness with a unique symptomatology and thus establish it as a recognizable clinical reality. On the other hand, as Freud admits, the "exclusively nosographical approach adopted at the School of the Salpêtrière was not suitable for a purely psychological subject" (SE 3:22 / GW 1:34). By identifying, classifying, and describing the symptoms of hysteria (the nosographical approach), Charcot missed the most important and only indispensable etiological factor of hysteria, according to Freud, namely the "sexual noxae [*sexuelle Schädigung*]" (SE 1:142 / N 164).

17. Freud does not reduce hysteria to a preexisting disposition, but neither does he preclude disposition from the etiology of hysteria. See, for example, Freud's discussion of disposition in *Studies on Hysteria*: "It should be understood that I do not mean by this a hysteria which is independent of *any* pre-existing disposition. It is probable that no such hysteria exists. But we do not recognize a disposition of this sort in a subject until he has actually become a hysteric; for previously there was no evidence of its existence" (SE 2:122 / GW 1:180–81). Or see his discussion of heredity in "An Autobiographical Study": "When I laid stress on the hitherto neglected importance of the part played by the accidental impressions of early youth, I was told that psychoanalysis was denying constitutional and hereditary factors—a thing for which I had never dreamt of doing" (SE 20:58 / omitted in GW 14:85, 1948 ed.). Freud will often speak of the reciprocal action between innate dispositions (heredity) and accidental experiences: "The determining cause of all the forms taken by human mental life, is, indeed, to be sought in the reciprocal action between the innate dispositions and accidental experiences [*in der Wechselwirkung von mitgebrachten Dispositionen und akzidentellen Erlebnissen*]" (SE 23:183 / GW 17:110).

18. In a lecture delivered at a meeting of the Vienna Medical Club on January 11, 1893, just ten days after the publication of the first part of the

"Preliminary Communication," Freud will again speak of "the accident which occurs in traumatic hysteria" as a "determining factor [*veranlassendes Moment*]" (SE 3:31/N 187).

19. For anyone who has read the "Preliminary Communication" in English, this statement may seem a little strange. This is because Strachey translates "das akzidentelle Moment" as "external events": "external events determine the pathology of hysteria to an extent far greater than is known and recognized" (SE 2:4). Though not technically incorrect, this interpretation of *akzidendell* seems precisely to underscore the point Freud and Breuer are making here: The accident has been missed. Its importance has been minimized in the study of hysteria.

20. I am indebted here to Derrida's analysis of suffering at the beginning of Session 6 in *The Death Penalty, Volume II* (DP2 29–30/53–54). Jean Laplanche will also speak of psychical trauma as the formation of a "kind of *internal-external* instance [*une espèce d'*externe-interne]." Jean Laplanche, *Life and Death in Psychoanalysis*, trans. Jeffrey Mehlman (Baltimore, MD: Johns Hopkins University Press, 1976), 42; *Vie et mort en psychanalyse* (Paris: Flammarion, 1970), 75. See also his interview with Cathy Caruth, where he speaks of Freud's theory of seduction as the "complex play between the external and the internal," between "external and internal causality." Cathy Caruth, "Traumatic Temporality: An Interview with Jean Laplanche," in *Listening to Trauma: Conversations with Leaders in the Theory and Treatment of Catastrophic Experience* (Baltimore, MD: Johns Hopkins University Press, 2014), 26.

21. What we find, in other words, is that whereas neurology may help us think the structure of the accident (the structure according to which we are all traumatizable according to "cerebral laws" [OA 34]), psychoanalysis helps us distinguish between the structure of the accident and something like an accidental structure, between the accident to which we are all vulnerable (logically, neurologically) and the accident whose occurrence *does not occur for* everyone. That is, in the case of psychical trauma, *it will always be an accident whether or not any particular "accident" becomes traumatizing*. For more on the accident to the second degree, see Chapter 2.

22. Catherine Malabou also draws attention to Freud's move to the language of "infiltrate," but she comes to a very different conclusion. Instead of seeing the infiltrate as a further and more radical expression of the unlocatability of trauma and thus precisely as the impossibility of synthesis, Malabou reads infiltration as a sign that the traumatic event can and has been "integrated" into the history of the subject. For Malabou, the unlocatability of the infiltrate makes the traumatic event something that is "proper [*propre*]" to the subject. Catherine Malabou, *The New Wounded: From Neurosis to Brain Damage*, trans. Steven Miller (New York: Fordham University Press, 2012), 93;

Les nouveaux blessés: De Freud à la neurologie, penser les traumatismes contemporains (Paris: Bayard, 2007), 159–60. For a reading of the "infiltrate" as a form of pathogenic resistance ("infiltrating resistance"), see John Fletcher, *Freud and the Scene of Trauma* (New York: Fordham University Press, 2013), 54–55.

23. In all of the cases, the damage in question was caused by cerebrovascular accidents in the distribution of the right middle cerebral artery (CS 148).

24. Malabou makes similar claims in *The New Wounded*, 52–53; *Les nouveaux blessés*, 99–102.

25. See Kaplan-Solms and Solms: "[These episodes] represented breakthroughs of suppressed feelings about the deficits that he had previously denied" (CS 166); "repressed feelings broke through into consciousness, in the form of uncontrollable tearfulness" (CS 171); "the fact that . . . depressive affects break through in this way" (CS 171); "defenses . . . breaking down momentarily" (CS 172).

2. TRAUMATIC TEMPORALITIES: FREUD'S OTHER LEGACY

1. I am thinking in particular of Jean Laplanche. See, for example, Jean Laplanche, "The So-Called Death Drive: A Sexual Drive," in *Between Seduction and Inspiration: Man*, trans. Jeffrey Mehlman (New York: The Unconscious in Translation, 2015), 159–82; "La soi-disant pulsion de mort: une pulsion sexuelle," in *Entre séduction et inspiration: L'homme* (Paris: PUF, 1999), 189–218. For more on Laplanche, see Chapter 5.

2. Thus, by "structural," as should be clear, I do not mean that we are all traumatized or that we are all traumatizable ("Everyone is subject to structural trauma"), nor do I mean that "all history is trauma." See Dominick LaCapra, *Writing History, Writing Trauma* (Baltimore, MD: Johns Hopkins University Press, 2001), 79, 64, hereafter abbreviated WHWT. On the contrary, as we will see in this chapter, the structure in question is always bound up with the accident, i.e., with an actual, concrete, life-threatening or integrity-threatening event.

3. As it turns out, this phrase was first used in a real estate classified ad in the *Chicago Tribune* in 1926.

4. See "Some Points for a Comparative Study of Organic and Hysterical Motor Paralyses," where Freud speaks of the ambiguity of this expression: "We have several times heard from M. Charcot that [the lesion in hysterical paralysis] is a cortical lesion, but one that is purely dynamic or functional. This is a thesis whose negative aspect we can well understand: it is equivalent to asserting that no appreciable tissue changes will be found *post mortem*. But in its positive aspect its interpretation is far from being unequivocal. What, after all, is a dynamic lesion? I am quite sure that many who read M. Charcot's works believe that a dynamic lesion is indeed a lesion . . . such as an oedema,

an anaemia or an active hyperaemia. These, however, although they may not necessarily persist after death, are true organic lesions even if they are slight and transitory" (SE 1:168/GW 1:50).

5. See Oliver Sacks, "The Other Road: Freud as Neurologist," in *Freud: Conflict and Culture*, ed. Michael S. Roth (New York: Knopf, 1998), 227–28. See also Michel Foucault's discussion of Charcot and "the body of pathological-anatomical localization" in the final session of *Psychiatric Power*: "In one of his courses, in 1879, Charcot said that the constitution, progress, and, in his view, culmination of neurology, was the triumph of the 'spirit of localization.'" Michel Foucault, *Psychiatric Power: Lectures at the Collège de France, 1973–1974*, ed. Jacques Lagrange, trans. Graham Burchell (New York: Picador, 2006), 297; *Le pouvoir psychiatrique: Cours au Collège de France, 1973–1974* (Paris: Seuil/Gallimard, 2003), 299.

6. See also the contemporaneous "The Aetiology of Hysteria" (1896): "I therefore put forward the thesis that at the bottom of every case of hysteria there are *one or more occurrences of premature sexual experience*. . . . I believe that this is an important finding, the discovery of a *caput Nili* in neuropathology" (SE 3:203/GW 1:439).

7. In his "Five Lectures on Psychoanalysis" (1910 [1909]), Freud points to the connection between the seduction theory and the influence of Charcot: "When . . . Breuer and I published our 'Preliminary Communication' on the psychical mechanism of hysterical phenomena, we were completely under the spell [*im Banne*] of Charcot's researches. We regarded the pathogenic experiences of our patients as psychical traumas, and equated them with the somatic traumas whose influence on hysterical paralyses had been established by Charcot" (SE 11:21/GW 8:17).

8. In his famous letter of September 21, 1897, Freud tells Wilhelm Fliess that he no longer believes in his "*neurotica*." *The Complete Letters of Sigmund Freud to Wilhelm Fliess 1887–1904*, ed. and trans. Jeffrey Moussaieff (Cambridge, MA: The Belknap Press of Harvard University Press, 1985), 264.

9. Jean Laplanche, "Notes on Afterwardsness," in *Seduction, Translation, and the Drives*, trans. Martin Stanton (London: Institute of Contemporary Arts Editions, 1993), 212–23.

10. Jean Laplanche, *Life and Death in Psychoanalysis*, trans. Jeffrey Mehlman (Baltimore, MD: Johns Hopkins University Press, 1985), 41, modified; *Vie et mort en psychanalyse* (Paris: Flammarion, 1970), 73, hereafter abbreviated LDP.

11. Hence, one might say, in rather provocative terms, that a trauma only has a pathogenic effect when it becomes *autotraumatic* or *autotraumatizing*.

12. In other words, there was always an incubation period for Freud, and this incubation period was directly related to the biphasic nature of

human sexuality. I will give two other examples of Freud's insistence on this temporal delay, both of which date from the years before his abandonment of the seduction theory: "The development of hysterical disorders often calls for a sort of incubation, or rather for a period of latency, during which the provoking cause continues to operate in the unconscious" (SE 1:52–53/N 85 [1888]). Or again: "It is precisely because the subject is in his infancy that the precocious sexual excitation produces little or no effect at the time; but its *psychical trace* is preserved. Later, when at puberty the reactions of the sexual organs have developed to a level incommensurable with their infantile condition, it comes about in one way or another that this unconscious psychical trace is awakened. Thanks to the change due to puberty, the memory will display a power which was completely lacking from the event itself. *The memory will operate as though it were a contemporary event.* What happens is, as it were, a *posthumous action by a sexual trauma*" (SE 3:154/GW 1:419 [1896]). There is no trauma properly speaking before the (re)awakening of the psychical trace. And perhaps more fundamentally: It is not until the moment or scene repeats itself that one can speak of trauma as such. In other words, when the moment or scene returns, it returns as something that was not there in the first place.

13. See also Lacan who paraphrases these lines as follows: "Why on earth is there an exception in this particular case [*Pourquoi diable y a-t-il une exception dans ce cas-là*]?" Jacques Lacan, *The Seminar of Jacques Lacan, Book II: The Ego in Freud's Theory and in the Technique of Psychoanalysis, 1954–1955*, trans. Sylvana Tomaselli (New York: Norton, 1988), 62; *Le Séminaire de Jacques Lacan, Livre II: Le moi dans la théorie de Freud et dans la technique de la psychanalyse, 1954–1955*, ed. Jacques-Alain Miller (Paris: Seuil, 1978), 90.

14. Cathy Caruth, *Unclaimed Experience* (Baltimore, MD: Johns Hopkins University Press, 1996), 132n7, my emphasis, hereafter abbreviated UC.

15. I am paraphrasing Jacques Derrida's definition of the "event" here: "The event is what comes and, in coming, comes to surprise me, to surprise and to suspend comprehension: the event is first of all *that which* I do not first of all comprehend. Better, the event is first of all *that* I do not comprehend. It consists in *that*, *that* I do not comprehend: *that which* I do not comprehend and first of all *that* I do not comprehend, the fact that I do not comprehend: my incomprehension" ("AI" 90/139). Although I will do no more than mention it here, it is striking that Derrida moves from a language of "incomprehension" to a language of "temporality" or "temporalization" when he begins to speak of the "traumatic event" six pages later.

16. As we will see, however—and this is where LaCapra's insistence on the distinction between "structural trauma" (to which "everyone is subject" [WHWT 79]) and "historical trauma" (to which "not everyone is subject" [WHWT 78]) misses what is crucial in *Beyond*—the structure of delay that determines a trauma is always the repetition, with a *traumatic* difference, of

an earlier, originating structure. Only in its repetition does this structure become "traumatic" properly speaking. Indeed, for Freud, as I am arguing here, there can be no *trauma* until this structure is repeated in a way that is both contingent and historical.

17. For empirical corroboration on this point, see "*Nachträglichkeit*: A Freudian Perspective on Delayed Traumatic Reactions," in which the authors review the data on the DSM Criterion A events (traumatic stressors): "Empirical research does not corroborate the idea that traumatic pathology is limited to a well-defined set of events . . . in a comprehensive review Ozer et al. (2003) concluded that less than 20% of the total variance in clinical outcome after experiencing a traumatic event can be explained by the combination of all hitherto-known predictors (particularities of both the event *and* the person). The other 80% is unaccounted for, which basically means that it is impossible to predict who will develop traumatic pathology after which event." Gregory Bistoen, Stijn Vanheule, and Stef Craps, "*Nachträglichkeit*: A Freudian Perspective on Delayed Traumatic Reactions," *Theory & Psychology* 24, no. 5 (2014): 670.

18. And here one might further distinguish between accidental structures. If death is an accident that is bound to occur, brain injury is an accident that may always fail to occur (see Chapter 1). We will all die, but we will not all suffer brain injury (although we all could). In this sense, psychical trauma is an accident of another order: neither a necessary accident (like death) nor a necessary possibility (like brain trauma, i.e., the destructive plasticity that belongs to the possible as existential structure). Psychical trauma gives us, as I have claimed, an accidentality to the second degree insofar as no given accident can be said to produce a trauma. Indeed, even for someone who, like Judith Herman, believes that "the most powerful determinant of psychological harm is the character of the traumatic event itself" and that "with severe enough traumatic exposure, no person is immune," there still remains an irreducible element of accidentality ("luck") in trauma and survival: "Though highly resilient people have the best chance of surviving [traumatic events] relatively unscathed, no personal attribute of the victim is sufficient in itself to offer reliable protection. The most important factor universally cited by survivors is good luck. Many are keenly aware that the traumatic events could have been far worse and that they might well have 'broken' if fate had not spared them." Judith Lewis Herman, *Trauma and Recovery: The Aftermath of Violence—from Domestic Abuse to Political Terror* (New York: Basic Books, 1997), 57, 59–60.

3. IS THERE SUCH A THING AS A PSYCHICAL ACCIDENT?

1. As Strachey indicates, Freud is quoting here from a postscript added to a letter to Wilhelm Fliess (letter of August 27, 1899). Statements

about Freud's belief in psychical determinism are frequent. See, for example, his claim in his "Five Lectures on Psychoanalysis" (1910 [1909]), where he says that "psychoanalysts are marked by a particularly strict belief in the determination of mental life. For them there is nothing trivial, nothing arbitrary or haphazard [*nichts Kleines, nichts Willkürliches und Zufälliges*]" (SE 11:38 / GW 8:38).

2. See, for example, his essay "Leonardo da Vinci and a Memory of his Childhood" (1910): "We are all too ready to forget that in fact everything to do with our life is chance [*Wir vergessen . . . gern, daß eigentlich alles an unserem Leben Zufall ist*], from our origin out of the meeting of spermatozoon and ovum onwards—chance [*Zufall*] which nevertheless has a share in the law and necessity of nature, and which merely lacks any connection with our wishes and illusions" (SE 11:137 / GW 8:210).

3. Jamieson Webster, "The Accidents of Psychoanalysis," *New York Times*, December 6, 2014, http://opinionator.blogs.nytimes.com/2014/12/06/the-accidents-of-psychoanalysis/.

4. For a reading of this downward movement, see "MC." As Derrida reminds us in this essay, this downward motion is also the case in German, i.e., outside of the Latin filiation of *cadere*: "But it is also the case, outside this linguistic family, of the *Zufall* or the *Zufälligkeit*, which in German means 'chance,' of *zufallen* (to fall due), of *zufällig*, the accidental, fortuitous, contingent occasional—and the word 'occasion' belongs to the same Latin descent. *Fall* is the case" ("MC" 348/357). "*Fall* is the case" not only because the German *Fall* means "case" but also because "case" (*casus*) means "fall," *a falling down*. In other words, all roads lead downward when it comes to accidents or chance, coincidence or contingency.

5. Catherine Malabou, *Ontology of the Accident: An Essay on Destructive Plasticity*, trans. Carolyn Shread (Cambridge, MA: Polity, 2012), 30; *Ontologie de l'accident: Essai sur la plasticité destructrice* (Paris: Léo Scheer, 2006), 33–34.

6. The example he gives is of missing a train "by mistake" in order to avoid going where one does not want to go.

7. For a discussion of this second medical blunder, which, it turns out, is Freud's own, see Chapter 4.

8. In both *The Psychopathology of Everyday Life* and the *Introductory Lectures*, the language of somnambulism is everywhere associated with dexterity, unerring aim, and above all "certainty."

9. See, for example, the end of Lecture 3 in the *Introductory Lectures*, where Freud tells us that "an act so often understands how to disguise itself as a passive experience" (SE 15:58 / GW 11:53).

10. Elsewhere Freud speaks of the "counter-current [*Gegenströmung*]" that is at work within us and whose force at the moment of execution might subtract from the force of our intention: "For we are only sure of complete

success if all our mental forces are united in striving towards the desired goal" (SE 6:259–60 / GW 4:288–89).

11. Once again, in other words, it is the voice of self-criticism that makes itself heard in the bungled action. As Freud demonstrates again and again, "a bungled action is quite specially suitable for use ... as a self-reproach: the present mistake seeks to re-present [*darstellen*] the mistake that has been committed elsewhere" (SE 6:166–67 / GW 4:184, modified).

12. Jacques Lacan, "Seminar on the 'Purloined Letter,'" in *Écrits*, trans. Bruce Fink, in collaboration with Héloïse Fink and Russell Grigg (New York: Norton, 2002), 21; "Le séminaire sur 'La lettre volée,'" in *Écrits* (Paris: Éditions du Seuil, 1966), 30.

13. Although I will do no more than mention it here (to do more would take us away from Freud and Freud's language), it would be interesting to think the Lacanian "real"—understood as that which resists symbolization—in relation to such an accident. For it may be, at least in the case of the carriage accident, that the "encounter with the real" is nothing if not an excess of symbolization. What would it mean, one might ask, for the "real" to be an *excess* of symbolization, a *jouissance* of symbolization to the point of overflowing? In short, what would it mean for the "real" to be an excess rather than a lack (*manque, ratage, béance, trou*)? Would it not mean that one had to rethink this excess in relation to earlier statements about full speech and contingency? See, for example, "The Function and Field of Speech and Language in Psychoanalysis," where Lacan says the following: "Let's be categorical: in psychoanalytic anamnesis, what is at stake is not reality, but truth, because the effect of full speech is to reorder past contingencies by conferring on them the sense of necessities to come, such as they are constituted by the scant freedom through which the subject makes them present" (*Écrits*, 213/256). Would it not mean that one had to rethink what, in 1973, Lacan called the "science of the real [*science ... du réel*]"? See Jacques Lacan, "L'étourdit," *Scilicet* 4 (Paris: Éditions du Seuil, 1973), 6. For more on the long and winding history of the "real" in Lacan, see François Roustang, *Lacan: De l'équivoque à l'impasse* (Paris: Éditions Payot & Rivages, 2009), 99–167; Tom Eyers, *Lacan and the Concept of the "Real"* (New York: Palgrave Macmillan, 2012). In another but not unrelated context, one also may wonder to what extent a linguistic accident goes further than Jung's notion of "meaningful coincidences [*Fälle von sinngemäßen Koinzidenzen*]" in representing "a special instance of randomness or chance" that is "*contingent* to causal determination." For Jung ends up appealing—in *his* "ontology of the accident"—to what are transcendental grounds: "The archetype *is* the introspectively recognizable form of *a priori* psychic orderedness [*die durch Introspektion erkennbare Form des* apriorischen *psychischen Angeordnetseins*]." In this way, Jung, like Catherine Malabou, ends up emphasizing both

the structure or "orderedness" of the accident and its necessary possibility. See C. G. Jung, *Synchronicity: An Acausal Connecting Principle*, trans. R. F. C. Hull (Princeton, NJ: Princeton University Press, 1973), ¶846, 24; ¶964–65, 99–100; *Synchronizität als ein Prinzip akausaler Zusammenhänge*, in *Die Dynamik des Unbewussten*, ed. Marianne Niehus-Jung, Lena Hurwitz-Eisner, Franz Riklin, Lilly Jung-Merker, and Elisabeth Rüf, *Gesammelte Werke*, 18 vols. (Zürich: Rascher Verlag, 1967), vol. 8, ¶846, 499; ¶954–55, 573–75.

4. WHAT ARE THE CHANCES? PSYCHOANALYSIS AND TELEPATHY: (FOREIGN BODIES II)

1. George Eliot, *Middlemarch*, ed. Bert G. Hornback (New York: Norton, 1977), 417.

2. George Eliot, *Daniel Deronda*, ed. Terence Cave (New York: Penguin, 1995), 19. I am indebted to Nicholas Royle for his discussion of these passages in Eliot as well as for all of his work on telepathy. See Nicholas Royle, *Telepathy and Literature: Essays on the Reading Mind* (Oxford: Blackwell, 1990); *After Derrida* (Manchester: Manchester University Press, 1995), 161–84; *The Uncanny* (Manchester: Manchester University Press, 2003), 256–76; "Telepathies" and "Ouijamiflip," in *Telepathies*, ed. Nicholas Royle, *Oxford Literary Review* 30, no. 2 (2008): v–x, 235–55.

3. Ernest Jones, *The Life and Work of Sigmund Freud*, 3 vols. (New York: Basic Books, 1957), 3, 375, hereafter abbreviated J3.

4. There are in fact two further allusions to Hamlet's familiar words in Freud's writings on telepathy. The first is to the posthumously published "Psychoanalysis and Telepathy" (1941 [1921]): "To this day psychoanalysis is regarded as savoring of mysticism, and its unconscious is looked upon as one of the things between heaven and earth which philosophy refuses to dream of" (SE 18:178 / GW 17:28). The second is to "Dreams and Occultism" (1933 [1932]): "Occultism asserts that there are in fact 'more things in heaven and earth than are dreamt of in our philosophy'" (SE 22:31 / GW 15:32). In other words, psychoanalysis aligns itself with occultism for better and for worse when it wants to think, perchance to dream, beyond philosophy (and science).

5. Although Freud specifically defines telepathy as communication between people who are "distant in space" (SE 22:36 / GW 15:38), he is constantly moving between cases in which individuals are at a distance from one another (telepathy) to cases in which individuals are present to one another (thought transference). That is, he uses the terms "telepathy" and "thought transference" almost interchangeably. It is as though the simple fact of mental processes "leaping" (SE 17:234 / GW 12:246) from one person to another had done away with the very conception of space that would be needed to separate telepathy from thought transference. When listing "events described

as occult" in "Dreams and Occultism," for example, Freud will see no difference between them: "There is, for instance, the phenomenon of thought-transference, which is so close to telepathy and can indeed without much violence be regarded as the same thing" (SE 22:39/GW 15:42). Or he will bring them together quite literally and speak of "the hypothesis of a telepathic thought-transference [*die Annahme telepathischer Gedankenübertragung*]" (SE 6:262/GW 4:291). It is also worth noting that Freud's 1922 paper "Some Neurotic Mechanisms in Jealousy, Paranoia and Homosexuality" was written at the same time as his first paper on telepathy ("Psychoanalysis and Telepathy"). Indeed, as we learn from Ernest Jones, Freud read both papers to a small group of friends in the Harz mountains in September 1921 (J3 81). This would seem to indicate that Freud was rethinking the question of the communication between unconsciouses more generally. People who are paranoid, he tells us in this paper, do not simply project onto others something that they do not wish to recognize in themselves. "Certainly they do this; but they do not project it into the blue [*ins Blaue*], so to speak, where there is nothing of the sort already" (SE 18:226/GW 13:199). That is, people who are paranoid do not just project randomly; they have an unconscious knowledge of the unconscious minds of others. For an excellent description of this unconscious knowledge, see Alan Bass, *Fetishism, Psychoanalysis, and Philosophy: The Iridescent Thing* (New York: Routledge, 2018), 123.

6. For a discussion of the systematic character assassination of Ferenczi that began with Ernest Jones's biography of Freud, see Pamela Thurschwell, *Literature, Technology, and Magical Thinking* (Cambridge: Cambridge University Press, 2001), 115–50.

7. This lecture, which happens to be the thirtieth of his *New Introductory Lectures*, is, like all of Freud's lectures on telepathy, a "fake lecture," as Jacques Derrida reminds us ("Tel" 241/251–52). Of course, all of Freud's *New Introductory Lectures* are also "fake lectures" (Derrida will refer to them as "the *New Introductory* fake *Lectures*" ["Tel" 254/264]). As Freud says in his preface, the lecture form was adopted as a mere "artifice of the imagination" (SE 22:5/GW 15:3). Perhaps, then, one could say that the "Dreams and Occultism" lecture is doubly fake or remarkably fake, i.e., fake to the second degree.

8. To understand the complicated editorial history of this essay, see Strachey's Editor's Note to "Some Additional Notes on Dream-Interpretation as a Whole" (SE 19:125–26) as well as Jones's biography (J3 394).

9. In his "Geopsychoanalysis 'and the rest of the world,'" Derrida describes psychoanalysis as a kind of state or "superstate [*super-État*]" ("Geo" 321/330) administering its relations with the rest of the world.

Notes to pages 50–53

10. See the conclusion of Jacques Derrida's "Telepathy" essay: "So psychoanalysis . . . resembles an adventure of modern rationality set on swallowing *and* simultaneously rejecting the foreign body named Telepathy, assimilating it and vomiting it up without being able to make up its mind to do one or the other" ("Tel" 261/270). Though Derrida does not mention Freud's remarkable response to Jones in this context, I would like to read Freud's response to Jones as a first attempt to contain this split by splitting his body from the body of psychoanalysis. Seven years later, in "Dreams and Occultism," what is alien to, or outside of, psychoanalysis will become the "foreign body" (*Fremdkörper*) *of* psychoanalysis.

11. References to the German are to Sigmund Freud, *Briefwechsel Sigmund Freud Ernest Jones 1908–1939* (Frankfurt am Main: Fischer, 1993), 43. For more on this odd triptych of telepathy, smoking, and Judaism, "each part perhaps disreputable," see Stephen Frosh, *Hauntings: Psychoanalysis and Ghostly Transmissions* (Houndmills: Palgrave Macmillan, 2013), 92–116, esp. 95–98.

12. See, for example, "Dreams and Telepathy" (SE 18:197–220/GW 13:165–91), which was published in 1922, or "The Occult Significance of Dreams" (SE 19:135–38/GW 1:569–73), which was published in 1925.

13. Peter Gay, *Freud: A Life for Our Time* (London: Papermac, 1989), 443.

14. Derrida gives no reference for this quotation, but it appears to be his own translation of Freud's words to Eitingon about what "always perplexed him to distraction" (J3 391), namely the Bacon-Shakespeare controversy and occultism. In his biography, Jones footnotes the phrase Freud uses: *bringen mich immer aus der Fassung*.

15. Derrida of course stages his own "resistance" in his first footnote to the "Telepathy" essay.

16. These would include, besides Freud's chapter on "Determinism, Belief in Chance, and Superstition—Some Points of View" in *The Psychopathology of Everyday Life*, the following four essays: "Psychoanalysis and Telepathy" (1941 [1921]), "Dreams and Telepathy" (1922), "The Occult Significance of Dreams" (1925), and "Dreams and Occultism," i.e., Lecture XXX of the *New Introductory Lectures on Psychoanalysis* (1933 [1932]).

17. Maria Torok, "Afterword: What Is Occult in Occultism? Between Sigmund Freud and Sergei Pankeiev Wolf Man," in Nicolas Abraham and Maria Torok, *The Wolf Man's Magic Word: A Cryptonymy*, trans. Nicholas Rand (Minneapolis: University of Minnesota Press, 1986), 91, hereafter abbreviated "A."

18. Strachey tells us that the original manuscript was left without a title. Sarah Kofman will refer to it as a "decapitated text" but also as a text "sans tête ni queue [without head or tail]," given, as we will see, its missing third

case. See Sarah Kofman, *"Il n'y a que le premier pas qui coûte"* (Paris: Galilée, 1991), 65, my translation. It should also be noted that Freud's essay, having been amputated of its third and final case, (inevitably?) ends with amputation, i.e., with Freud's discussion of the decapitation of Saint-Denis (SE 18:193/GW 17:44).

19. And this would be just as true for Lacan as it was for Freud, according to Derrida: "This tradition has continued. For example, Lacan follows Freud to the letter on this point, when he says that a letter always arrives at its destination" ("MC" 369/377).

20. See also "MC" 368–69/376–77.

21. See also "MC" 365–66/373–75.

22. Jacques Lacan, "Tuché and Automaton," in *The Seminar of Jacques Lacan, Book XI: The Four Fundamental Concepts of Psychoanalysis*, ed. Jacques-Alain Miller, trans. Alan Sheridan (New York: Norton, 1998), 54; "Tuché et automaton," in *Le séminaire, livre XI: Les quatre concepts fondamentaux de la psychanalyse*, ed. Jacques-Alain Miller (Paris: Éditions du Seuil, 1973), 54.

23. See also "MC" 367–68/375–76. Derrida does not mention the second prequel.

24. And not only of communication between human individuals. Freud also speculates about the communication between insects: "If only one accustoms oneself to the idea of telepathy, one can accomplish a great deal with it—for the time being, it is true, only in imagination. It is a familiar fact that we do not know how the common purpose comes about in the great insect communities: possibly it is done by means of a direct psychical transference of this kind" (SE 22:55/GW 15:59).

25. For one of the most elaborate and original readings of the telephonic communications in Freud, see Avital Ronell, *The Telephone Book: Technology, Schizophrenia, Electric Speech* (Lincoln: University of Nebraska Press, 1989), esp. 84–94, 423–24n48, 449–50n140, hereafter abbreviated TB.

26. Or perhaps one could say, making use of Elissa Marder's neologism, that all analysis is "techno-analysis." See Elissa Marder, *The Mother in the Age of Mechanical Reproduction* (New York: Fordham University Press, 2012), 112.

27. For more on telepathy at the intersection of deconstruction and psychoanalysis, see Maud Ellman, "Deconstruction and Psychoanalysis," in *Deconstructions: A User's Guide*, ed. Nicholas Royle (New York: Palgrave, 2000), 211–37; John Forrester, *The Seductions of Psychoanalysis: Freud, Lacan, and Derrida* (Cambridge: Cambridge University Press, 1990), 243–59; J. H. Miller, *The Medium Is the Maker: Browning, Freud, Derrida, and the New Telepathic Ecotechnologies* (Sussex: Sussex Academic Press, 2009); Martin McQuillan, *Deconstruction after 9/11* (New York: Routledge, 2009), 47–64; Michael Naas, *Taking on the Tradition: Jacques Derrida and the Legacies of Deconstruction*

(Stanford, CA: Stanford University Press, 2003), 76–92; Marc Redfield, "The Fictions of Telepathy," *Surfaces* 2, no. 27 (1992): 4–20; Avital Ronell, *Dictations: On Haunted Writing* (Lincoln: University of Nebraska Press, 1986); David Wills, *Prosthesis* (Stanford, CA: Stanford University Press, 1995), 92–129; Sarah Wood, "Let's Start Again," *Diacritics* 29, no.1 (1999): 4–19.

28. For an exemplary instance of the unconscious telephoning itself to itself, see Avital Ronell's discussion of the "phony call" received by Jacques Derrida from Martin (Martine or martini) Heidegger in *The Post Card* (TB 82; "Env" 21n1/25–26n1). See also Samuel Weber, *Institution and Interpretation*, expanded ed. (Stanford, CA: Stanford University Press, 2001), 103–4.

29. Although Freud is far more focused on the miraculous quality of thought transference in his writings on telepathy, we must not forget its essential "uncanniness": "In other words, there is a doubling, dividing and interchanging of the self [*Ich-Verdopplung, Ich-Teilung, Ich-Vertauschung*]" (SE 17:234/GW 12:246).

30. François Roustang also points to this case as the only one in which Freud "personally implicates himself as analyst." See François Roustang, . . . *Elle ne le lâche plus* (Paris: Éditions Payot & Rivages, 2009), 91.

31. In her 1983 "Afterword to the English Edition" of *The Wolf Man's Magic Word*, Maria Torok argues that P. is none other than Sergei Pankeiev: "For reasons that will become clear, the patient seems to me none other than Sergei Pankeiev, called the Wolf Man in Freud's case study of 1918" ("A" 85). For a truly masterful reading of this "Afterword," see Elissa Marder, *The Mother in the Age of Mechanical Reproduction*, esp. 49–52.

32. François Roustang suggests that it is Freud—and not P.—who associates the nightmare with Jones. After all, Roustang contends, "this story of telepathy" would have been a "nightmare" for Jones—"and Freud knows it." Roustang, . . . *Elle ne le lâche plus*, 94.

33. In order to bolster her claim that Herr P. is indeed "Sergei Pankeiev Wolf Man" ("A" 86), Torok adds parenthetically that Galsworthy and Bennett were "both notoriously influenced by Russian literature, notably the writings of Turgenev" ("A" 87).

34. See Maria Torok, who suggests, in her own way, that "P. is a Forsyte" too—namely, "the hero of a saga . . . written by Freud and called by him *The History of an Infantile Neurosis*" ("A" 87).

35. To this list, Torok would certainly add both *Versicherung* and *prévoyance*. According to Torok, Mr. Pankeiev, alias M. P., was able to get employment in an insurance agency while undergoing his second analysis with Freud in Vienna (from September 1919 to Easter 1920): hence "*Versicherung*, insurance; cf. foresight, *Vorsicht*" ("A" 88). In her very next paragraph, she also adds a reference to Rousseau: "This man—who in his memoirs quotes

Rousseau: 'La prévoyance, la prévoyance, voilà la source de toutes mes souffrances' ('Foresight, foresight is the source of all my suffering')—how could he be anybody else but Mr. P., the third man whose case was forgotten at the Gastein meeting in 1921? Definitely, Mr. P. is Pankeiev Wolf Man, a foresightful insurance agent" ("A" 88).

36. In his "Telepathy" essay, Derrida leafs through *The Forsyte Saga* but comes up empty-handed: "At the start of the 'modern comedy' there's a magnificent 'Forsyte family tree' spread out over five pages. But I reread the *Forsyth-Forsyte-von Vorsicht-foresight-Freund-Freud* story in the *New Introductory Lectures*, I read it and reread it in three languages but without results, I mean without picking up, behind the obvious, any scent I can follow [*quelque chose que je flaire*]" ("Tel" 233/244). And yet, as always, Derrida is on the scent . . . of scent, as it turns out. For, on the very first pages of The *Forsyte Saga*, there is "the sniff": "The Forsytes were resentful of something . . . this resentment expressed itself in an added perfection of raiment, an exuberance of family cordiality, an exaggeration of family importance, and—the sniff. Danger . . . was what the Forsytes scented; the premonition of danger put a burnish on their armor." John Galsworthy, *The Forsyte Saga* (Oxford: Oxford University Press, 1995), 16, hereafter abbreviated FS.

37. For more on Freud's use of the term "foreign body" in *Studies on Hysteria*, see Chapter 1.

38. George Eliot, *Romola* (London: Penguin, 1996), 407.

5. THE SPECULATIVE TURN:
PLATO'S PLACE IN THE THEORY OF THE DRIVES

1. http://www.sipp-ispp.org/index.php?language=_L4&menu_id=185#/185.

2. After my paper was delivered (I can only assume!), the English website was changed to match the French.

3. J. L. Austin, *How to Do Things with Words*, ed. J. O. Urmson and Marina Sbisà (Cambridge, MA: Harvard University Press, 1962), 22, hereafter abbreviated HTDT.

4. In the final session of *Psychiatric Power*, Michel Foucault points to this story of belated discovery (which Freud recounts in both "On the History of the Psychoanalytic Movement" and "An Autobiographical Study") in order precisely to indict Freud for not seeing and not speaking sooner. See Michel Foucault, *Psychiatric Power: Lectures at the Collège de France, 1973–1974*, ed. Jacques Lagrange, trans. Graham Burchell (New York: Picador, 2006), 321–22; *Le pouvoir psychiatrique: Cours au Collège de France, 1973–1974* (Paris: Seuil/Gallimard, 2003), 322–23.

5. See Freud's letter to Georg Groddeck in which Freud, while reproving Groddeck for his unrestrained ambition, also refers to his own "originality"

in this way. Sigmund Freud, *The Meaning of Illness: Selected Writings by Georg Groddeck Including His Correspondence with Sigmund Freud*, ed. Lore Schact, trans. Gertrud Mander (London: Karnac, 1988), 37, hereafter abbreviated GG. For the German letters, see *Sigmund Freud: Briefe 1873–1939* (Frankfurt am Main: Fischer, 1980), 333, hereafter abbreviated B.

6. In "Some Elementary Lessons in Psychoanalysis" (1940 [1938]), Freud makes it clear that psychoanalysis was not alone in proposing an alternative view of the "psychical," one that would include the unconscious: "[It need not] be supposed that this alternative view of the psychical is an innovation due to psychoanalysis. A German philosopher, Theodor Lipps, asserted with the greatest explicitness that the psychical is in itself unconscious and that the unconscious is the truly psychical" (SE 23:286/GW 17:147).

7. See, for example, "An Outline of Psychoanalysis" (1940 [1938]), where Freud says: "Yet more than a century before the emergence of psychoanalysis the French philosopher Diderot bore witness to the importance of the Oedipus complex by expressing the difference between the primitive and the civilized world in this sentence: 'Si le petit sauvage était abandonné à lui-même, qu'il conservât toute son imbécilité, et qu'il réunît au peu de raison de l'enfant au berceau la violence des passions de l'homme de trente ans, il tordrait le col à son père et coucherait avec sa mère'" (SE 23:192/GW 17:119).

8. See also a similar passage in "The Resistances to Psychoanalysis" (1925 [1924]), where Freud concedes that Schopenhauer may also have been the first to recognize the phenomenon of sublimation, i.e., the fact that sexual components diverted from their immediate aims can be directed to other things like cultural achievements: "These views were not entirely new. The incomparable significance of sexual life had been proclaimed by the philosopher Schopenhauer in an intensely impressive passage" (SE 19:218/GW 14:105).

9. The great irony here is that "Schopenhauer" is the name Freud uses to illustrate the difference between a superficial, intellectual knowledge and a real, affective knowledge: "The waiters who used to serve Schopenhauer at his regular restaurant 'knew' him in a certain sense, at a time when, apart from that, he was not known either in Frankfurt or outside it; but they did not 'know' him in the sense in which we speak today of 'knowing' Schopenhauer" (SE 10:196n1/GW 7:418n1). The irony, of course, is that Schopenhauer is someone whom Freud does not really "know": "The large extent to which psychoanalysis coincides with the philosophy of Schopenhauer . . . is not to be traced to my acquaintance with his teaching. I read Schopenhauer very late in my life" (SE 20:59–60/GW 14:86).

10. In fact, Freud will himself draw the comparison between his peculiar relation to philosophy and his peculiar relation to Breuer, Charcot, and Chrobak in a discussion on April 1, 1908, of the meeting of the Vienna Psychoanalytic Society, devoted to a discussion of the third section of Nietzsche's *The*

Genealogy of Morals: "Prof. FREUD stresses above all his peculiar [*eigentümliches*] relation to philosophy whose abstractions were so uncongenial to him that he finally decided to give up the study of philosophy. He also does not know Nietzsche; an occasional attempt to read him was stifled by an excess of interest. In spite of the much noted similarities, he could assure us that Nietzsche's thought had had absolutely no influence on his own work. To show how complex, and at times strange [*seltsam*], the origin of new ideas can be, he recounts, on this occasion, the development of his idea of the sexual etiology of the neuroses: three great physicians, Breuer, Charcot, and Chrobak, had expressed this idea in his presence. Yet he recalled this fact only later when, faced with the [general] repudiation of this idea, he attempted to justify himself. Apart from infantilism, the mechanism of displacement is *not* recognized by Nietzsche." *Minutes of the Vienna Psychoanalytic Society*, vol. 1: *1906–1908*, ed. Herman Nunberg and Ernst Federn, trans. M. Nunberg (New York: International Universities Press, 1962), 359–60, modified; *Protokolle der Wiener Psychoanalytischen Vereinigen*, vol. 1 (Frankfurt am Main: Fischer, 1976), 338. Samuel Weber also draws attention to these minutes in the context of Freud's denial of Nietzsche (and of philosophy) and his extraordinary "kettle logic": "'No, I haven't read Nietzsche—he is too interesting. No, he hasn't influenced my work and I know nothing of his. Moreover, he has completely failed to recognize the mechanism of displacement.'" Samuel Weber, *Institution and Interpretation*, expanded ed. (Stanford, CA: Stanford University Press, 2001), 110.

11. Cited in Paul Roazen, *Freud: Political and Social Thought* (New Brunswick, NJ: Transaction, 1999), 3–4.

12. See "On the History of the Psychoanalytic Movement," where Freud makes the facts of transference and resistance the sine qua non of what goes by the name of "psychoanalysis": "Any line of investigation which recognizes these two facts and takes them as the starting-point of its work has a right to call itself psychoanalysis, even though it arrives at results other than my own" (SE 14:16/GW 10:54).

13. Freud's very first use of the word "speculation" at the end of "The Aetiology of Hysteria" (1896) already makes this point: "Whatever you may think about the conclusions I have come to, I must ask you not to regard them as the fruit of idle speculation [*die Frucht wohlfeiler Spekulation*]. They are based on a laborious [*mühseliger*] individual examination of patients which has in most cases taken up a hundred or more hours of work" (SE 3:200/GW 1:458).

14. This conception of psychoanalysis as painstaking or laborious may also help explain why Freud was so extraordinarily sensitive about the unacknowledged appropriation of his ideas and concepts by his followers. Although Otto Rank may have once jokingly remarked that "Freud distributed references

to other analysts' writings on the same principle as the Emperor distributed decorations, according to the mood and fancy of the moment" (J2 412), Freud shows a scrupulousness—even a scrupulosity—in citing the whole scientific literature in his neurological works and in early texts such as *The Interpretation of Dreams*. Thus, having done his best to recognize and acknowledge his own "cryptomnesia," he expects others to do the same. And when they do not, there are consequences. See, for example, Paul Roazen, *Brother Animal: The Story of Freud and Tausk* (New York: Knopf, 1969), 59–93. Of course, any discussion of plagiarism or cryptomnesia must lead us back to the question of debt and to the astonishing ease with which Freud refuses to assume his debt to Nietzsche and to philosophy in general. For a discussion of this debt, see Derrida, "SoF" 262–73/280–91; and Samuel Weber, *Institution and Interpretation*, 105–8.

15. Translating *mühsam* as *pénible*, which in French means painful as well as painstaking, Derrida muses: "What is most painful and least bearable (brief sigh), is that that which has been paid for with so much pain (what is most painful), to wit, the laborious findings of psychoanalysis, is given to the philosopher without pain, gratuitously, graciously, as if by playing, for nothing. What is most painful is that the painful is not painful for others, thereby risking the loss of its value: counterfeit coins, in sum, produced by this unworthy ancestor of psychoanalysis. As if it had cost him nothing" ("SoF" 263/281).

16. I have only included the examples of Groddeck and Adler, but one might also include that of Jung. For a discussion of Jung and the pleasures of speculation, see Sarah Kofman, "'It's Only the First Step That Counts,'" trans. Sarah Wykes, in *Speculations after Freud: Psychoanalysis, Philosophy, and Culture*, ed. Sonu Shamdasani and Michael Münchow (London: Routledge, 1994), 99–107; "*Il n'y a que le premier pas qui coûte*": *Freud et la spéculation* (Paris: Galilée, 1991), 15–39.

17. Sigmund Freud, *Sigmund Freud and Lou Andreas-Salomé: Letters*, ed. Ernst Pfeiffer, trans. William and Elaine Robson-Scott (New York: Norton, 1985), 61; *Sigmund Freud Lou Andreas-Salomé Briefwechsel*, ed. Ernst Pfeiffer (Frankfurt am Main: Fischer, 1980), 68, hereafter abbreviated LAS.

18. See Freud's letter of July 13, 1917, to Lou Andreas-Salomé, where he refers to Jung and Adler as "system-builders [*Systembauern*]" (LAS 61/68).

19. Or as he writes to Lou Andreas-Salomé on April 2, 1919: "The systematic working through of material [*das systematische Bearbeiten eines Stoffes*] is not possible for me; the fragmentary nature of my experiences and the sporadic character of my insights do not permit it" (LAS 95/105).

20. It is hard not to be reminded here of Jacques Derrida's discussion of Giorgio Agamben in *The Beast and the Sovereign, Volume I*. Agamben, Derrida tells us, wants to be not just first but *twice first*: "the first to see and announce,

and the first to remind: he wants both to be the first to announce an unprecedented and new thing . . . and also to be the first to recall that in fact it's always been like that, from time immemorial. He is the first to tell us two things in one: it's just happened for the first time, you ain't seen nothing yet, but nor have you seen, I'm telling you for the first time, that it dates from year zero" (BS1 330/439).

21. And here we must look to Donald J. Trump, who presents us with what is perhaps the purest form of *phallic narcissism*. In boasting to Howard Stern about his daughter Ivanka's breasts, it is clear that her breasts are no longer her breasts: (1) they are no longer *hers*, and (2) they are no longer *breasts*. Rather her breasts are an extension of his phallic power. That is, his daughter's breasts are a supplement for his penis—a sign of his superior (that is to say, if we follow Adler here, of his inferior) endowment. See also Samuel Weber, who makes an explicit connection between narcissism and the system: "Thus, what Freud 'rejects,' here . . . is not simply a debt to philosophy as such . . . but rather a debt to a philosophy that masks its own constitutive indebtedness with narcissistic claims to construct systematic explanations or arguments." Samuel Weber, *Institution and Interpretation*, 122.

22. Jacques Lacan, "Tuché and Automaton," in *The Seminar of Jacques Lacan, Book XI: The Four Fundamental Concepts of Psychoanalysis*, ed. Jacques-Alain Miller, trans. Alan Sheridan (New York: Norton, 1981), 53; "Tuché et automaton," in *Le séminaire, livre XI: Les quatre concepts fondamentaux de la psychanalyse*, ed. Jacques-Alain Miller (Paris: Seuil, 1973), 53.

23. In a letter to Lou Andreas-Salomé, dated May 25, 1916, Freud will speak of his eyes being "adapted . . . to the dark" and refer to himself as a "mole [*Maulwurf*]" (LAS 45/50). Of course, Nietzsche will also refer to himself as a "subterranean man" and a "mole" in his preface to *Daybreak*: "In this book you will discover a 'subterranean man' at work, one who tunnels and mines and undermines. You will see him—presupposing you have eyes capable of seeing this work in the depths." Friedrich Nietzsche, *Daybreak: Thoughts on the Prejudices of Morality*, ed. Maudemarie Clark and Brian Leiter, trans. R. J. Hollingdale (Cambridge: Cambridge University Press, 1997), 1. As Sarah Kofman notes in "'It's Only the First Step That Counts,'" Freud's "right to obscurity" (102/26) should here be contrasted with the lynx-eyed ideal of philosophical vision.

24. In his famous essay "Fear of Breakdown," D. W. Winnicott begins, in his poetic way, by channeling Freud: "Naturally, if what I say has truth to it, this will already have been dealt with by the world's poets, but the flashes of insight that come in poetry cannot absolve us from our painful task of getting step by step away from ignorance towards our goal." D. W. Winnicott, "Fear of Breakdown," in *In One's Bones: The Clinical Genius of Winnicott*, ed. Dodi Goldman (Northvale, NJ: Jason Aronson, 1993), 39.

25. See also Sarah Kofman's discussion of these letters in "'It's Only the First Step That Counts,'" 99–107/15–39.

26. Ernest Jones, *The Life and Work of Sigmund Freud*, 3 vols. (New York: Basic Books, 1957), 1:29, hereafter abbreviated J1. See also Freud's early letter of September 9, 1875, to Eduard Silberstein, where he says "I am more suspicious than ever of philosophy." Sigmund Freud, *The Letters of Sigmund Freud to Eduard Silberstein, 1871–1881*, ed. Walter Boehlich, trans. Arnold J. Pomerans (Cambridge, MA: The Belknap Press of Harvard University Press, 1990), 128; *Sigmund Freud Jugendbriefe an Eduard Silberstein 1871–1881*, ed. Walter Boehlich (Frankfurt am Main: Fischer, 1989), 145, hereafter abbreviated ES. Or his letter of January 30, 1917, to Werner Achelis: "The other deficiencies in my nature surely wounded me and made me modest, but it is otherwise with metaphysics; not only do I have no organ (no 'capacity') for it, but I also have no respect for it. Secretly—one mustn't say these things out loud—I think that one day metaphysics will be condemned as 'a nuisance,' as an abuse of thought, as a 'survival' [relic] from a period characterized by a religious Weltanschauung" (B 389, my translation: the words "nuisance" and "survival" are in English in Freud's text).

27. In an interesting essay, Patricia Herzog returns to Freud's repeated citation of the two-line fragment from Heine's poem "Die Heimkehr" and shows that even Freud's disparagement of the speculative philosopher/system builder—the one who "With his nightcap and the tatters of his dressing gown ... patches up the gaps in the structure of the world [*Stopft ... die Lücken des Weltenbaus*]"—must be juxtaposed with his own account of the own psychoanalytic enterprise, which is precisely "to stop up" or "fill in" the gaps in consciousness ("die Lücken in der bewussten Wahrnemung auszufüllen"; "die Lücken unserer Bewusstsein-phänomene auszufüllen"). See Patricia Herzog, "The Myth of Freud as Anti-Philosopher," in *Freud: Appraisals and Reappraisals, Contributions to Freud Studies*, ed. Paul E. Stepansky (Hillsdale, NJ: Analytic Press, 1988), 2:182–83.

28. This is why Freud will often associate "speculative systems" with paranoid delusions. Again and again Freud will point to an affinity between paranoia and philosophy's "artificially constructed systems" (SE 19:217/GW 14:104): "This may have some bearing on the characteristic tendency of paranoiacs to construct speculative systems" (SE 14:96/GW 10:164); "It might be maintained that a case of hysteria is a caricature of a work of art, that an obsessional neurosis is a caricature of a religion and that a paranoiac delusion is a caricature of a philosophical system" (SE 13:73/GW 9:91); "the delusions of paranoiacs have an unpalatable external similarity and internal kinship to the systems of our philosophers" (SE 17:261/GW 12:327).

29. See also the parallel passage in "To Speculate—on 'Freud'": "But let us not be too quick to interpret. If there is avoidance, if it [*ça*] is avoided with

so much insistence, it is because there is tendency, temptation, inclination. Freud acknowledges this" ("SoF" 289–90/272, modified).

30. See Peter Gay, *Freud: A Life for Our Time* (London: Papermae, 1976), 367. In his letter of March 15, 1875, to Eduard Silberstein, Freud reports that Brentano has just warned him against reading certain philosophers (Kant, Schelling, Fichte, and Hegel) because reading them may lead to madness: "'And so you want to let us off without reading them?' I asked [him]. More than that, I want to warn you against reading them; do not set out on these slippery paths of reason [*auf diese schlüpfrigen Wege des Verstandes*]—you might fare like doctors at insane asylums, who start out thinking people there are quite mad but later get used to it and not infrequently pick up a bit of dottiness themselves" (ES 101/117–18).

31. See Derrida's comments in both his 1975–1976 seminar *Life and Death* and in "To Speculate—on 'Freud'": "First, as regards the speculative: the speculative is not the philosophical. These are speculative *hypotheses* that are not formed a priori, neither in a pure a priori nor in a descriptive a priori. The origin of this speculation is not philosophical and, in the end, such speculation expects nothing from philosophy. . . . Speculation is thus foreign to philosophy or to metaphysics; it is not, for example, the speculative in Hegel" (LVLM 286); "The 'speculative assumptions,' therefore, would not be of a philosophical order. The speculative—here—is not the philosophical. The speculative assumptions are not formed *a priori*, neither in a formal nor a material *apriori*, whether they are inferred or offered for immediate description. Here speculation would have nothing to expect from philosophy. . . . Speculation, *this* speculation thus would be foreign to philosophy or metaphysics. . . . The speculation which is in question in this text cannot purely and simply refer to the speculative of the Hegelian type, at least in its dominant determination" ("SoF" 276–77/295–96).

32. In both his 1975–1976 seminar *Life and Death* and in "To Speculate—on 'Freud,'" Derrida will speak of the essentially nonpositional or nonthetic structure of *Beyond the Pleasure Principle*, "its *a-thetic* functioning" ("SoF" 279/261), its "fictional drift [*dérive*]" (LVLM 275).

33. In German, *Lösung* means both solution and dissolution (one speaks, for example, of the dissolution of a bond: *Lösung einer Bindung*). In English there is also an archaic use of the word "solution," in which solution means dissolution: "the solution of the British supremacy in South Africa" (*OED*).

34. The theory of the drives had a difficult labor. As Freud writes in *Civilization and Its Discontents* (1930 [1929]): "Of all the slowly developed parts of analytic theory," the theory of the drives is "the one that has felt its way the most painfully forward [*am mühseligsten vorwärts*]" (SE 21:117/GW 14:476).

35. Summarizing the conclusions he reached in *Beyond*, Freud again refers to the "phenomena of life" in *Civilization and Its Discontents*: "As well as Eros there was a death drive. The phenomena of life [*die Phänomene des Lebens*] could be explained from the concurrent or mutually opposing action of these two drives" (SE 21:119/GW 14:478, modified).

36. See a very similar passage in "SoF" 377/402. For Lacan's discussion of *Beyond* in terms of this back-and-forth movement, see Jacques Lacan, *The Seminar of Jacques Lacan, Book II: The Ego in Freud's Theory and in the Technique of Psychoanalysis, 1954–1955*, trans. Sylvana Tomaselli (New York: Norton, 1988), 27–90; *Le séminaire de Jacques Lacan, Livre II: Le moi dans la théorie de Freud et dans la technique de la psychanalyse, 1954–1955*, ed. Jacques-Alain Miller (Paris: Seuil, 1978), 43–128, hereafter abbreviated S2.

37. In his "Pulling Strings Wins No Wisdom," David Farrell Krell refers to the "original" *fort/da* game of Freud's grandson Ernst as "serious play": "Ernst is the oldest of Freud's grandchildren. His game with the spool or bobbin, while pleasureful, is serious play—*ernst* in German means serious or earnest, as in the importance of being earnest." David Farrell Krell, "Pulling Strings Wins No Wisdom," *Mosaic* 44, no. 3 (2011): 29.

38. See also Derrida: "by playing so seriously (by speculating) at writing *Beyond*" ("SoF" 302/323).

39. For more on Freud's pleasure in thinking beyond the pleasure principle, see Appendix A.

40. In his chapter entitled "Freud et Platon," Paul-Laurent Assoun begins by situating Chapter 6 of *Beyond* "at the heart [*au cœur*]" of his speculative endeavor. Paul-Laurent Assoun, *Freud, la philosophie et les philosophes* (Paris: PUF, 1976), 187–94.

41. Indeed, Peter Gay describes Freud's relation to speculation as something that might best be called "speculation-envy," an envy that would apply both to writers and philosophers. See Peter Gay, *Freud: A Life for Our Time*, 317.

42. When we remember that the German neuropsychiatry of the 1880s from which Freud emerged and from which he separated himself (in particular when it came to the work of his teacher Theodor Meynert) was criticized "as being based on 'brain mythology' rather than on reliable anatomical insight," we might wonder about Freud's decision to reinscribe the language of "mythology" in his later works. To what extent, in other words, does the language of "mythology" already suggest a game of return and departure? For a discussion of the expression "brain mythology," see Katja Guenther, "Recasting Neuropsychiatry: Freud's 'Critical Introduction' and the Convergence of French and German Brain Science," *Psychoanalysis and History* 14, no. 2 (2012): 210n18.

43. I am of course referring to the game played by Freud's eighteen-month-old grandson in Chapter 2 of *Beyond*. This game consists in repeatedly throwing a wooden reel on a string over the edge of a curtained cot while uttering the sound "o-o-o-o" (*fort* ["gone"]) and then pulling the reel out of the cot again with a joyful "a-a-a-a" (*da* ["here"]). For more on this game, see Appendix A.

44. Of the fourteen or so references to Plato in Freud's work, eleven of them are to the *Symposium* either directly, i.e., specifically by name, or indirectly. But the earliest mention of the *Symposium* is no doubt the one we find in Freud's letter of August 28, 1883, to his then fiancée Martha Bernays: "I cannot stand anyone's company for long, least of all that of the family; I am really only half a person in the sense of the old Platonic fable which you are sure to know, and the moment I am not active my cut hurts me [*Ich kann's in keiner Gesellschaft mehr lange aushalten, am wenigsten in der Familie, ich bin ja nur ein halber Mensch im Sinne der alten platonischen Fabel, die Du gewiß kennst, und meine Schnittfläche schmerzt mich, sobald ich außer Beschäftigung bin*]." *Letters of Sigmund Freud, 1873–1939*, ed. Ernst L. Freud, trans. Tania Stern and James Stern (London: Hogarth, 1961), 63/B 55.

45. See also Sarah Kofman's discussion of Freud's misreading of Plato's "dictum" in *The Interpretation of Dreams*. Sarah Kofman, *Séductions: De Sartre à Héraclite* (Paris: Galilée, 1990), 61–86.

46. Jean Laplanche, *Life and Death in Psychoanalysis*, trans. Jeffrey Mehlman (Baltimore, MD: Johns Hopkins University Press), 27; *Vie et mort en psychanalyse* (Paris: Flammarion, 1970), 48, hereafter abbreviated LDP.

47. Many have argued that Freud exaggerates the resistance generated by his insistence on the primacy of sexuality and infantile sexuality. See, for example, Philippe Van Haute and Tomas Geyskens, *Confusion of Tongues* (New York: Other Press, 2004), xvi–xvii.

48. Jean Laplanche offers a very different reading of Freud's pansexualism, which he defends on the contrary: It is not that sexuality *is* everything but that there is sexuality *in* everything (LDP 26/47).

49. After 1920, Freud will not hesitate to flaunt his philosophical pedigree (especially when articles comparing him to Plato begin to appear, e.g., Nachmansohn's "Freuds Libidotheorie verglichen mit der Eroslehre Platos" [1915] or Pfister's "Plato als Vorläufer der Psychanalyse" [1921]). For other examples of Freud's identification with Plato, see *Group Psychology and the Analysis of the Ego* (1921): "[Psychoanalysis] has done nothing original in taking love in this 'wider' sense. In its origin, function, and relation to sexual love, the 'Eros' of the philosopher Plato coincides exactly with the love-force, the libido of psychoanalysis" (SE 18:91/GW 13:99); "The Resistances to Psychoanalysis" (1925 [1924]): "What psychoanalysis called sexuality . . .

had far more resemblance to the all-inclusive and all-preserving Eros of Plato's *Symposium*" (SE 19:218/GW 14:105); and "Why War?" (1933 [1932]): "According to our hypothesis human instincts are of only two kinds: those which seek to preserve and unite—which we call 'erotic,' exactly in the sense [*ganz im Sinne*] in which Plato uses the word 'Eros' in the *Symposium*, or 'sexual,' . . . —and those which seek to destroy and kill and which we group together as the aggressive or destructive instinct" (SE 22:209/GW 16:20).

50. There is only one earlier reference to Plato in Freud's work, and it is to Plato's *Republic*, in *The Interpretation of Dreams* (SE 5:620/GW 2/3:625). There are also two references to Plato that were added by Freud to the original text of *The Interpretation of Dreams* in 1914 and 1925 respectively: The first is a reference to *The Republic* (SE 4:67/GW 2/3:70), and the second is a reference to "Eros" (SE 4:160–61n1/GW 2/3:166–67n1). Thus the "poetic fable" at the beginning of the *Three Essays* is, chronologically speaking, the second reference to Plato in Freud's published work (I have not counted the one very generic reference to Eros that is not attributed to Plato and is made by Breuer in *Studies on Hysteria*).

51. Plato, *Symposium*, trans. Alexander Nehamas and Paul Woodruff (New York: Hackett, 1989), 189e–190a. All references will be to this edition unless otherwise noted.

52. In fact, Freud will use the very same trope of soldering in the Dora case (1905 [1901]) to describe the hysterical symptom. Like the soldering of the sexual object to the sexual drive in the case of sexuality, a psychical meaning is soldered to a somatic origin in the case of hysteria: "The hysterical symptom does not bring with it this meaning, but the meaning is lent to it, soldered to it, as it were [*Diesen Sinn bringt das hysterische Symptom nicht mit, er wird ihm verliehen, gleichsam mit ihm verlötet*]; and in every instance the meaning can be a different one, according to the nature of the suppressed thoughts which are struggling for expression" (SE 7:40–41/GW 5:200, modified). Just as the sexual object was neither simply innate nor simply acquired in the *Three Essays*, so too the hysterical symptom is neither simply somatic nor simply psychical. The hysterical symptom cannot be reduced to an alternative whose terms would be exclusive. Although I will do no more than mention it here, Derrida is also very fond of this figure and uses it often in his writing; for an example of this, see Chapter 7.

53. Plato, *Symposium*, trans. W. R. M. Lamb (London: Loeb, 1983), 143–45.

54. See the fascinating discussion of Imre Hermann and the dream of unity with the primal object in Philippe Van Haute and Tomas Geyskens, *From Death Instinct to Attachment Theory* (New York: Other Press, 2007), 97–132.

55. Samuel Weber offers an even more "imposing" reading of Hephaestus's silence in the *Symposium*: "But if Hephaistos thus ties up the loose ends of the story into a seemingly neat knot, the lovers, it should be observed, remain silent. And since they cannot say what it is they want, Hephaistos must do it for them. For he does not merely pose his question, he *imposes* the response, putting his answer into the mouths of the lovers just as Plato, according to Freud at least, put his story into the mouth of Aristophanes." Samuel Weber, *The Legend of Freud* (Stanford, CA: Stanford University Press 1982), 202.

56. David Wills, *Inanimation: Theories of Inorganic Life* (Minneapolis: University of Minnesota Press, 2016), 58.

57. Jean Laplanche, *The Temptation of Biology: Freud's Theories of Sexuality*, trans. Donald Nicholson-Smith (New York: The Unconscious in Translation, 2015); "Le fourvoiement biologisant de la sexualité chez Freud," in *Problématiques VII* (Paris: PUF, 2006), 11–126, hereafter abbreviated TB.

58. Jean Laplanche, "The *Three Essays* and the Theory of Seduction," in *Freud and the Sexual: Essays 2000–2006*, ed. John Fletcher, trans. John Fletcher, Jonathan House, and Nicholas Ray (New York: The Unconscious in Translation, 2011), 249; "Les *Trois essais* et la théorie de la séduction," in *Sexual: La sexualité élargie au sens freudien 2000–2006* (Paris: PUF, 2007), 241.

59. Jean Laplanche, "The So-Called Death Drive: A Sexual Drive," in *Between Seduction and Inspiration: Man*, trans. Jeffrey Mehlman (New York: The Unconscious in Translation, 2015), 160; "La soi-disant pulsion de mort: une pulsion sexuelle," in *Entre séduction et inspiration: L'homme* (Paris: PUF, 1999), 190, hereafter abbreviated "SDD."

60. The more Freud insists on the importance of the death drive, the more diagrams of planes, spirals, and dihedrals proliferate in the pages of Laplanche's books.

61. Unlike Laplanche, Deleuze considers *Beyond the Pleasure Principle* to be Freud's "masterpiece" precisely because of its philosophical—and ultimately transcendental—turn. In his *Présentation de Sacher-Masoch*, Deleuze claims that the death drive (or what he prefers to call the "death instinct [*instinct de mort*]"), in its aporetic conception and its groundlessness, is the sign of a "specifically philosophical reflection," the essence of which is to be "transcendental." Gilles Deleuze, "Coldness and Cruelty," in *Masochism*, trans. Jean McNeil (New York: Zone, 1989), 111–21; *Présentation de Sacher-Masoch: Le froid et le cruel* (Paris: Éditions de Minuit, 1967/2007), 96–105. For a discussion of the unconscious as a "transcendental" subject and the dissolution of the specificity of psychoanalytic thinking that results from such an equation, see Weber, *The Legend of Freud*, 159–74.

62. See Jean Laplanche, "Freud and Philosophy," in *Freud and the Sexual*, 272/262.

63. Indeed, one might contrast the seriousness with which Laplanche takes Freud's reading of Aristophanes's myth with Lacan's own discussion of Aristophanes's speech in his seminar on "Transference," where he develops the thesis that love is comic: "L'amour est un sentiment comique [love is a comical feeling]." Jacques Lacan, *The Seminar of Jacques Lacan, Book VIII: Transference, 1960–1961*, trans. Bruce Fink (New York: Polity, 2017), 33, 77–94; *Le séminaire de Jacques Lacan, Livre VIII: Le transfert, 1960–1961*, ed. Jacques-Alain Miller (Paris: Seuil, 2001), 46, 99–118.

64. Here I am greatly indebted to Cathy Caruth's reading of the life drive: "Freud thus reintroduces the language of departure not as the origin of the death drive, but as the way it repeats itself, differently, as the drive for life. . . . It is a language of departure, that is, that does not repeat the unconscious origin of life as death, but creates a history by precisely departing toward survival." Cathy Caruth, *Literature in the Ashes of History* (Baltimore, MD: Johns Hopkins University Press, 2013), 9.

65. See also Weber, *The Legend of Freud*, 200.

66. For a brilliant reading of this awakening into life from the "side" of the "inanimate," see David Wills: "What we call life begins as a rupture vis-à-vis itself, an interruption of inanimate by an animate that has somehow lain inert, or inanimate, within the inanimate" (*Inanimation*, 69).

6. FOR THE LOVE OF PSYCHOANALYSIS: DECONSTRUCTION AND PSYCHOANALYSIS

1. Geoffrey Bennington, "Circanalyse (la chose même)," in *Depuis Lacan*, ed. Patrick Guyomard and René Major (Paris: Aubier, 2000), 272.

2. See also Derrida's larger discussion of friendship in his *Politics of Friendship*. Indeed, Derrida will himself refer to this book in these pages: "Of course, it will not surprise you if I say that I implicitly load this word 'friendship' with all the worries, questions, affirmations, even mutations that are at work in my book *Politics of Friendship*" (FWT 168/272).

3. For a discussion of Derrida and love more generally, see Peggy Kamuf's "Deconstruction and Love," where she argues that a "loving movement" is the "indispensable key" to understanding what deconstruction does. Peggy Kamuf, *Book of Addresses* (Stanford, CA: Stanford University Press, 2005), 26. See also the transcription of Derrida's improvised responses in *The Ear of the Other*, where Derrida defines deconstruction in terms of love: "I tried to determine this concept ['deconstruction'] in my own manner, which I did by insisting on the fact that it was not a question of a negative operation. I don't feel that I'm in a position to *choose* between an operation that we'll call negative or nihilist, an operation that would set about furiously dismantling systems, and the other operation. I love very much everything I deconstruct

in my own manner; the texts I want to read from the deconstructive point of view are texts that I love, with that impulse of identification which is indispensable for reading. They are texts whose future, I think, will not be exhausted for a long time. . . . My relation to these texts is characterized by loving jealousy and not at all by nihilistic fury (one can't read anything in the latter condition)" (EO 87/118–19).

4. Of course, just a few pages later, Derrida will go on to say that the concepts of *Nachträglichkeit* and *Verspätung* are a little different: "The irreducibility of the 'effect of deferral [*du à-retardement*]'—such, no doubt, is Freud's discovery" ("FSW" 203/303). In other words, Freud, like Derrida, recognizes *differance* at the origin: "It is thus delay [*retard*] which is in the beginning" ("FSW" 203/302).

5. In his final presidential debate against the former Massachusetts governor Mitt Romney, Barack Obama responded to Romney's familiar attack about the Navy having fewer ships than under past presidents by saying: "Governor, we also have fewer horses and bayonets because the nature of our military has changed. We have these things called aircraft carriers where planes land on them. We have these ships that go underwater, nuclear submarines." Kathleen Hennessy, "With 'Horses and Bayonets,' Obama Casts Romney as Out of Touch," *Los Angeles Times*, October 22, 2012.

6. Paul de Man, "The Resistance to Theory," in *The Resistance to Theory* (Minneapolis: University of Minnesota Press, 1986), 11.

7. This gesture should be contrasted with Alain Badiou's attempt to erase Derrida's name from the title of René Major's talk at this very same conference. For a brief account of this ignominious act, see Benoît Peeters, *Derrida* (Paris: Flammarion, 2010), 503–9, as well as the "Appendix" to the conference proceedings published in *Lacan avec les philosophes* (Paris: Albin Michel, 1991), 423–52.

8. See in particular the long note to Lacan at the end of Derrida's interview with Jean-Louis Houdebine and Guy Scarpetta ("Pos" 107–113n44/112–119n33), where Derrida points to Lacan's "philosophical facileness [*facilités philosophiques*]" ("Pos" 108n44/114n33), his "art of evasion [*art de l'esquive*]" ("Pos" 110n44/115n33), or his "reinstallation of the 'signifier,' and of psychoanalysis in general, in a new metaphysics" ("Pos" 109n44/115n33).

9. See, for example, *The Post Card*: "A letter does *not always* arrive at its destination, and from the moment that this possibility belongs to its structure one can say that it never truly arrives, that when it does arrive its capacity not to arrive [*son pouvoir-ne-pas-arriver*] torments it with an internal drifting" ("FV" 489/517).

10. William Shakespeare, *The Tragedy of Hamlet, Prince of Denmark*, act 3, scene 4, 178, in *The Riverside Shakespeare*, ed. G. Blakemore Evans (Boston: Houghton Mifflin, 1974), 1169.

11. Derrida clearly speaks of the psychoanalytic revolution as a force (*puissance*) rather than a power (*pouvoir*): "This reaffirmation of reason can go against a certain state or a certain historical concept of reason, and this force [*puissance*] can provoke thought beyond even 'power [*pouvoir*]' and the 'drive for power' identified by Freud and therefore the drive for sovereignty" (FWT 172–73/280). On the difference between *puissance* and *pouvoir* as one of Hélène Cixous's gifts to Derrida, see Peggy Kamuf, *To Follow: The Wake of Jacques Derrida* (Edinburgh: Edinburgh University Press, 2010), 127.

12. To do so, we would have to begin with the 1905 version of the *Three Essays on the Theory of Sexuality*, where Freud says that "the impulses of cruelty arise from sources which are in fact independent of sexuality, but may become united with it at an early stage owing to an anastomosis [cross-connection] near their points of origin" (SE 7:193n1). We would also have to think cruelty with the *Bemächtigungstrieb* (drive for mastery, *pulsion d'emprise*) but without sadism: "The origin of infantile cruelty is sought in a drive for mastery whose original aim is not to make the other person suffer—rather, it simply fails to take the other person into account (this phase precedes pity as well as sadism). ... The drive for mastery is said to be independent of sexuality, even though it 'may become united with it at an early stage owing to an anastomosis near their points of origin.'" Jean Laplanche and J.-B. Pontalis, *The Language of Psychoanalysis*, trans. Donald Nicholson-Smith (New York: Norton, 1973), 217, modified.

13. One might say that Derrida has become a kind of analytic witness to psychoanalysis's failure to witness. For more on the demand to witness in analysis, see Claire Nouvet, "Nothing to Say: The Negative Phrase of Affect," *Paragraph* 40, no. 3 (2017): 294–309.

14. See also Session 8 of *The Death Penalty, Volume II*, where, in posing the question, "Who will have been the crueler of the two, Kant or Robespierre?" (DP2 186/251), Derrida returns both to "Psychoanalysis Searches the States of Its Soul" and to the obscurity of the word "cruelty": "If each [Kant and Robespierre] appears crueler than the other, then, the obscurity surrounding the question of knowing what cruelty is only increases. Indeed, the psychoanalytic recourse to these words, cruel, cruelty (a recourse about which I briefly commented elsewhere, in "Psychoanalysis Searches the States of Its Soul"), is perhaps not adequate to dispel the obscurity and draw a genuine concept of cruelty from the confusion of its everyday usage. In our present context, the fact remains that . . . one cruelty [can always be] more cruel than another which always means that when we think we are less cruel,

when we abstain from cruelty, we risk being even more cruel, etc." (DP2 204/274).

15. This beyond (the beyond of) *Beyond the Pleasure Principle* would also be a thinking of what "overflows power" ("SoF" 405/432). See the end of "To Speculate—on 'Freud,'" where Derrida points to what would be the *pas au-delà*, the step (not) beyond power and the drive for power: "We will not say . . . beyond the death drive—power [though he will say 'Beyond the pleasure principle—power']. . . . For it is equally the case that everything described under the heading of the death drive or the repetition compulsion, although proceeding from a drive for power, and borrowing all its descriptive traits from this drive, no less overflows power [*n'en déborde pas moins le pouvoir*]. This is simultaneously the reason and the failure [*la raison et l'échec*], the origin and the limit [*l'origine et la limite*] of power" ("SoF" 404/432).

16. See, for example, what Derrida says of Freud's attempt to reappropriate the aneconomy of death and destruction: "In truth, Freud works constantly to reintegrate this aneconomy, thus to take it into account, to bring reason to bear on it, in a calculable fashion, in an economy of the possible" ("PSS" 275/81).

17. As Derrida himself notes, this originary affirmation of beyond the beyond is associated with other figures in other texts (e.g., hospitality, the gift, forgiveness).

18. In the French edition of *États d'âme de la psychanalyse*, the subtitle "Adresse aux États Généraux de la Psychanalyse" appears on the front cover of the book (where it appears as the only subtitle). In the English edition, "Address to the [E]states General of Psychoanalysis" ("PSS" 238) appears in parentheses and in a smaller font following the title and subtitle of the essay.

19. I am speaking here of the text of "Psychoanalysis Searches the States of Its Soul"; the "Postscript" appears to have been written one week later, on July 16, 2000.

20. And he mentions at least two of them by name in his lecture: Élisabeth Roudinesco and René Major ("PSS" 263/57). It should also be noted, in this context, that Derrida's *Politics of Friendship* famously begins with a vocative to his "friends": "'O my friends, there is no friend [*O mes amis, il n'y a nul amy*]'" (PoF 1/17).

7. CRUELTY AND ITS VICISSITUDES

1. The nineteen states to have abolished or overturned the death penalty are the following: Alaska (1957), Connecticut (2012), Delaware (2016), Hawaii (1957), Illinois (2011), Iowa (1965), Maine (1887), Maryland (2013), Massachusetts (1984), Michigan (1846), Minnesota (1911), New Jersey (2007), New Mexico (2009), New York (2007), North Dakota (1973), Rhode Island

(1984), Vermont (1964), Washington (2018), West Virginia (1965), and Wisconsin (1853), and the District of Columbia (1981). http://www.deathpenalty info.org/states-and-without-death-penalty.

2. http://www.cbsnews.com/news/maryland-governor-signs-repeal-of -death-penalty/.

3. https://deathpenaltyinfo.org/recent-legislation-governors-signature -makes-connecticut-fifth-state-five-years-end-death-penalty.

4. https://deathpenaltyinfo.org/documents/FactSheet.pdf.

5. Immanuel Kant, *The Conflict of the Faculties*, in *Religion and Rational Theology*, ed. Paul Guyer and Allen W. Wood, trans. Mary J. Gregor and Robert Anchor, in *Cambridge Edition of the Works of Immanuel Kant* (Cambridge: Cambridge University Press, 1992–), 301; *Kants gesammelte Schriften*, ed. Königliche Preussische (later Deutsche) Akademie der Wissenschaften (Berlin and Leipzig: Walter de Gruyer, 1902), 7:84, hereafter abbreviated CoF for the English and Ak for the German, followed by volume and page number.

6. Peggy Kamuf, *To Follow: The Wake of Jacques Derrida* (Edinburgh: Edinburgh University Press, 2010), 193, hereafter abbreviated TF.

7. For more on this "strange and stupefying and shocking fact" (DP2 2/20), see Chapter 8.

8. In the margin of the typescript of the first session of *The Death Penalty, Volume I*, Derrida writes: "(No philosophy against the death penalty)" (DP1 17n25/43n2).

9. See Robert Badinter, *L'Exécution* (Paris: Grasset, 1973), 212, my translation.

10. The question of nonreproductive (and thus terrifying) female sexuality is bound up with the guillotine, whether in the form of the feminized noun "guillotine," which turns the guillotine into the (castrating) daughter of Dr. Guillotin, or in the nickname "la Veuve" (the Widow), whose voracious, postreproductive sexuality is clearly an issue for Hugo here.

11. Quoted in Daniel Arasse, *The Guillotine and the Terror*, trans. Christopher Miller (New York: Allen Lane/Penguin, 1989), 11.

12. Badinter, *L'Exécution*, 89, my translation.

13. "Before coming to the sign by which Hugo recognizes this imminent end" (DP1 202/280); "The sign by which Hugo recognizes this imminent end" (DP1 204/282).

14. *Cruor* is not *sanguis*, which designates both the blood circulating in bodies and that shed by wounding; only the blood that flows from a wound is *cruor*.

15. As we saw in Chapter 6, this "beyond" is a very difficult thing to think. It requires that we think not only the "transcendental predicate" of

power (*Bemächtigung*) that attaches to every drive as such (whether life or death) but also that which lies "beyond" it, namely, "the origin and the limit of power" ("FSW" 405/432). For—and Derrida will insist on this at the very end of "To Speculate—on 'Freud'"—although the death drive (or the repetition compulsion) proceeds from a *Bemächtigungstrieb*, although it proceeds from a drive for power and mastery and borrows all of its descriptive traits from this drive, "everything described under the heading of the death drive or the repetition compulsion . . . no less overflows power" ("FSW" 405/432). Once again, in other words, we must read this overflowing. For an excellent discussion of the *Bemächtigungstrieb* in Freud and Derrida, see David Farrell Krell, "Pulling Strings Wins No Wisdom," *Mosaic* 44, no. 3 (2011): esp. 33. For more on the question of cruelty in both Freud and Derrida, see Simon Morgan Wortham, "Survival of Cruelty," *Southern Journal of Philosophy* 51 (Spindel Supplement, 2013): 126–41; Robert Trumbull, "Derrida and the Death Penalty: The Question of Cruelty," *Philosophy Today* 59, no. 2 (2015), 317–36.

16. Peggy Kamuf, "Introduction: Event of Resistance," in *Without Alibi*, 27.

17. I am indebted to Elissa Marder for reminding me of this phantasy.

18. Victor Hugo, *Les Misérables* (Paris: Pléiade, 1956), 968, my translation.

8. THE "QUESTION" OF THE DEATH PENALTY

1. In the opening session of *The Death Penalty, Volume II*, Derrida muses on the homonymic locutions *cerf-volant* (kite) and *cerveau lent* (slow brain) in order to raise the question of the multiplicity of ages and aptitudes in each of us: "What is an age and at what age is a subject legally responsible? What is the age of the responsible legal subject? . . . This question is not only unsettled, exposed to the winds by the multiplicity of mental and social ages in each of us, but also <by> the more serious <existence> of the difference between the age of so-called mental, social consciousnesses, etc., and the age, if there is one, of the unconscious. Is there a history, a time, and an age of the unconscious?" (DP2 11/31–32). Just two years later, as if in response to Derrida's questions, the US Supreme Court ruled in *Atkins v. Virginia* (2002) that it was unconstitutional to execute "mentally retarded persons." https://www.law.cornell.edu/supct/html/00-8452.ZO.html.

2. Thus, when it comes to the death penalty, the choice is not between life and death but between "two modes and two times of an unavoidable and always imminent death" (DP2 6/25). What this means, as I show in Chapter 9, is that what we oppose when we oppose the death penalty is not death. It is the "calculating decision" (DP1 256/347).

3. See FWT 139–65 and "PMS" 13–38.

4. Pope Francis has issued the most forceful call yet to abolish the death penalty, one that goes beyond current church teaching. In a letter to the president of the International Commission against the Death Penalty on March 20, 2015, Francis declared the death penalty to be "inadmissible, no matter how serious the crime committed." See "Pope Francis: No Crime Ever Deserves the Death Penalty," Vatican Radio, March 20, 2015; "Pope Francis: The Death Penalty Is Inadmissible," Vatican Information Service, March 20, 2015, https://deathpenaltyinfo.org/node/6086.

5. "Pope Backs Initiatives to Abolish the Death Penalty," http://www.youtube.com/watch?v=Qg-S3mnNYEY.

6. http://www.priestsforlife.org/magisterium/bishops/04-07ratzingerommunion.htm. My emphasis.

7. Peggy Kamuf, *To Follow: The Wake of Jacques Derrida* (Edinburgh: Edinburgh University Press, 2010), 187–88. See the discussion of this passage in Chapter 7.

8. Sophocles, *Oedipus Tyrannus*, ed. and trans. Hugh Lloyd-Jones (Cambridge, MA: Loeb/Harvard University Press), ll. 806–9.

9. In *La peine de mort*, Jean Imbert tells us that the Inquisition borrowed the torture known as "la question" (*quaestio*) from Roman law. "La question" then became the technical term for torture in the pre-Revolutionary French judicial system. *La Question* is also the title of book by Henri Alleg, published in 1958, notorious for describing in great detail the methods of torture used by French paratroopers during the Algerian War (*La Question*, the book, was censored in France after selling sixty thousand copies in two weeks). See Jean Imbert, *La peine de mort* (Paris: PUF, 1989). See also Elisabeth Weber, who goes even further: "In French (just as in Latin) . . . torture is sometimes simply called *la question*, just as in German, *peinliche Frage* is synonymous with *Folter*." Elisabeth Weber, *Kill Boxes: Facing the Legacy of US-Sponsored Torture, Indefinite Detention, and Drone Warfare* (Brooklyn, NY: Punctum, 2017), esp. 49–75.

10. Kant, Heidegger, and Freud are the three figures whose thinking offers a kind of resistance to the thinking of the principle of reason as the principle of calculability. In Heidegger, Derrida will take up another accentuation, another understanding of the principle of reason that leads to the abyss of *Abgrund* and the historical future of *Dasein*; in Kant, the incomparable dignity of a rational being is a dignity that by definition defies comparison; in Freud, decapitation is a mere substitute for a unique, originary, irreplaceable thing, namely, castration.

11. For other references to psychoanalysis as a question of reason and the principle of reason, see "Let Us Not Forget—Psychoanalysis" and "For

the Love of Lacan." In his largely improvised introductory remarks to a talk by René Major ("La raison depuis l'inconscient: René Major"), Derrida says the following: "People are starting to behave as though [psychoanalysis] was nothing at all, as though nothing had happened, as though taking into account the event of psychoanalysis, a logic of the unconscious, of 'unconscious concepts,' even, were no longer *de rigueur*, no longer even had a place in something like the history of reason: as if one could calmly continue the good old discourse of the Enlightenment, return to Kant, call us back to the ethical or juridical or political responsibility of the subject by restoring the authority of consciousness, of the ego, of the reflexive cogito, of an 'I think' without pain or paradox; as if, in this moment of philosophical restoration that is in the air—for what is on the agenda, the agenda's moral agenda, is a sort of shameful, botched restoration—as if it were a matter of flattening the supposed demands of reason into a discourse that is purely communicative, informational, smooth; as though, finally, it were again legitimate to accuse of obscurity or irrationalism anyone who complicates things a little by wondering about the reason of reason, about the history of the principle of reason or about the event—perhaps a traumatic one—constituted by something like psychoanalysis in reason's relation to itself" ("LNF" 4). Similarly, in "For the Love of Lacan," Derrida tells his audience that it was never about opposing Lacan or showing Lacan to be wrong. Rather, he says, "The question lies elsewhere: it is the question of reason and of the principle of reason" ("LL" 63/81).

12. I would like to thank Cathy Caruth for this reference. See Cathy Caruth, "Orphaned Language: Traumatic Crossings in Literature and History," in *A Companion to Comparative Literature*, ed. Ali Behdad and Dominic Thomas (West Sussex: Blackwell, 2011), 239–53.

13. Charles Dickens, *David Copperfield* (New York: Norton, 1990), 179, hereafter abbreviated DC.

9. A NEW PRIMAL SCENE: DERRIDA AND THE SCENE OF EXECUTION

1. "Abolitionist and Retentionist Countries," Death Penalty Information Center, http://www.deathpenaltyinfo.org/abolitionist-and-retentionist-countries?scid=30&did=140. My numbers do not include the Cook Islands, Niue, or Taiwan, since these countries are not yet member states of the United Nations and do not have observer status.

2. The psychoanalytic definition of anal erotism would point the way to sadism here: "How should the link between sadism and anal erotism be understood? The suggestion is that sadism, being essentially bipolar (since its self-contradictory aim is to destroy the object but also, by mastering it, to preserve it) corresponds par excellence to the biphasic functioning of the anal

sphincter (evacuation/retention) and its control." See the entry for "Anal-Sadistic Stage (or Phase)," in Jean Laplanche and J.-B. Pontalis, *The Language of Psychoanalysis*, trans. Donald Nicholson-Smith (New York: Norton, 1973), 35–36.

3. "Abolitionist and Retentionist Countries," Death Penalty Information Center, http://www.deathpenaltyinfo.org/abolitionist-and-retentionist-countries?scid=30&did=140.

4. Alexis de Tocqueville, *Democracy in America* (New York: Penguin, 2003), 525, my emphasis.

5. The only other "retentionist country" in the Americas is Saint Kitts and Nevis.

6. See Ernest Jones, *The Life and Work of Sigmund Freud*, 3 vols. (New York: Basic Books, 1955), 2:60.

7. Norman Mailer, *The Presidential Papers* (New York: Bantam, 1964), 11, hereafter abbreviated PP.

8. "The Executioner's Song" had also been used as a title in two earlier works by Mailer: first as the title of a poem in *Cannibals and Christians* (1966) and then as a chapter heading in his documentary novel *The Fight* (1975).

9. In the end, Mailer's article was published not in *Esquire* but in *Dissent*, in the winter of 1960 (PP 305).

10. Norman Mailer, *The Executioner's Song* (New York: Grand Central, 2012), 1012, hereafter abbreviated ES.

11. Michel Foucault, *Discipline and Punish: The Birth of the Prison*, trans. Alan Sheridan (New York: Random House, 1977), 9; *Surveiller et punir: Naissance de la prison* (Paris: Gallimard, 1975), 14, hereafter abbreviated DP.

12. Michel Foucault, *The Punitive Society: Lectures at the Collège de France, 1972–1973*, ed. Bernard E. Harcourt, trans. Graham Burchell (New York: Palgrave Macmillan, 2015), 11; *La société punitive: Cours au Collège de France, 1972–1973*, ed. Bernard E. Harcourt (Paris: Seuil/Gallimard, 2013), 12.

13. It is interesting to note that the work of the Groupe d'information sur les prisons (GIP) to which Foucault alludes in *Discipline and Punish* (DP 30–31/35) had, as its working principle, to expose the material conditions of prison life to the public ("to make the invisible visible," as my colleague Kevin Thompson has put it). Though this work of revealing the deplorable conditions of detention (overcrowding, poor sanitation, lack of medical care, lack of privacy, etc.) certainly did make "visible" what was "hidden" and "invisible" to the public, the notions of visibility/publicity to which the GIP appealed were, importantly, literal: The public must (be made to) see with its own eyes the material conditions of the prisons. Indeed, this literality was its force. But it is precisely this literal notion of visibility that Derrida challenges here.

14. There is only one explicit reference to Foucault in *The Death Penalty, Volume I*. In *The Death Penalty, Volume II*, there are two. The first is in a parenthetical remark: "again the question of spectacle and visibility, of the voyeurism that we raised last year with and against Foucault, while also reading Hugo and Camus" (DP2 45/73). The second reference is the one I cite in my third example. In *The Death Penalty, Volume II*, there is also a short comment on bio-power and Kant. If, for Kant, as Derrida explains, to put to death a guilty citizen according to law and justice is "in no way . . . to dispose sovereignly of his body," then there is in Kant a logic that resists "everything that is today called—in an often confused way—bio-power" (DP2 42/69). Later, in his interview with Élisabeth Roudinesco, Derrida makes explicit reference to his critique of Foucault in *The Death Penalty* seminars (see FWT 12, 146, 159/28, 237, 256). He also makes an implicit reference to Foucault in the list of philosophers who have secondarized the death penalty: "Others believed, rightly or wrongly, that they saw in [the death penalty] a particular phenomenon or a mere exacerbation of the penal system, even of imprisonment in general" (FWT 146/238).

15. Frank Main, "Chicago Top Cop Says Police Body-Camera Project off to Solid Start," *Chicago Sun Times*, February 13, 2015, http://chicago.suntimes.com/news/chicago-top-cop-says-police-body-camera-pilot-program-off-to-solid-start/.

16. The first year of *The Death Penalty* seminar did not have its own title; it was simply the continuation of the years 1997–1998 and 1998–1999, both of which had as their subtitles "Perjury and Pardon." It was not until the second year of the seminar in 2000–2001 that the subtitle "The Death Penalty" appeared in the *EHESS Annual Report* ("Editorial Note," DP1 xiii/13–14).

17. DP 15/21. And to make matters worse, the same remains *fundamentally* true of torture. In fact, Foucault repeats the word "fond" in both cases: Just as "capital punishment remains fundamentally [*en son fond*] . . . a spectacle" so too "there remains . . . a trace of 'torture' [*un fond 'suppliciant'*] in the modern mechanisms of criminal justice" (DP 16/21). Both spectacle and torture will have continued; they still continue today.

18. Charles Baudelaire, "L'heautontimoroumenos," in *Œuvres complètes*, ed. Claude Pichois (Paris: Pléiade, 1975), 1:78–79; "Heautontimoroumenos," in *Flowers of Evil*, trans. Wallace Fowlie (New York: Bantam, 1964), 71.

19. Michel Foucault, "Right of Death and Power over Life," in *The History of Sexuality: Volume 1, An Introduction*, trans. Robert Hurley (New York: Random House, 1978), 140; "Droit de mort et pouvoir sur la vie," in *Histoire de la sexualité 1: La volonté de savoir* (Paris: Gallimard, 1976), 184, hereafter abbreviated HS.

20. In this context, one might read Foucault's turn away from death and the death penalty in *The History of Sexuality* as another example of this

"recognition." It is as if Foucault had pinpointed the very condition of impossibility of his theory and had then simply excluded it. Foucault will argue that the procedures of power must turn away from death in order to focus on the management of life: "How could power exercise its highest prerogatives by putting people to death, when its main role was to ensure, sustain, and multiply life, to put this life in order? For such a power, execution was at the same time a limit, a scandal, and a contradiction.... Now it is over life... that power establishes its dominion; death is power's limit, the moment that escapes it; death becomes the most secret aspect of existence, the most 'private'" (HS 138/181–82). In a sense, then, by drawing attention to the death penalty in *The Death Penalty* seminars, Derrida begins with Foucault's disavowal; that is, he begins with the limit case that Foucault has excluded from consideration and asks if the death penalty is not precisely the quasi-transcendental condition of sovereignty: included as excluded.

21. Harry Blackmun dissented from the US Supreme Court's decision denying review in a Texas death penalty case (*Callins v. Collins*) on February 22, 1994. See https://www.law.cornell.edu/supct/html/93-7054.ZA1.html.

22. For a wonderful discussion of literature and the "heart of the other," see Peggy Kamuf, "At the Heart of the Death Penalty," *Oxford Literary Review* 35, no. 2 (2013): 241–51.

23. One may think of Freud here and his description of the death drive in *Civilization and Its Discontents*: "Even where it emerges without any sexual purpose, in the blindest fury of destructiveness, we cannot fail to recognize that the satisfaction of the drive is accompanied by an extraordinarily high degree of narcissistic enjoyment, owing to its presenting the ego with a fulfillment of the latter's old wish for omnipotence" (SE 21:121 / GW 14:480, modified).

24. As both primal scene and phantasm, the scene in which I give myself death would be both a scene of origin and a scene of closure. In this it would differ interestingly from Freud's three primal phantasms, all of which are scenes of origin: the "primal scene," which is the scene of the origin of the subject; "castration," which is the scene of the origin of the distinction between the sexes; and "seduction," which is the scene of the origin of sexuality.

25. In other words, the phantasm of the end of finitude—and here, I would argue, Derrida is adding a new chapter to *Beyond the Pleasure Principle*—is the trace of "my life" attempting (but forever failing) to return to the moment before there was the other in me, that is to say, to the moment before life began.

26. Indeed, I would argue that the profound racialization of the death penalty in the United States is the most outrageous and visible expression of this literalizing violence.

27. The official time of death turned out to be 8:07 a.m.
28. http://mytikker.com.
29. Anne Hodgekiss and Victoria Woollaston, "How Long Have You Got Left to Live?" *Daily Mail*, October 1, 2014, http://www.dailymail.co.uk/health/article-2776230/How-long-YOU-got-left-live-New-Death-Watch-claims-calculate-life-expectancy-based-lifestyle-counts-death.html.

APPENDIX A. WHAT IS AT PLAY IN PLAY?
DERRIDA'S *FORT/DA* WITH FREUD'S *FORT/DA*

1. The Derrida Seminars Translation Project was formed in 2006 to start planning an English-language edition of the Seminars of Jacques Derrida. This edition, coedited by Geoffrey Bennington and Peggy Kamuf, began appearing in 2009. To date, the six founding members of DSTP—Geoffrey Bennington, Pascale-Anne Brault, Peggy Kamuf, Michael Naas, Elizabeth Rottenberg, and David Wills—have translated seven volumes of the Seminars of Jacques Derrida. See http://www.derridaseminars.org/.

2. The *Standard Edition* is now in the process of being revised—of being revised and expanded. Mark Solms, who is overseeing the *Revised Standard Edition* (RSE), has given some indication as to what these revisions will look like. See Mark Solms, "Notes on the Revised Standard Edition," *Psychoanalytic Review* 100 (2013): 201–10. Not only has Solms updated Strachey's editorial introductions and footnotes and explained new and/or controversial translations (e.g., the use of "drive" for *Trieb*), but he has also provided lengthy discussions of the history of the English translation of technical terms and specific words or phrases (e.g., "where id was there shall ego be [*wo Es war, soll Ich werden*]"). But perhaps most importantly he has added four volumes of neuroscientific writings to the now *Revised Standard Edition of the Complete Psychological Works of Sigmund Freud*. Thus, the new *Standard Edition*, if we can still call it this, will comprise twenty-four volumes (i.e., the *Revised Standard Edition of the Complete Psychological Works of Sigmund Freud*) plus four volumes (i.e., *The Complete Neuroscientific Works of Sigmund Freud*), which is not exactly the same thing as twenty-eight volumes. To integrate or not to integrate the neuroscientific work with the psychological work, this has been Solms's question and indeed the question par excellence of neuropsychoanalysis of which Solms is an outspoken proponent, as we saw in Chapter 1.

3. For more on the question of pleasure and play, including the play that takes us beyond the pleasure principle, see my "Intimate Relations: Psychoanalysis Deconstruction / La psychanalyse la déconstruction," *Derrida Today* 11, no. 2 (2018): 178–95.

4. D. W. Winnicott, *Playing and Reality* (New York: Routledge, 1989), 54.

APPENDIX B. DEVOURING FIGURES: LITTLE RED RIDING HOOD
AND THE FINAL SEMINARS OF JACQUES DERRIDA

1. For more on DSTP, see Appendix A.
2. IMEC is the state-supported archive that houses the papers of Jacques Derrida. See http://www.imec-archives.com/.
3. As David Farrell Krell reminds us, the two buccal activities of vociferation and devourment were already the subject of Derrida's (still unpublished) seminars of 1989 and 1990, "Eating the Other" and "Rhetoric of Cannibalism." See David Farrell Krell, *Derrida and Our Animal Others: Derrida's Final Seminar, "The Beast and the Sovereign"* (Bloomington: Indiana University Press, 2013), 13.
4. Charles Perrault, *Contes de ma mère Loye* (Paris: Claude Aveline, 1923), 31, my translation.
5. Jacob Grimm, *Kinder- und hausmärchen gesammelt durch die Brüder Grimm*, ed. Paul Neuburger, 2 vols. (Berlin: Bong, n.d.), 1:100, my translation.

INDEX

Abraham, Karl, 53
Abraham, Nicolas, 103, 215n17
accident, accidental, accidentality, 1, 3–5, 12, 16–17, 22, 25–26, 30–31, 33–34, 35–46, 52, 54–57, 59–60, 64, 66–67, 68, 81, 152, 167, 191, 205n15, 206nn18–19, 207n23, 210n18, 212–13n13; happy, 1, 3, 6; linguistic, 46, 64, 212n13; lucky, 41; necessary, 17, 26, 34, 37, 44, 210n18, 213n13; psychical, 35–46; structural, 22, 25–26, 33–34, 210n18; traumatic, 26, 33–34, 38, 46. See also *Unfall*
Achelis, Werner, 223n26
Adler, Alfred, 76–80, 82, 221nn16,18, 222n21
Agamben, Giorgio, 221n20
agent provocateur, 16, 18, 204n15. *See also* Charcot, Jean-Martin
alibi, 11, 104–7, 111–12, 114, 123, 131–32
Alleg, Henri, 235n9
America, American, 89, 120–22, 128, 138, 151–55, 158, 174, 181–83, 185, 237n5. *See also* United States
Andreas-Salomé, Lou, 221nn17–19, 222n23
après coup, 25, 72. See also *Nachträglichkeit*
Arasse, Daniel, 233n11
Aristophanes, 85–86, 89–97, 228n55, 229n63. *See also* Plato
Aristotle, 86
Assoun, Paul-Laurent, 225n40
Atkins v. Virginia, 121, 234n1
Augustine, 86
Austin, J. L., 218n3

Bacon, Francis, 192, 215n14
Badinter, Robert, 124, 126, 129, 233n9
Badiou, Alain, 130n7
Bass, Alan, 214n5
Baudelaire, Charles, 165, 238n18
belief, 48, 51, 55–57, 166, 211n1; occult, 48; scientific, 55; superstitious, 56, 59
Bemächtigungstrieb. *See* drive: drive for mastery
Benedict XVI (pope), 143–44. *See also* Cardinal Ratzinger
Bennington, Geoffrey, 182, 185, 190–91, 229n1, 240n1

Bergson, Henri, 202–3n7
Berkeley, George, 86
bête, bêtise, 190–91
biopower, biopolitics, 160, 238n14
Blackmun, Harry, 170, 239n21
Blanchot, Maurice, 94
Bloechl, Jeffrey, 68–70
blood, 123, 126–28, 130–31, 135–36, 141, 233n4
Bontems, Roger, 126
Brault, Pascale-Anne, 190, 240n1
Brentano, Franz, 86, 224n30
Breuer, Josef, 14–18, 71–72, 75, 203n10, 204n14, 206n19, 208n7, 219–20n10, 227n50
Buffet, Claude, 126, 129
bungled actions, 37, 39–44, 57–59, 212n11. See also *Vergreifen*

calculate, calculating, calculation, calculability, 5, 20, 65, 118, 133, 141, 145–48, 150, 163, 166, 168–73, 175, 232n16, 234n2, 235n10, 240n29. *See also* decision
Callins v. Callins, 170, 239n21
Camus, Albert, 124, 126, 238n14
Caruth, Cathy, 206n20, 209n14, 229n64, 236n12
chance, 1, 3–6, 35–46, 47–67, 72, 74, 132, 135, 159, 170, 179, 189, 196, 210n18, 211n2, 212n13; incalculable, 132, 170. See also *Zufall*
Charcot, Jean-Martin, 2–4, 12, 16–18, 26–27, 52, 71–72, 75, 81, 201n3, 204–5n15, 205n16, 207n4, 208nn5,7, 219–20n10
Christian, Christianity, 124, 126, 135, 143–44, 152
Chrobak, Rudolf, 71–72, 75
Cicero, Marcus Tullius, 86
Cixous, Hélène, 3–4, 201n4, 231n11
coincidence, 36–37, 48, 110, 116, 175, 183, 211n4, 212n13
Colting, Fredrik, 174–75
contingency, 1, 3–4, 6, 37, 55, 91, 179, 211n4, 212n13; demonic, 37; positive, 1, 6. *See also* chance
correlate, correlation, 10–13, 19, 23, 201–2n3

243

credulity, 47–48, 57, 111
Cronenberg, David, 24
cruelty, 5, 107, 110–19, 120–38, 140–42, 150, 156, 170, 231n12, 231–32n14, 234n15

Danton, Georges Jacques, 134
David-Ménard, Monique, 1, 201n1
death drive (*Todestrieb*). See drive: death drive
death penalty, 5, 113, 120–27, 129–30, 132–35, 137–38, 139–50, 151–53, 155–56, 158–62, 166–70, 172–73, 175–76, 183, 233nn1–4,8, 234n2, 235nn4–5, 236n1, 237n3, 238nn14,16, 238–39n20, 239nn22,26
decision, 5, 72, 83, 143, 169–72, 225n42, 234n2; calculating, 5, 170–72, 234n2, 239n21
deconstruction, 4, 101–19, 121, 123, 125, 132, 134, 142, 144, 148–49, 158, 166–74, 191, 198, 216n27, 229n3, 240n3; dream of, 166–74; and psychoanalysis, 4, 101–19, 134, 204n3; of the death penalty, 121, 123, 125, 132, 142
Defoe, Daniel, *Robinson Crusoe*, 194–96
delay, 29–30, 33–34, 73, 209n12, 230n4; structure of, 30, 33–34; temporal, 29–30, 209n12. See also *Nachträglichkeit*
Deleuze, Gilles, 2, 228n61
Democritus, 86
Derrida, Jacques, works by: "And Say the Animal Responded," 103; *Archive Fever*, 103; "Autoimmunity: Real and Symbolic Suicides," 116, 209n15; *The Beast and the Sovereign, Volume I*, 190–97, 221–22n20; *The Beast and the Sovereign, Volume II*, 182, 191, 194–97; *The Death Penalty, Volume I*, 114, 121, 123–31, 132–33, 136–38, 140–42, 150, 152, 155–62, 166–75, 223nn8,13, 234n2, 238n16; *The Death Penalty, Volume II*, 4–5, 111, 121–23, 130–31, 135–36, 138, 140–42, 144, 146–48, 152, 155–56, 162, 167–69, 183, 206n20, 231–32n14, 233n7, 234nn1–2, 238n14; "Du tout," 103; *The Ear of the Other*, 104, 229–30n3; "Envois," 3, 217n28; "Le facteur de la vérité," 103, 109, 230n9; "Fors: The Anglish Words of Nicolas Abraham and Maria Torok, 103; "For the Love of Lacan," 61, 103, 105, 107–13, 235–36n11; *For What Tomorrow . . . A Dialogue*, 11, 101–7, 111–12, 117, 119, 121–25, 127, 129–30, 132, 142–44, 148, 152, 156, 161–62, 166, 229n2, 231n11, 235n3, 238n14; "Freud and the Scene of Writing," 103–5, 158, 202n6, 230n4, 233–34n15; "Geopsychoanalysis 'and the rest of the world,'" 65, 103, 214n9; "Implications: Interview with Henri Ronse," 102, 112; "In Praise of Psychoanalysis," 101, 106; *Learning to Live Finally*, 6, 102, 149, 184; "Let Us Not Forget—Psychoanalysis,"

103, 235–36n11; *Life Death*, 82–85, 95, 180, 184–89, 224nn31–32; *Monolingualism of the Other*, 182; "Me—Psychoanalysis," 103; "My Chances/*Mes chances*," 52, 55, 57–58, 103, 211n4, 216nn19–21,23; "Peine de mort et souveraineté," 145, 235n3; *Politics of Friendship*, 108, 229n2, 232n20; *Positions*, 109; "Positions," 105, 230n8; *The Post Card*, 103, 110, 217n28, 230n9; "Psychoanalysis Searches the States of Its Soul," 11, 102–3, 107, 111–18, 123, 126, 130–32, 135, 142, 158, 166, 174–75, 231n14, 232nn16,19; *Resistances of Psychoanalysis*, 102; "Resistances," 102, 103; *Rogues*, 116; "Telepathy," 51, 66, 103, 214n7, 215n10, 218n36; "To Do Justice to Freud," 103; "To Speculate—on 'Freud,'" 75–76, 84–85, 103, 184–85, 187–89, 221n14, 223–24n29, 224n32, 225n36, 232n15, 234n15; "The University without Condition," 116–17; *Without Alibi*, 132
Descartes, René, 86
despectacularization, 155, 160–61, 163. See also Foucault, Michel
destinerrance, 109–11
determinism, 55, 67, 211n1; psychical, 55, 211n1
devourment, 193–98, 241n3
Dickens, Charles, 149, 236n13
Diderot, Denis, 86, 219n7
differant, differance, 4–5, 97, 106, 230n4
disseminal, dissemination, 147–48, 150
dream, 10, 15, 24–25, 30–31, 48, 54, 58–59, 80, 83, 85, 91, 132–35, 155, 165, 166–74, 213n4; of deconstruction, 166–74; traumatic, 15, 25, 30–31, 83
drive, 5–6, 12, 25–26, 28, 33, 40, 43–44, 55–56, 68–98, 81–87, 92–98, 115–17, 125, 129, 131, 141, 181, 184–85, 224–25n34, 225n35, 227n52, 228nn60–61, 229n64, 231n11–12, 232n15, 234n15, 239n23, 240n2; death drive (*Todestrieb*), 5–6, 25–26, 28, 33, 81–87, 92–98, 115–17, 129, 131, 184–85, 225n35, 228nn60–61, 229n64, 232n15, 234n15, 239n23; drive for mastery (*Bemächtigungstrieb*), 115, 231n12, 234n15; drive for power, 115–16, 132, 231n11, 232n15, 234n15; life drive (*Lebenstrieb*), 25, 92–98, 229n64, 234n15; sexual drive, 25, 89–94, 96, 125, 181, 227n52
DSTP (Derrida Seminars Translation Project), 179–80, 182, 190, 240n1, 241n1
Duchenne de Boulogne, Guillaume, 201n3

Einstein, Albert, 86
Eitingon, Max, 51, 53–54, 215n14
Eliot, George, 47–48, 67, 213nn1–2, 218n38
Ellman, Maud, 216n27
Emma (case of), 28–30
Empedocles, 86

Index

Eros, 84, 88–89, 91–98, 225n35, 226–27n49, 227n50. *See also* sexuality
Europe, European, 114, 124, 126, 134–35, 152, 154
event, 12–13, 15–18, 20, 22, 28, 30–34, 36–37, 40, 42–44, 52–53, 55–57, 63, 93, 103, 108, 113–14, 116–19, 122, 132, 153, 158, 175, 192, 206n19, 207n2, 209nn12,15, 210nn17–18, 213n5, 236n11; chance, 36–37, 43, 57; neurological, 22, 26; psychical, 52; traumatic, 13, 18, 26, 33, 209n15, 210nn17–18
execution, 121, 126–29, 133, 142, 149, 151–76; 239n20; scene of 151–76
Eyers, Tom, 212n13

famille névropathique, 16, 204–5n15
fantasy, 18, 92, 134, 180–82, 186. *See also* phantasy
Ferenczi, Sándor, 42, 49, 53, 214n6
Fichte, Johann Gottlieb, 86, 224n30
Fletcher, John, 207n22
Fliess, Wilhelm, 208n8, 210n1
foreign body (*Fremdkörper*), 5, 18–19, 21–22, 26, 66–67, 215n10, 218n37
Forrester, John, 202n5, 216n27
fort/da, 83, 86, 97, 179–89, 225n37
Foucault, Michel, 156, 159–67, 170, 202–3n7, 203n9, 205n15, 208n5, 218n4, 237nn11,12, 238nn14,17, 238n19, 238–39n20; *Abnormal*, 203n9; *The Birth of the Clinic*, 202–3n7; *Discipline and Punish*, 159–66, 237n11, 238n17; *The History of Sexuality: Volume 1*, 238n19, 238–39n20; *Psychiatric Power*, 203n9, 205n15, 208n5, 218n4; *The Punitive Society*, 159, 237n12
Francis (pope), 235n4
Frank, Alvin, 204n14
Freud, Anna, 51
Freud, Sigmund, works by: "The Aetiology of Hysteria," 16, 204n13, 208n6, 220n13; "Analysis of a Phobia in a Five-Year-Old Boy," 78; "Analysis Terminable and Interminable," 76, 86; "An Autobiographical Study," 14, 70–74, 76, 80–84, 205n16,17, 218n4, 219n9; *Beyond the Pleasure Principle*, 15, 25–27, 29–34, 70, 75, 82–87, 91–98, 115, 131, 184–89, 209n16, 228n61, 239n25; "Charcot," 12–13, 16–17, 52, 205n16, 224n32; *Civilization and Its Discontents*, 84, 165, 224–25n34, 225n35, 239n23; "The Claims of Psychoanalysis to Scientific Interest," 75; "A Difficulty in the Path of Psychoanalysis," 74, 76; "Dreams and Occultism," 47–54, 60–67, 213n4, 213–14n5, 214n7, 215nn10,16, 216n24; "Dreams and Telepathy," 215nn12,16; "The Dynamics of Transference," 158; *The Ego and the Id*, 82; "Five Lectures on Psychoanalysis," 78, 81, 208n7, 211n1; "Fragment of an Analysis of a Case of Hysteria," 227n52; "From the History of an Infantile Neurosis," 78; "Further Remarks on the Neuro-Psychoses of Defense," 17; *Group Psychology and the Analysis of the Ego*, 82, 226n49; "Heredity and the Aetiology of the Neuroses," 16–17, 27, 204n13, 209n12; "Humour," 135; "Hysteria," 209n12; *The Interpretation of Dreams*, 25, 54, 76, 133–34, 202n6, 221n14, 226n45, 227n50; *Introductory Lectures on Psychoanalysis*, 40–41, 43, 55–56, 75, 81, 211nn8,9; *Jokes and Their Relation to the Unconscious*, 71, 136; "Leonardo da Vinci and a Memory of his Childhood," 211n2; "Negation," 135; "The Neuro-Psychoses of Defense," 16, 204n13; *New Introductory Lectures on Psychoanalysis*, 74, 86, 214n7, 215n16; "Notes upon a Case of Obsessional Neurosis," 219n9; "The Occult Significance of Dreams," 49, 54, 215nn12,16; *On Aphasia*, 10–11, 202n5; "On the History of the Psychoanalytic Movement," 70–76, 79–82, 218n4, 220n12; "On Narcissism: An Introduction," 223n28; "On the Psychical Mechanism of Hysterical Phenomena: A Lecture," 18, 204n13; "An Outline of Psychoanalysis," 86, 98, 205n17, 219n7; "The Papers on Technique," 61; "Preface and Footnotes to the Translation of Charcot's *Tuesday Lectures*," 204–5n15, 205n16; "Preface to Reik's *Ritual: Psychoanalytic Studies*," 223n28; "Preliminary Communication," 14–15, 17–19, 25, 66–67, 203n10, 206nn18,19, 208n7; "Project for a Scientific Psychology," 28–29; "Psychoanalysis and Telepathy," 51, 53–54, 80, 213n4, 214n5, 215n16, 215–16n18; *The Psychopathology of Everyday Life*, 35, 37, 39–45, 52, 55–59, 76, 211n8, 211–12n10, 212n11, 214n5, 215n16; "Report on my Studies in Paris and Berlin," 205n16; "The Resistances to Psychoanalysis," 75, 219n8, 223n28, 226–27n49; "Some Additional Notes on Dream-Interpretation as a Whole," 54, 214n8; "Some Character-Types Met with in Psychoanalytic Work," 74; "Some Elementary Lessons in Psychoanalysis," 219n6; "Some Neurotic Mechanisms in Jealousy, Paranoia and Homosexuality," 214n5; "Some Points for a Comparative Study of Organic and Hysterical Motor Paralyses," 13–14, 21, 204n11, 207–8n4; *Studies on Hysteria*, 14–15, 17–19, 25–28, 44, 66–67, 68, 203n10, 204nn10,14, 205n17, 206nn18,19, 208n7, 218n37, 227n50; *Three Essays on the Theory of Sexuality*, 25, 84, 86–94, 227n52, 231n12; *Totem and Taboo*, 65, 223n28; "The Uncanny,'" 213n5, 217n29; "Why War?," 84, 86, 227n49

friend, friendship, 64, 72, 74, 88, 101–9, 111–15, 117–19, 176, 214n5
Frosh, Stephen, 215n11

Galsworthy, John, 63–65, 217n33, 218n36
game, 61, 85–86, 141, 146–48, 180, 185–89, 202n3, 225n37, 226n43; of *fort/da*, 86, 180, 185–89, 225nn37,42, 226n43; of telephone, 61; of the goose, 146
Gay, Peter, 215n13, 224n30, 225n41
Gazzaniga, Michael S., 202n4
Genet, Jean, 126
Geyskens, Thomas, 226n47, 227n54
Gilmore, Gary, 153, 174
Grimm, Jacob, 197–98, 241n5
Groddeck, Georg, 76–78, 82, 218–19n5, 221n16
Guenther, Katja, 204n11, 225n42
Guillotin, Joseph Ignace, 123, 128–29, 233n10
guillotine, 123, 126–30, 133–34, 137, 167, 170, 233n10. *See also* phantasy

Hamlet, 213n4
Hegel, G. W. F., 86, 95, 111, 124, 144–45, 224nn30–31
Heidegger, Martin, 3, 95, 105, 111, 142, 146–47, 217n28, 235n10
Heine, Heinrich, 223n27
Hephaestus, 91–92, 288n55
Heraclitus, 86
heredity, 16–17, 27, 38, 205n17. *See also* Charcot, Jean-Martin
Herder, Johann Gottfried, 86
Herman, Judith Lewis, 210n18
hermeneutic, hermeneutics, 38, 40, 52, 55–56, 141; hermeneutic circle, 141; hermeneutic drive, 40, 55–56
Herzog, Patricia, 203n27
Hippocrates, 201n3
Hobbes, Thomas, 86, 192
Hugo, Victor, 120, 122–24, 126–27, 129–30, 137–38, 144, 233nn10,13, 234n18, 238n14
hysteria, hysteric, hysterical, 2, 10, 12–18, 21, 24–29, 34, 71–73, 203n9, 204nn11,14, 204–5n15, 205nn16,17, 206nn18,19, 207n4, 208nn6,7, 209n12, 223n28, 227n52

Imbert, Jean, 235n9
IMEC (Institut Mémoires de l'Édition Contemporaine), 190, 241n2
incalculable, incalculability, 67, 116, 132, 170–72
infiltrate (*Infiltrat*), 19, 26, 29, 206–7n22
ISPP (International Society of Psychoanalysis and Philosophy), 68–70, 218n1

Jewish, 50, 123, 135–36
joke, 49, 72–73, 123, 135–36, 186; Jewish, 123, 135–36

Jones, Ernest, 47–54, 62–64, 81, 152, 213n3, 214nn5–6, 214n8, 215n10, 217n32, 223n26, 237n6
Judaism, 215n11
Jung, Carl Gustav, 76, 212–13n13, 221nn16,18

Kamuf, Peggy, 111, 124, 190, 229n3, 231n11, 233n6, 234n16, 235n7, 239n22, 240n1
Kant, Immanuel, 86, 122, 124, 144–45, 147, 224n30, 231n14, 233n5, 235n10, 236n11, 238n14
Kaplan-Solms, Karen, 9, 12–13, 19–21, 201n1, 207n25
kite, 140, 142, 149, 234n1
Kofman, Sarah, 215–16n18, 221n16, 222n23, 223n25, 226n45
Kojève, Alexandre, 111
Krell, David Farrell, 225n37, 234n15, 241n3

Lacan, Jacques, 46, 57, 80, 85, 104–5, 107–11, 204n12, 209n13, 212nn12–13, 216nn19,22, 222n22, 225n36, 229n63, 230n8, 236n11
LaCapra, Dominick, 207n2, 209n16
La Fontaine, Jean de, 192
Laplanche, Jean, 27–28, 88, 93–96, 206n20, 207n1, 208nn9–10, 226nn46,48, 228nn57–62, 229n63, 231n12, 237n2
laws, 13, 22, 38, 51, 206n21; cerebral, 13, 22, 38, 206n21
lesion, 13–14, 19–22, 26–27, 203n7, 204n11, 207–8n4
Levinas, Emmanuel, 142
libido, 24, 93, 226n49
life drive (*Lebenstrieb*). *See* drive: life drive
Lipps, Theodore, 219n6
literature, 4, 10, 62–67, 150, 190, 217n33, 239n22
Little Red Riding Hood, 190–98
localization, localizationalist, localizationism, 11–13, 21, 26–27, 202n6, 202–3n7
Lucretius (Titus Lucretius Carus), 86
Luther, Martin, 142

machine, 106, 126–29, 146, 163–64, 166, 169–71, 175–76
Mailer, Norman, 153–56, 174, 237n7
Maine de Biran (François-Pierre-Gontier de Biran), 86
Major, René, 230n7, 232n20
Malabou, Catherine, 13, 20, 203n8, 206n22, 207n24, 211n5, 212n13
Marder, Elissa, 216n26, 217n31, 234n17
mastery, 105, 111, 115, 148, 164, 166, 168, 171, 173–74, 231n12, 234n15. *See also* drive: drive for mastery
Maury, Alfred, 133–34
maw (*gueule*), 191, 193–98
McQuillan, Martin, 216n27

Index

memory, 14–16, 18–19, 28–29, 53, 122, 133, 204n12, 209n12; disturbance of, 14, 204n12
Miller, J. Hillis, 216n27
MMPI (Minnesota Multiphasic Personality Inventory), 1–2, 6, 201n2
Molière (Jean-Baptiste Poquelin), 88, 95
Montaigne, Michel de, 192
mythology, 86–87, 104, 225n42

Naas, Michael, 176, 190, 216–17n27, 240n1
Nachträglichkeit, nachträglich, 25, 27–30, 33, 72, 210n17, 230n4
Nancy, Jean-Luc, 1
narcissism, narcissistic, 68, 79, 184, 239n23; phallic narcissism, 80, 222n21. *See also* Trump, Donald J.; Trump, Ivanka
neologism, 181–82, 216n26
neurology, neurological, 10–14, 19, 21–22, 26–27, 38, 48, 104, 201–2n3, 202nn5,6, 202–3n7, 206n21, 208n5, 220–21n14
neuropsychiatry, 225n42
neuro-psychoanalysis, neuro-psychoanalytic, 10, 12–13, 19, 22, 201n1, 201–2n3, 240n2
neuroscience, neuroscientific, 9–23, 107, 201n2, 201–2n3, 240n2
Nietzsche, Friedrich, 74–76, 81–82, 86, 130, 219–20n10, 221n14, 222n23
Nouvet, Claire, 231n13

occult, occultism, 47–53, 63, 213n4, 213–14n5, 215n14. *See also* telepathy
Oedipus, Oedipal, 9–13, 58–59, 73, 150, 219n7; Oedipus complex, 58–59, 219n7
ontology, 38, 124, 212n13; of the accident, 38, 212n13
orality, 191–94

Pankeiev, Sergei, 62, 215n17, 217nn31,33, 217–18n35. *See also* Wolf Man
paranoia, paranoid, 2, 22, 214n5, 223n28
parapraxis (*Fehlleistung*), 35, 40–41, 43–44, 53–55, 58–59
Peeters, Benoît, 230n7
Perrault, Charles, 193, 197–98, 241n4
phantasm, phantasmatic, 78, 113, 132–35, 142, 155, 162, 165–66, 168, 171–74, 194–98, 239nn24–25; phantasm of devourment, 194–98; phantasm of the end of finitude, 172–73; phantasm of sovereignty, 113, 132; primal phantasm, 132, 239nn24–25
phantasy, 28, 59, 70, 86, 133–34, 153–55, 158, 165, 234n17; guillotine phantasy, 133–34; primal phantasy, 28; ready-made phantasy, 133, 155
Plato, 68, 85–98, 124, 144–45, 192, 226nn44–45, 226–227n49, 227nn50–51, 227n53, 228n55
Plautus (Titus Maccius Plautus), 192

pleasure, 24, 31, 79–80, 82, 85–86, 97, 129–30, 135, 183–86, 221n16, 225n3n7,39, 240n3. *See also* speculation
pleasure principle. *See* principle: pleasure principle
Plotinus, 87
Pompidou, Georges, 129
Pontalis, Jean-Bertrand, 231n12, 237n2
principle, 30–31, 65, 68–80, 83, 85, 93, 97, 115–16, 124, 132, 139, 144–46, 148, 150, 162–64, 165, 170–71, 180, 184, 232n15, 235n10, 235–36n11, 240n3; of calculability, 145, 150, 235n10; of compulsory visibility, 163–64; of the death penalty, 124, 144–45, 150; of indetermination, 132, 170–71; pleasure principle, 30–31, 68–80, 83, 85, 97, 115, 180, 184, 232n15, 240n3; possessive principle, 65; power principle, 162, 164; reality principle, 70, 115; of reason, 139, 145–46, 148, 150, 235n10, 235–36n11
psychosis, psychotic, 2, 10, 21, 204n12
puberty, 28–30, 33, 209n12. *See also* sexuality

Rabelais, François, 192
random, randomness, 40, 43, 45, 52, 55–56, 212n13, 214n5
Rank, Otto, 53, 74, 220–21n14
Ratzinger, Cardinal, 143, 235n6. *See also* Benedict XVI (pope)
Redfield, Marc, 217n27
reminiscences (*Reminiszenzen*), 14–17, 29, 204n14
repetition, 28, 30, 68, 73, 83, 116, 183, 184, 209–10n16, 232n15, 234n15; repetition compulsion, 28, 30, 83, 116, 184, 232n15, 234n15
repression, repressed, 4, 16, 20–22, 25, 29, 39, 41, 43, 56–57, 61, 74–76, 79, 81, 85, 87–88, 104, 153, 155, 181, 204n14, 207n25
resistance, 5, 12, 21, 42, 44, 51–55, 60, 65, 75, 88, 108, 111, 203n9, 207n22, 215n15, 220n12, 226n47, 235n10
revolution, revolutionary, 11, 52, 102–3, 107, 111–14, 131–32, 135, 147, 148, 231n11; French Revolution, 122
Roazen, Paul, 220n11, 220–21n14
Robinson Crusoe, 182, 194–96
Ronell, Avital, 216n25, 217nn27–28
Roper v. Simmons, 121
Roudinesco, Élisabeth, 101–2, 106, 110, 148, 161, 232n20, 238n14
Rousseau, Jean-Jacques, 87, 124, 144–45, 192, 217n35, 218n35
Roustang, François, 212n13, 217nn30,32
Royle, Nicholas, 213n2, 216n27
Russia, Russians, 66, 153, 217n33

Sachs, Hanns, 53
Sacks, Oliver, 20, 208n5
sadism, 113, 153, 155, 231n12, 236n2

Sartre, Jean-Paul, 111
scene, 11, 28, 31, 58, 63, 71, 132, 135, 137–38, 142, 151–76, 181, 184, 186–88, 209n12, 239n24; Oedipal, 58; primal, 11, 151–76, 239n24; sexual, 71
Schelling, Friedrich Wilhelm Joseph, 87, 224n30
Schiller, Friedrich, 87
Schleiermacher, Friedrich, 87
Schopenhauer, Arthur, 74–76, 81, 87–88, 219nn8–9
seduction theory, 16, 27–28, 206n20, 208n7, 209n12
sexuality, 4, 24–28, 30, 73–76, 78–79, 87–96, 208–209n12, 226nn47–49, 227n52, 231n12, 233n10, 239n24. *See also* Eros
Shakespeare, William, 215n14, 231n10
sign, 16, 37, 80, 122–32, 135–38, 150, 158, 172, 206n22, 222n21, 228n61, 233n13; deconstructive, 122–23; historical (*Geschichtszeichen*), 122
Silberstein, Eduard, 223n26, 224n30
SIPP (Société Internationale de Psychanalyse et Philosophie), 68–70, 218n1
Smith, Adam, 87
solder, soldering, 90–92, 124–26, 227n52
Solms, Mark, 9–13, 19–21, 201nn1,2, 202n5, 207n25, 240n2
Sophocles, 145, 235n8
sovereignty, 113–15, 124–26, 132, 136, 139–40, 145–46, 157–58, 164, 167, 231n11, 239n20
spatialization, 203n7
spectacle, 153–57, 159–63, 166–67, 173–74, 238n14; public, 153–54. *See also* theater
speculation, 26, 33, 42, 45, 75, 80–87, 92, 96–97, 184, 220n13, 221n16, 224n31, 225n41
St. Germain, Mark, 24
Strachey, James, 53–54, 58, 83, 179–82, 185, 206n19, 210n1, 214n8, 215n18, 240n2
structure (accidental), 25, 34, 206n21
suffering, 13, 18, 112, 114, 123, 130–31, 160–61, 206n20, 218n35; psychical, 13, 112, 123, 131
superstition, superstitious, 47–48, 52, 55–57, 59, 66

technology, technological, 61, 146, 198, 203n9
telepathy, telepathic, 47–67, 213n2, 213–14nn4–5, 214n7, 215nn10–11, 216nn24,26, 217n29. *See also* occult
telephone, telephonic, 60–62, 216n25
temporality 5, 24–34, 209n15; traumatic, 5, 24–34. *See also* trauma
theater, 45, 103, 118, 130, 142, 155–56, 158–60, 167–68, 173–74
Thomas, D. M., 24, 68
Thompson, Kevin, 237n13
thought transference, 47, 49–50, 52–53, 60, 62–63, 75, 213–14n5, 217n29

Thurshwell, Pamela, 214n6
Tikker, 174–76, 240n28
Tocqueville, Alexis de, 152, 237n4
Todestrieb. *See* drive: death drive
Torok, Maria, 62, 103, 205n17, 217nn31,33,34,35
translation, 10–11, 54, 101, 179–83, 185, 187–91, 194, 198, 215n14, 240n1
trauma, 4, 13, 17–19, 22, 25–34, 38, 44, 54, 73, 204n11, 206nn20–21, 207n2, 208n11, 209n12, 210n18; psychical, 18, 27, 32, 206n20, 210n18; sexual, 26–27, 29, 73, 209n12; war, 29, 33
Trumbull, Robert, 234n15
Trump, Donald J., 222n21. *See also* narcissism: phallic narcissism
Trump, Ivanka, 222n21. *See also* narcissism: phallic narcissism
Turnbull, Oliver, 201n2

unconscious, unconsciousness, 4, 20–21, 24–25, 35, 37–45, 48, 51, 53, 55, 59–63, 69–71, 73–76, 87, 106, 148, 187, 202n6, 209n12, 213n4, 214n5, 217n28, 219n6, 234n1, 236n11
Unfall, 17, 35, 38–40, 44–45, 55. *See also* accident
United Nations, 151, 236n1
United States, 121, 124, 130, 143, 151–53, 155, 158, 239n26
unlocatability, 5, 13, 18, 19–22, 26–27, 29, 206n22; spatial, 5, 13, 18, 22, 26–27; temporal, 22, 26, 29–34. *See also* infiltrate

Vaihinger, Hans, 87
Van Haute, Philippe, 226n47, 227n54
Vergreifen, 41, 58–59. *See also* bungled actions
Villers de l'Isle Adam, Auguste, 137–38
virtuality, 38, 116, 157, 172, 198
virtualization, 155, 159–67
vociferation, 191, 193–94, 196
Voltaire (François-Marie Arouet), 87, 124

Weber, Elisabeth, 235n9
Weber, Samuel, 217n28, 220n10, 221n14, 222n21, 228n55, 229n65
Webster, Jameson, 36–40, 44, 211n3
Weismann, August, 85
Wills, David, 217n27, 228n56, 229n66, 240n1
Winnicott, D. W., 183, 222n24, 240n4
wolf, 192–94, 197–98. *See also* Little Red Riding Hood
Wolf Man, 62, 192, 217nn31,33, 217–18n35. *See also* Pankeiev, Sergei
Wood, Sarah, 217n27
Wortham, Simon Morgan, 224n15

Zufall, zufällig, 35–36, 38–45, 55–57, 64, 67, 211nn2,4. *See also* chance

Elizabeth Rottenberg is Professor of Philosophy at DePaul University and a practicing psychoanalyst in Chicago. She is the author of *Inheriting the Future: Legacies of Kant, Freud, and Flaubert* and the editor and translator of many books by Maurice Blanchot, Jacques Derrida, and Jean-François Lyotard.

www.ingramcontent.com/pod-product-compliance
Lightning Source LLC
Chambersburg PA
CBHW030437300426
44112CB00009B/1052